THE TOWER OF BABBLE

RICHARD STURSBERG

THE TOWER OF BABBLE

SINS, SECRETS AND SUCCESSES INSIDE THE CBC

Douglas & McIntyre
D&M PUBLISHERS INC.
Vancouver/Toronto/Berkeley

Douglas & McIntyre
An imprint of D&M Publishers Inc.
2323 Quebec Street, Suite 201
Vancouver BC Canada V5T 4S7
www.douglas-mcintyre.com

Cataloguing data available from Library and Archives Canada
ISBN 978-1-926812-73-1 (cloth)
ISBN 978-1-926812-74-8 (ebook)

Editing by Trena White
Jacket and interior design by Jessica Sullivan
Jacket illustration of hand © Antar Dayal/Getty Images
Printed and bound in Canada by Friesens
Distributed in the U.S. by Publishers Group West

We gratefully acknowledge the financial support of the Canada Council
for the Arts, the British Columbia Arts Council, the Province of British
Columbia through the Book Publishing Tax Credit and the Government
of Canada through the Canada Book Fund for our publishing activities.

For my father.

CONTENTS

I shoot the Hippopotamus
With bullets made of platinum,
Because if I use the leaden ones
His hide is sure to flatten 'em.
Hilaire Belloc, "The Hippopotamus,"
The Bad Child's Book of Beasts

one
THE PUBLIC OF PUBLIC BROADCASTING

THE ROOM WAS packed. Everyone from the broadcasting and film communities in Montreal was there. It was the luncheon talk of the Académie canadienne du cinéma et de la télévision, the French-Canadian equivalent of the Academy of Motion Picture Arts and Sciences. The most important producers, directors and writers were in attendance, along with various television personalities, stars and broadcasting executives. The murmur of industry talk and the clinking of ice in glasses filled the hall.

The president of the Académie rose to introduce me as the luncheon speaker, the guest from Toronto, the head of English services at the Canadian Broadcasting Corporation (CBC). I knew most of the people in the room, since three years earlier I had been the head of Telefilm Canada and had financed many French films. They knew me and, with the exception of a few malcontents whose films did not get financed, liked me well enough. Certainly they liked the fact that a broadcasting executive would come from Toronto and address them in French.

My topic was "The Strategy for English Television at the CBC." The president finished his introduction, the room stilled and a polite hush fell over the crowd. On either side of the podium from which I was to deliver my remarks were two huge screens. The best way to explain strategy is always to start with the problem.

I began by projecting a chart showing the names of the twenty most popular television shows in English Canada. Beside each name I had placed a little flag showing its country of origin. There was nothing but American flags.

"*Voici le problème*," I intoned.

There were cries of disbelief, shock and bewilderment; calls of "*non*" and "*impossible*." The Quebec producers, directors and executives simply could not believe that English Canadians preferred foreign shows to their own. It must be humiliating. How do the writers and actors hold their heads up? How can people show their faces in public?

When I explained that American shows had dominated since the dawn of television in English Canada, there were fresh cries of outrage and disbelief. Strong men could be seen gasping for air; beautiful women fanned themselves in dismay. When I explained that this did not seem to bother the cultural elites in English Canada, people started passing out. One of Quebec's most distinguished screenwriters had to be revived with smelling salts.

The French television and film community was, of course, right to be scandalized. In Quebec, the most popular television shows are all Canadian. The truth is that English Canada's situation is unique in the industrialized world. Nowhere else—not in France, Britain, Germany, the United States, Italy, Ireland, Australia—do the citizens overwhelmingly prefer the television shows of a foreign country. Everywhere else, they prefer their own television shows, the shows that speak to their particular cultural sensibilities, their sense of humour, their traditions and history, and their narrative preoccupations.

If English Canada had a number one cultural challenge, this was it. The situation of the other mass media is dramatically different. English Canadians prefer their own newspapers, magazines and sports teams. They read with avidity their own novels and listen to their own music. When it comes to these other popular media,

Canadians like domestic fare as least as well as, if not more than, what is available from the United States.

For its part, the Canadian Broadcasting Corporation has historically been ambivalent about the problem. Although it may seem self-evident that Canada's largest and best-financed cultural institution should take on Canada's biggest cultural challenge, the CBC has never really screwed up its courage and focused on making popular TV shows. Instead, it has focused on information programs: news, talk, documentaries, current affairs and sports. When it comes to entertainment, it has contented itself with producing dramas and comedies deemed "distinctive," "higher quality" or "edgy," rather than embracing the extraordinarily demanding work of making shows that Canadians might actually want to watch.

This failure represents a deep misunderstanding about the nature of television. Television is fundamentally about entertainment. It is the medium par excellence that people consume to be told stories, to be made to laugh, to be thrilled, frightened, moved, charmed or excited. It is a narrative medium, like the novel or the feature film. Its great strength is its immersive grip: its ability to command the emotional attention of audiences while it elaborates plots, creates characters and carries the viewer along the structure of its chosen stories.

It is true that private television networks also show documentaries, news and public affairs programs. Other than on specialty networks, however, these are almost always reserved for the non-prime time hours of the schedule. From eight o'clock in the evening until eleven at night, from Sunday to Friday every week, when dinner is done and it is time to relax and watch television, the big networks offer schedules that are built almost exclusively of entertainment shows of one variety or another. They command enormous audiences, numbering in the millions and dwarfing the consumption of anything else. Only as the day winds down do the big networks move away from entertainment. Later in the evening, after eleven o'clock, the news and talk shows appear.

The CBC seems never to have been comfortable with the idea that its television mandate should be to create and exhibit distinctively

Canadian entertainment shows. At the height of its power and wealth, in the late 1970s and early 1980s, its prime-time schedule featured almost no Canadian drama or comedy. Instead, prime time was a mix of U.S. entertainment shows, with Canadian news, documentaries and public affairs filling up the schedule. This was surprising not simply because the CBC made little or no attempt to address English Canada's greatest cultural challenge, but also because—even then—there was no shortage of Canadian news available elsewhere.

Over the 1980s and 1990s, this approach continued. At one point, the CBC became so dominated by the news that it attempted to move the major nightly newscast—*The National*—from its traditional prime-time slot at 10:00 PM to an even primer slot at 9:00 PM. The result was a fiasco. Ratings plummeted as Canadians declined to watch news in the middle of the evening. Regardless of this experience, the CBC continued to resist making popular Canadian entertainment shows, and continued to pursue its factual and educational approach to programming.

As a result, the CBC saw its audience share collapse over the thirty years leading up to 2004. As choice increased with the emergence of specialty channels, Canadians abandoned the Corporation in droves. While its great rival CTV also lost audience share, it lost it at half the speed of the CBC. As the decades went by, the CBC seemed incapable of changing strategy. Despite the fact that Canadians clearly preferred a different television diet to the CBC's, the Corporation—the "public" broadcaster—continued to ignore the public's obvious preferences. By 2004, the CBC's prime-time share was the lowest in its history.

Throughout this discouraging descent, the CBC's news audience also abandoned it. The irony was that in compromising its entertainment strategy in favour of news, the Corporation did nothing well. In the 1980s the CBC had been the number one or two local newscaster in all the major English markets, but then its position eroded. In response to budgetary difficulties, the Corporation started to abandon local news in the early 1990s. From Halifax through

Toronto, Calgary, Edmonton and Vancouver, it saw a plunge in viewership, to the point where it had the least-watched local newscasts everywhere except Charlottetown. This was devastating, since over two-thirds of news viewing in English Canada is local and—not surprisingly—two-thirds of news advertising revenue is local as well.

By 2000, the situation had become so severe that it seemed pointless to continue. The then-president of the CBC, Robert Rabinovitch, proposed to the board that the Corporation exit local news altogether. He argued that there was no point spending large amounts of money on local newscasts that nobody was watching. The board, as is typical of CBC boards, sought a compromise, and a compromise was created. A new show was produced—called *Canada Now*—with only half an hour of local news instead of the original hour. It was launched in 2000, and like its unhappy predecessors, saw its audience decline year over year. At its nadir, it had less than 200,000 viewers across the entire country. By way of contrast, CTV's supper-hour newscasts were drawing 1.5 million viewers every night.

It was not as though the de-emphasis of local news strengthened the performance of *The National* or the CBC's specialty news network, Newsworld. *The National* continued to see its share erode too. In the 1980s *The National* had utterly eclipsed the CTV national newscast, but it now found itself posting numbers significantly inferior to those of its great competitor. Worse still, its reputation eroded. Canadians had historically ranked it as the most trustworthy and authoritative newscast, but by the early twenty-first century, public opinion studies showed that the gap with CTV had almost completely vanished.

The story at Newsworld was no happier. Founded in the early 1980s as an all-day news network, it had enjoyed an effective monopoly for almost twenty years as the only Canadian all-news specialty channel. It had no domestic competitors, only foreign ones, including CNN and ultimately MSNBC and Fox. Despite these advantages, it struggled with strategy (*Antiques Roadshow* was a staple of its breaking news) and audiences. Most of the time CNN's audiences in Canada were bigger than Newsworld's, often twice as large.

It was embarrassing to see Canadians choose foreign news sources over their own.

By 2004 CBC news was drawing the lowest audiences in its history. It had become—with the exception of the weakened but still important *National*—a sideshow to the ongoing public debate, drawing only 12 percent of all viewers of Canadian news, whereas Global drew 33 percent and CTV, 55 percent. This was an astonishing collapse for what had once been the dominant news broadcaster in the country.

The only part of the CBC that retained anything of its former glory in 2004 was the sports department. *Hockey Night in Canada* continued to draw very respectable audiences and generate considerable profits. The Corporation had produced well-received Olympic Games in 2000, 2002 and 2004. The Canadian Football League was still a great property, producing strong ratings and impressive numbers for the annual Grey Cup.

But even for Sports, the writing was on the wall. The National Hockey League had locked out its players for the entire 2004–05 season, thus cancelling *Hockey Night in Canada*. The new Olympic bid was due in early 2005, and the CFL contract had only two years to run. The other networks and the sports specialty channels were circling these properties, hoping to snatch them from the CBC. At the zenith of its success, the future of the sports department was uncertain.

IN EARLY 2004, at the very worst point of CBC television's misfortunes, I received a call from a headhunter asking whether I would be interested in becoming the next head of English television. At the time, I was happily running Telefilm Canada and attempting to finance Canadian movies that Canadians might actually want to watch. The government had set a target of 5 percent of the domestic box office for our own films, and amid cries of outrage and disbelief, I was busy attempting to do just that. Where the Canadian feature film industry had historically focused on making art-house movies, the new policy required them to make commercially successful ones. Concerns were expressed in many quarters that we would end up "dumbing them down." The resulting changes in our approach to the financing and distribution of Canadian movies had made me a vilified figure in the English feature film community.

The headhunter explained that Harold Redekopp, the distinguished head of television and former head of CBC radio, was retiring, and they were looking for a replacement. I allowed that I knew the president of the CBC, Robert Rabinovitch, very well. I advised the headhunter that if his call was simply a fishing trip, I was uninterested. It was unfair to call me unless Robert knew he was going to do so and approved the call. He told me that he did and that he had.

When I discussed the possibility of going to the CBC with friends in the industry whose judgment I trusted, they argued sharply against it. "Why would you want to go?" they asked. "It is unsalvageable." They pointed to its thirty years of continuous decline. They noted, as well, that it had an acrimonious and undisciplined culture, that it was self-absorbed and indifferent to audiences, and that it had terrible judgment. Even my ancient father, Peter Stursberg, who had been a war correspondent for the CBC during the Second World War and its first correspondent at the United Nations in the 1950s, dismissed the idea. "My dear boy," he said, "do not go there. It is a snake pit."

And yet. Amidst the flops, wonderful things were produced. There were sparkling radio shows: *Quirks & Quarks*, *As It Happens*, *Sunday Morning*, *The House*, *Writers & Company*, *Metro Morning*. And on television too, there were remarkable shows. The brilliant *Rick Mercer Report*, the excellent *Fifth Estate*, often *The National*, the iconic *Hockey Night in Canada*, CBC News: *Sunday Night*, *Canada: A People's History*. All great.

And the people working there. The CBC still had some of the most gifted, dedicated and imaginative programmers in Canada. They toiled away producing gems of originality and creativity. They wrote, produced, voiced, directed, edited, acted and hosted with intelligence and authority. They were the Corporation's great underused and under-loved assets.

And it was, after all, the CBC. Bowed and diminished, but still the CBC. Still English Canada's most important cultural institution and the great hope for asserting ourselves as a sophisticated people. For years, like most Canadians, I had loved and despised it, admired and ridiculed it. From my earliest memories, it had been there. It had occupied our house when I was a child, like an unseen guest at the table. My father's CBC, from the war and his days at the United Nations. My CBC, as a child and teenager, watching *Wayne & Shuster* and listening to *Rawhide*. My CBC, as an adult, through all the years of news and current affairs, and the occasional great show (CODCO, *Street Legal*, *The Kids in the Hall*, *Traders*). It was woven through my life and memory like an invisible thread, connecting the tissue of my family with the broader character of the country.

The key question for me was: why had the CBC declined so far? Why did it find itself in its precarious situation? Why was it incapable over the course of thirty years of finding a better strategy? Why could it not save itself? Were the problems a result of external factors over which CBC television had no control, or were they problems of the Corporation's own making? There was, after all, no point in even considering going if its fate was already sealed. Then my father and friends would be right: it would be truly unsalvageable.

If, on the other hand, the reasons for its decline were managerial and strategic, rather than external, there might be some hope. If the long decline was a result of poor judgments and mistaken plans, then it might be possible to rectify them. Then maybe, just maybe, there would be a chance to turn things around. Everything depended on what the real problem was.

Traditionally, CBC supporters argue that the problem is successive governments' mean-spirited approaches to financing. They note—correctly—that the CBC is the worst-financed public broadcaster in the industrialized world, apart from PBS in the United States, and TVNZ in New Zealand (which is a public broadcaster in name only, since it receives no money from the government). The BBC, they point out, receives seven times as much money per capita as the CBC to provide broadcasting services in only one language and one time zone. By comparison, Canada's population is scattered over five-and-a-half time zones and must be fully served in two languages and partially served in seven aboriginal ones.

These supporters further note that the Corporation has been subjected to repeated cuts, most notably the reductions by Jean Chrétien and Paul Martin in the mid-1990s, which removed almost 25 percent of the public subsidy. The cuts have been compounded every year since by the water torture of inflation that erodes the real value of the fixed amount being received. Even when the last Liberal government put up an extra $60 million, it was done on a one-time basis. The subsidy has been renewed every year since, but the Corporation never knows from one year to the next whether it will continue.

The CBC's financial woes may partly account for its decline, but others argue that they are certainly not the whole story. The Corporation's problems, they believe, are more of its own devising than the government's. The wounds it has suffered over the years are largely self-inflicted. They are brought on in great measure by weak management and a corrosive internal culture.

The more I looked into the matter, the more that seemed to be the case. It appeared, in fact, that CBC television's decline had been as much a result of poor strategy as anything else. The Corporation was the victim of its own weird sets of ideas and the elitist directions they suggested.

The first and most important issue was the belief that popular success was inherently incompatible with quality. It was widely felt that a choice must be made between producing programs that were popular and making those that were good. There was no middle ground. A show with broad appeal must by its very nature be coarse, stupid or vulgar; a high-quality show will inevitably be too complicated, intelligent and refined to attract a significant number of viewers.

The language that the CBC used to discuss this disjunction was revealing. Popular shows were inevitably denigrated as "commercial," as mere "entertainments." Quality shows were seen, however, as "mandate" shows, at the root of what the CBC should be.

The private sector should concern itself with attracting audiences by pandering to baser tastes. The CBC, though, would address itself to a much more sophisticated, albeit much smaller, audience that was capable of appreciating more demanding fare.

In this view, the world was divided into groups. On the one hand, there was the public at large, living in their dreary suburbs, consuming American TV and besotted by crime reporting and sports. There they were: the middlebrow members of the middle class, content in their self-regard, indifferent to the higher arts, obsessed only with money and sentimentality. On the other hand, there was the more sophisticated elite, those who—like the CBC—lived for higher purposes.

Throughout its history, various presidents and senior managers of the Corporation have bemoaned CBC television's reliance on advertising revenue. They have complained that it inevitably pulls the network's programming in the direction of more popular shows at the expense of the more important ones. If CBC television could be released from the constraints of finding advertising revenues—as had happened with CBC radio in the 1970s—the Corporation could take greater creative and artistic risks. No longer having to pander to the gods of the market, CBC television would be able—like CBC radio—to occupy the sunlit uplands of high culture, where programming choices were based on nothing but artistic and intellectual merit.

As Al Johnson, a distinguished former president of the CBC, said to legendary broadcaster Knowlton Nash: "We at the CBC were always trapped with the tensions between commercials and public service." According to Nash, Johnson was distressed by the ethos of commercialization that he felt had polluted public broadcasting and created a split personality between the CBC's mandate to reflect Canada and its need to earn ever-higher commercial revenue. Like many CBC presidents before and after, he felt the CBC would have been better off never having started getting into commercials.

This view was widely shared at all levels of the Corporation. The employees of the news department, for example, would look at their sadly diminished audiences and console themselves with the thought that they were producing a higher-quality product. They did not—unlike their competitors at CTV and Global—"chase ambulances." Rather they produced much more "in-depth" news. The fact that the Canadian population was heartily uninterested in their higher-quality news simply confirmed the dim standards of the public at large and the more challenging and cerebral quality of the CBC's efforts. The same attitude prevailed in the drama department. The fact that Canadians yawned with indifference at their offerings confirmed that they must be on the right track. If the public was not watching, it must be because the shows were too demanding, too hard-hitting or too sophisticated. It could not possibly be because they were badly made, poorly written or boring.

This attitude, in turn, led to an indifference about what the other television networks were doing, whether Canadian or American. Why, after all, would one want to watch second-rate shows, designed for the tastes of a mass audience? Doing so would be pointless and disturbing. Watching CTV or Global's programs or news would be as relevant as studying the work of broadcasters in Congo or Peru. Indifference to the efforts of its competitors also had the effect of safeguarding the esteem of the management and staff. If one did not watch the competitors' shows, one remained unchallenged in the notion that they were inferior.

This created an impossible problem: no matter what was done, it would inevitably be a failure. If the show attracted large audiences—witness *Hockey Night in Canada* and its boisterous host Don Cherry—it must be vulgar and stupid. If it did not, then while people might console themselves with the belief that the show was high quality, it also failed. This created a profound schizophrenia within the CBC culture. People felt like superior losers.

The entire ideological structure was wrong. The most popular American entertainment shows that Canadians watched in their millions were not poorly made rubbish. To the contrary, they were often beautifully realized, well written, well acted, well directed and well produced. The top shows—*Law & Order*, *CSI*, *Desperate Housewives*—were exceptionally good by any standard. In fact, so good was American television in the mid-1990s and into the twenty-first century that critics spoke of it as a Golden Age. Many of the top writers and directors in Hollywood abandoned making movies for the pleasures of working in the more creative environment of television.

The same was true of news. Even a cursory comparison of CBC news with that of its competitors revealed the superior journalism of the private networks. Watching the local newscasts in any major market showed the privates to be faster to the stories, broader in their coverage, better in their presentation and deeper in their analysis. Much of this was, of course, invisible to the CBC news reporters and producers because they did not watch their competitors.

If it was untrue that a trade-off had to be made between quality and popularity, one could begin to think about the CBC's future success. If the internal culture could be changed, if CBC television could be reoriented toward the audience—to the public it was to serve—then perhaps the long slide into irrelevance could be countered.

OVER THE NEXT few months, Robert Rabinovitch and I had a number of long, searching conversations. I liked and admired him very much. During the 1980s I had worked with him briefly when I was the head of policy and strategy at the Department of Communications in Ottawa, where he had been the deputy minister.

When he left the government, he fell back on his training and moved into investment banking. Robert has a PhD in Finance from the Wharton School of the University of Pennsylvania. He ended up at Claridge, Charles Bronfman's holding company in Montreal. While there, he became involved in the buying and selling of the Cineplex Odeon cinema chain, the building and selling of the Sports Network (TSN) and the Discovery Channel, along with a number of other media assets. Eventually he rose to be chief operating officer at Claridge and made enough money to do as he pleased.

He was appointed CBC president by Jean Chrétien's government in 2000. He had excellent relationships with all levels of government. Eddie Goldenberg, Chrétien's principal policy advisor, was a personal friend, as were many members of the mandarinate. He was an old Ottawa hand and knew when he took the job that the

CBC would have to pass two essential tests before any more money would be forthcoming from the federal government. First, it had to prove that it could operate efficiently; second, it had to prove that it was fair in its political coverage. It was clear that the prime minister himself was doubtful that the CBC was capable of meeting the tests. He, like most members of the Liberal Party, was convinced that the French network was infested with separatists. He had also cut the CBC savagely just four years earlier as part of the deficit-busting efforts of then-finance minister Paul Martin. He had apparently asked Goldenberg if Rabinovitch really wanted the job. He could not quite understand why any sensible person would want to do it. Robert took the job without demanding any new money from the government. Rather, he planned to prove that the CBC could meet these tests and then ask for the cheque. He ultimately became the first president in over thirty years to receive any new funding.

Our first major discussion took place at Beckta, a small restaurant in Ottawa, much favoured by the top echelons of the civil service. It was the middle of Ottawa's unending winter, and snow was falling heavily as a storm began. The room twinkled with the warmth of dinner and conversation. Robert was at a table at the back. He is shortish, a little round, extremely clever, lively and sociable. He rose to greet me, smiling and gesturing to the other chair. He speaks quickly, his mind darting along like a fish in a rapid river.

"So, how are you?" he began. "How are the kids?"

We talked about our personal lives for a while, about our children, our wives, mutual friends. Then we came to the meat of it. His preoccupations were efficiency and the news, the two ineluctable tests.

He had spent considerable time over the three years he had been at the Corporation trying to force more businesslike behaviour on the place. He had made significant progress rationalizing the Corporation's real estate holdings, selling some of them and leasing out the unused space in others. Eventually he would make $100 million in sales and gain an additional $60 million in annual revenues.

Still, there was much more to be done. The fact that the CBC had four news services, two in French and two in English, cut no ice with anyone.

"The trucks," he opined. "Every time CBC and Radio-Canada show up at a press conference with four cameras and four trucks, we look fat. Ministers count them. Everyone else is there with one."

He warmed to his theme. "It is impossible to convince anyone that the Corporation is lean and mean when we cannot figure out how to share resources for the same event."

He ate a little and sipped his wine. The muffled chatter in the restaurant and the clink of glasses gave his lamentations a strange intimacy. Outside, the wind picked up in intensity.

"The studios," he went on. "The biggest studios in the country on the tenth floor of the Broadcast Centre in Toronto are mostly dark. How does that make sense? Why can't we rent them out?"

He could not understand why the CBC was not run sensibly, and why the internal culture was hostile to good management. He could not understand why the employees would not want the most efficient possible operation, since it would then allow them to make more and better programs.

"The news," he continued, sipping his wine, clattering his knife and fork and fixing me with his most rapt look. "What can one say? There is no business coverage of any value. It is as though they do not understand that most people in Canada are employed by private companies. Worse still, the news department appears actively hostile to business.

"And the French news! It's not even so much the actual content, it's the story selection, the eyeball rolling, the shoulder shrugging…" He trailed off on the French news, realizing we were talking about English television.

I agreed with all this. The CBC's legendary inability to meet the most elementary tests of good management, and its soft left, anti-business, Toronto-centric, politically correct cultural assumptions created significant problems for the Corporation. They were clearly key concerns. I then added my own.

"Who does it serve?" I asked. "Is the CBC there to serve the chatterati, the cultural elites—or the public at large? Is it supposed to make art-house fare or Canadian entertainment shows that Canadians might actually find entertaining?"

Outside the restaurant, the snow picked up in ferocity. The storm started to rage. The windows rattled.

I explained that I shared Robert's views, but I was also deeply concerned about the CBC's entertainment offerings. Nobody was watching the shows. Sure there had been great programs in the past but the Corporation hadn't had a hit in more than a decade.

"My thing, Robert, is audiences. I only have one idea. Audiences matter."

"Well, of course," he replied.

"No. No," I said. "This is regarded as a radical notion. Making popular shows is regarded as a betrayal in English Canada. It's a sign of vulgarity."

He paused. He knew what I was talking about. He wiped his glasses. The waiter came by with coffee. The wind picked up further.

"If I come, I want to focus on audiences, on making dramas and comedies that people will actually watch, on rebuilding the news so it has some viewers. If we don't reverse the decline, the CBC will collapse into complete irrelevance."

We went on for much longer. We talked about the labour situation. He had already taken two strikes and locked out the on-air staff in French. He described being trapped in a crowd of angry employees and how they had started to rock the car he was in, planning to push it over. He talked about the upcoming negotiations with the English unions and how difficult they would be.

We talked about Ottawa and the government, the board of directors, the mood of the Corporation—the endless myriad challenges and problems that confronted CBC television. We understood that if we were to be successful, if we were to rebuild CBC television, the task would be very difficult. We were certain to be resisted within, attacked without and made to feel generally wretched.

It was an appealing prospect.

"You know," I went on, "if you were to offer me the job and I were to accept it, you would compound your problems."

"How so?" he asked. "How could it be worse?"

"Well, I have an unattractive reputation, and worse still, I am not from the CBC. What fresh hell will this be for CBC television? Was there nobody within the organization worthy of running it? You understand the message you would be sending people?"

"Yup," he said. His eyes twinkled with enthusiasm. The great thing about Robert is that he has no fear of controversy. He would prefer to avoid fights, but if they are inevitable and necessary, he is a happy warrior.

Finally, we walked out into the Ottawa winter night.

ON JULY 27, 2004, I walked into the CBC's head office for the first time as the new head of English television. The date seemed propitious. It was my birthday, and the day was sunny and lovely. Despite all my misgivings and fears, I was filled with optimism and excitement. It was an extraordinary moment, the best moment, when everything was still possible and the inevitable mistakes and failures had not yet occurred. The first day on the job, the best day on the job.

Over the course of the next couple of months, I toured the organization, visiting the regions, looking at the financial situation, watching the shows, getting briefed by the various departments and finding the bathrooms. What I saw confirmed much of what I had believed was the problem with the organization. Now I saw the corporate culture in action.

When I visited the regional newsrooms, I was astonished to discover that no local CBC newsroom watched the competitors' shows. Despite the fact that the local supper-hour newscasts were collapsing, all the monitors were turned to BBC World or CNN or CBC Newsworld. None of them were tuned to the local shows of Global and CTV, who were beating them every day. Normal companies focus relentlessly on what their successful competitors are doing to try to understand how to do better themselves. Not at the CBC. They were making a superior product for a better-informed audience.

This indifference to competitors and hostility to the public at large also meant it was unnecessary to study audience data. When I met with the producers of *The National*, they said that they heard I was big on audiences. I allowed that I was. They asked what performance I would like for *The National*. I replied that 750,000

Canadians a night watching would be good. They asked how they were doing. I asked why they were asking me the question. They must see the audience numbers—called "overnights"—every afternoon, just like me. No, they replied. They had never seen them. Although the overnights are available every afternoon, nobody in the Corporation had access to them except the top four or five officials in English television.

Returning to my office, I inquired whether it was true that the producers did not see the overnights. I was advised that it was so, since top management did not want them to be discouraged by what they might see. We decided, then, to change course and post the overnights on the intranet, so that everyone at CBC television could see not only how they were doing, but how all the other networks were doing. The first day the numbers went up, demand to see them was so high that the intranet crashed.

This, of course, exposed the more difficult problem. Everyone secretly knew that the numbers did matter. In their heart of hearts they knew that it was important to attract large audiences, that there was little or no point spending hundreds of millions of dollars to make shows that nobody watched. They knew that success with audiences mattered, and that there could not be a public broadcaster without a public.

It soon became clear that there were no objective performance standards. And without objective measures, it was impossible to say whether the Corporation was succeeding or failing. Not surprisingly, management claimed that it was doing a great job, that the programs were terrific and the news a towering success. Equally unsurprisingly, the employees wanted to believe that was true. Like everyone in the world, they wanted to believe that they were doing a good job, indeed a superior job.

To try to understand how the CBC management had approached the problem in the past, I looked at the strategic plans that underpinned the last repositioning of the CBC in the late 1990s and that continued to inform the programming policies in 2004. The documents of the period and the resulting plan were revelatory.

Tremendous amounts of work had been done by many very clever people. They had established task forces, organized think-ins and retreats, and written position papers. Finally they concluded that the real problem was that the CBC was not "distinctive" enough and that the solution to its problems was to become more "distinctive."

When it came time to define the concept of "distinctiveness," they drew two conclusions, one sensible and one catastrophic. Sensibly they concluded that they should—to the maximum extent possible—eliminate American programs from the schedule. While that may seem an obvious principle, it had never been articulated as clearly before.

The second conclusion was that they should actively not do whatever the private networks were doing. If the private local newscasts offered hard news, they would do local current affairs. If the privates provided weather reports, they would not. If the privates provided multi-episode dramatic series, they would focus on miniseries and movies of the week. If the privates offered entertainment, they would offer the higher arts. If the privates preferred mainstream formats, they would emphasize edgier and more experimental fare. If the privates revelled in reality television, they would not.

Merely making the network Canadian would have made it distinctive. To go further and define programming strategy in opposition to what the privates were showing was unnecessary. The privates were, after all, extremely successful. To suggest that the CBC should make shows that were alien to what Canadians knew and liked seemed almost perverse.

The most interesting thing about the plan and the various studies underpinning it was what was missing. Nowhere had the diligent planners asked the Canadian public what it might like. Nor did they note that the public must have been dissatisfied with the CBC since they were turning away in droves.

Not surprisingly, the distinctiveness strategy failed. The collapse continued.

The cultural elitism of the CBC and its self-destructive strategies were compounded by what amounted to a war of all against all. Years of budget cuts and reductions had pitted the different parts of the Corporation against each other. The fundamental management challenge for each of the big departments had been to resist having the cuts fall in one's area of responsibility: if the news department suffered, then perhaps the sports department would not have to.

The competitors were within the walls of the Corporation. As the available resources shrank, each department eyed the others warily. Clearly somebody would have to be cut, and the key thing was to make sure it was somebody else. Each department pooh-poohed the others' accomplishments and denigrated their efforts as inadequate and unworthy, arguing that they were not real public broadcasters. No, the core of public broadcasting, the central and key part of its mandate was... well, wherever the person making the argument happened to work.

The result was a cacophony of snubs and disparagements. The radio department sneered at the sports department. The music department looked down on the sales department. The drama department belittled the regions. And the lordly news department looked down on everyone, refusing even to cover their activities, save to mock them.

In this cantankerous and unhappy atmosphere, there was no sharing or mutual support. The idea that radio would promote TV, or that TV would promote radio, was unthinkable. Why help the enemy? The result, of course, was that the CBC was much less than the sum of its parts.

The war of all against all reinforced the Corporation's inward-looking tendencies. Rumours circulated wildly, the small politics of position and office dominated conversation, myths were polished into truths, vendettas were pursued across generations of producers. Newcomers who fell afoul of one of the rival gangs could become unwitting victims of the savage turf wars. The entire place felt like a Hall of Angry Mirrors.

Perhaps not surprisingly, the continuing problems led to a certain backward-looking nostalgia. There was a Golden Age, which was now gone. The shades of Wayne and Shuster, Knowlton Nash, *The Friendly Giant* and *This Hour Has Seven Days* haunted the hallways.

The great atrium on the ground floor of the Toronto Broadcast Centre was converted into a shrine. There were display cases full of prizes from the Lucerne Television Festival of 1962, and a little museum with old microphones and tape recorders. There was the Graham Spry Theatre that showed almost-forgotten documentaries. And in one of the corridors, there was a player piano that produced songs from the Happy Gang in the 1940s.

What there was not, anywhere, was the faintest hint that it was 2004. There were no posters celebrating the shows or the big on-air personalities. There were no displays documenting the CBC's most recent triumphs. There were no hortatory slogans championing its new direction. There was nothing of the present, nothing to indicate that one was standing in the lobby of Canada's largest and most important contemporary cultural institution. Nothing but the faint bugles of past glories.

FOLLOWING MY VISITS and briefings, I worked out a plan for how to approach the job ahead: the rebuilding of CBC television's audiences. The challenge would be to try to make important changes without being slaughtered in the process. The Corporation is famous for its ability to resist the bright ideas of new management. Many strategies would be deployed. There would be passive resistance, where everyone would say "yes, yes" but really mean "no, no" and do nothing. There would be whispering campaigns, where bad rumours would be leaked to the press, sabotaging my reputation or initiatives. There would be outright rebellion and threats, complete with petitions, resistance and barricades. It was essential, therefore, to approach the problem gingerly and with cunning. The elephant should be eaten one slice at a time.

The first year would inevitably be a loss. Just getting to know the four thousand employees scattered across the country, the detailed budgets, the innumerable shows and the abilities of the different managers would take time. I would have to tour the stations, meet the staff, get briefed on their activities and try to understand their worries and preoccupations. It would be essential to immerse myself in the economics of the business to see what was possible and what was not. All of this would take time.

The next twelve months looked particularly grim. The negotiations between the National Hockey League and the players' union were going badly. It looked as though the NHL would lock out the players and cancel the season. If they did, we would have to cancel *Hockey Night in Canada*, the CBC's biggest show. *Hockey Night in Canada* was also the Corporation's largest money earner, producing almost half of the total advertising revenue. Without it, there would be huge financial and programming challenges.

Then there was the union. The negotiations for the contract's renewal had already begun by the time I arrived. There had, however, been no progress. The parties met but agreed to nothing. The CBC has a history of poisonous labour relations, dating back to the 1950s and the producers' strike at Radio-Canada (the French arm of the CBC) that galvanized the Three Wise Men, Pierre Trudeau, Jean Marchand and Gérard Pelletier. It had laid the foundations for the acrimonious contempt that much of the CBC staff felt for management. More recently, the Corporation had been rocked by strikes and lockouts nearly every year for the last twenty. The discussions with the union would likely result in industrial action.

The plan began, therefore, in the second year, 2005–06. The first order of business would be to secure the sports properties. Bidding would begin shortly for the 2010 and 2012 Olympic Games. With the exception of the Calgary and Lillehammer Games, the CBC had always produced the Olympics. A key part of its sports brand was its amateur-sport strategy: it promised Canadians that they would already know the athletes when they mounted the podium. Being in Vancouver, the 2010 Games would be the most important Olympics for Canada in a generation.

The other great sports contracts were also coming to an end. The most important of these was *Hockey Night in Canada*. Since the dawn of time, before the beginning of television, when the CBC was radio only—during the Pleistocene Era—*Hockey Night in Canada* had been there. It was the oldest continuing media property in the world, the signature show of the Corporation, its one great bond with the general public in its entirety. The French loss of *La Soirée du hockey* to the Réseau des sports had been the subject of bitter denunciations. Parliamentary committees had looked into the matter, excoriating the president and my counterpart at Radio-Canada. Whatever else might happen, *Hockey Night in Canada* had to be renewed.

The second year would also be the year to start reforming the entertainment shows. This would take a while. Making a new drama series or a new comedy is complicated, expensive and time-consuming. After the development of scripts and bibles, the shooting of pilots and the making and financing of series, it typically takes two to three years before a new show gets on air. We would have to start pretty much from scratch, with a new team and a brand new approach to the shows. It was hard to imagine that anything could reach the airwaves before the fall of 2007. As an impatient person, I had trouble accepting the idea that two-and-a-half years would pass before I could make even a preliminary mark. I worried that it was far too slow.

The third year would focus on news. This was without doubt the most dangerous part of the job. The news department—Fort News, as it was known inside the CBC—had a fearsome reputation. It regarded itself as a law unto itself, independent not just of the government of the day but of the CBC board, the president and the head of English television. Attempts to change the news department would be extremely ill-received. Fort News would feel honour-bound to take down any management impertinent enough to try. In fact, it treated the taunting and destruction of management as a much-loved blood sport.

My predecessor, the genial and cautious Harold Redekopp, had made it his policy to leave it alone. He rarely, if ever, showed up on the fourth floor of the Broadcast Centre, where the newsroom had its headquarters. He was well aware of how dangerous it could be when provoked.

Thus, the plan for news was to approach it cautiously. The best strategy would be to engage in a flanking movement, starting with Fort News' peripheral positions, the most lightly guarded of its redoubts, then moving on to its most heavily defended keeps and bunkers. This meant starting with local news, the unloved but essential supper hours, where the journalists and hosts had toiled for many years without honour and success. By approaching the local news first, it might be possible to build some allies in the regions and establish the principle that it was not altogether inappropriate for me to express a view about news.

By the end of year three, 2006–07, I hoped we would have concluded the labour issues, secured the sports rights, made progress on our entertainment shows and begun chipping away at the local news. If all went well, and if a few big fish could be landed, then maybe the employees of the CBC would believe that change was possible, that it was in fact happening and that success might result. This would then set the stage for the final assault, the breaching of Fort News' watchtowers and defensive walls, and the entry into the city itself, where the hand-to-hand combat would occur. With luck, only mopping-up operations would be left by 2008.

That, then, was my plan. I hoped that if it worked we would be able to reverse the thirty years of decline and begin to make the CBC relevant to Canadians again. There would be only one measure for success: audiences. If Canadians did not watch, it meant they did not care. If they watched, I was sure that the Corporation's fortunes would reverse. Everything would be pinned on rebuilding the audiences. In the words of the BBC, whose slogans are plastered all over the walls of White City, their great studio complex in west London, "Audiences mean everything to us."

It would be a brutal standard. It would contradict much of the Corporation's rhetoric for the last fifty years. It would no longer allow the Corporation to fudge the meaning of success by talking vaguely about "mandates" and "quality." It would be absolutely clear whether we succeeded or failed. It would be an ineluctable standard, but one that everyone could understand. It would be the standard by which shows, producers, stars and executives would be judged. If Canadians did not like what was offered, it would be axed. If Canadians said yes, it would be kept. It would sort clearly and simply the quick from the dead.

This too would be controversial and resisted. It would be mocked as the triumph of commercialism, vulgarity and American values. As the bearer of this standard, I would certainly be reviled. I would inevitably be accused of "dumbing down" the CBC and breaking faith with its great traditions. I knew that I would pay a price for saying that audiences mattered above all. I knew all that. But if not audiences, then what?

> Man is born free, and
> everywhere he is in chains.
> Jean-Jacques Rousseau,
> *The Social Contract*

two
LABOUR

MIDNIGHT. THE DARK hour. August 14, 2005. The unionized employees of the Canadian Media Guild (CMG) left quietly. There was no shouting, no singing, no cursing. They turned off their computers, closed the doors to central control and the edit suites, shut off the lights and walked silently into the Toronto summer night.

Fred Mattocks and I watched them leave from ten stories above the atrium floor. Mattocks, the head of operations and master mechanic of the CBC, dressed always in black, gloomy and brilliant, had been preparing for months for this moment. He had created contingency plans to keep the place running in the case of a strike or lockout. And now it had begun. The first test of the plan would start at 12:01 AM, but the real test would begin the next morning, when the picket lines would go up and management would take over day-to-day operations.

As the CMG employees left, security moved in. Our first fear had been sabotage: corrupted programs, damaged trucks, inoperable control rooms, smashed studios. It can be done in a minute, the minute just before departure. But nothing. Everything was intact. The employees left as they would any night, calmly, as though anticipating their return to work the next day. They would not be back for almost two months.

Outside Toronto, in Halifax, St. John's, Winnipeg, Regina, Calgary, Edmonton, Vancouver, Victoria and the dozens of smaller offices across the country, the doors were locked as the employees left. The buildings were completely vacated, the studios darkened, the edit suites and camera and control rooms turned off. Power was shut down altogether. When the employees arrived the next morning to set up their picket lines, they would be marching around vacant buildings. There would be nobody inside to read their signs, see their shaking fists or hear their angry, bewildered denunciations.

All the regional management staff had been moved to Toronto. For months, we had retrained them so that they could operate the organization. People who had not handled a camera or put together a radio show in years were going to be called upon to do it again. We needed to make sure they understood the new systems and procedures. It was essential that the CBC stay on the air if we were to survive.

Our ambitions were not great. Radio would consist almost exclusively of music and repeats of old shows, interspersed with a little weather, rudimentary news and station identifications. It would certainly not be the usual CBC radio, with its endless stream of brilliant talk shows, current affairs programs and news. When Canadians tuned in, they would find something to listen to—not much, perhaps, but something. CBC radio might be in the intensive care unit, but it would at least be able to smile wanly and reassure everyone that it was still alive. We expected to see massive audience erosion.

Television was another matter. If anything, it was much easier to manage. Summer is the dead zone. Networks typically offer repeats of the season's best shows along with movies and other chewed-over fare. The only live programming is news and sports. We had worked particularly hard to make sure that The National would continue to appear and that we could broadcast the football games on weekends.

For the news, we hauled two old anchors out of their management positions, dusted them off, made them up and put them back in front of a camera. We provided them with a "rip and read" made up of items torn from the wire services, supplemented with agency footage and news from the BBC. It would not be The National, but it would be news. Our plan was to start with a few minutes on the first day and grow as time went by. If you came every night to the CBC for news at 10:00 PM, it would be there.

Football was more difficult. To cover the games, we needed to take our trucks to the venues. Fortunately we had the assistance of the much smaller of CBC's two unions, the Association of Professionals and Supervisors (APS). Although the APS represents only about 5 percent of the Corporation's workforce, it is essential to the operation of the trucks that contain the mobile production studios. With them, we would be able to put the games on television. The only problem was that we had no idea how to provide the play-by-play and colour commentary. Nevertheless, if Canadians tuned in to watch the games, the games would be there.

It was important to hold the audiences for television. We needed to maintain as much of our advertising revenue as we could. We needed, as well, to send the union a message. If the audiences held up reasonably well, it would be harder for the union to hold out. We were fairly confident we could maintain most of our television audiences. Nobody else was.

The next morning, the picket lines went up around the CBC buildings across the country. The CMG had signs and placards ready to go. They were simple but effective. The best of them showed black-and-white photographs of famous on-air personalities, gagged, with the single word *Silenced* written across them. They stared balefully out of their pictures like Solzhenitsyn imprisoned in the gulag. There were Peter Mansbridge, Ian Hanomansing, Heather Hiscox and Wendy Mesley with black tape across their mouths, mute and oppressed. Management was going to lose the public relations war utterly.

At 1:30 that afternoon, the head of the Canadian Media Guild, Arnold Amber, arrived to make a speech and rally the troops. He stood on a platform constructed in the park adjacent to the Toronto Broadcast Centre. He is short, with a bald head and bull-like appearance. He resembles a retired wrestler. In his speech, he defined the union's plan, explaining that the Paul Martin Liberal government was "not only a minority government in this country, but there is a pending federal election promised by the prime minister. This means that the views of every MP are important."

He urged everyone listening to contact their MPs and apply political pressure to stop the lockout. He played the first card in the union's attempt to conclude the negotiations in the press and in Ottawa, rather than at the bargaining table.

It was clear from the beginning that the union's strategy was to seek a government-imposed resolution. To that end, it was essential for them to get the press on-side, as well as the members of Parliament. In the fall of 2005, the government was in a minority. The House of Commons was electric with pre-election manoeuvring. No rational MP would want to be off-side with the media.

That evening, management was able to cobble together a fifteen-minute newscast for the 10:00 PM time slot. *The National* was still on the air. It might be a little ramshackle and heavy on BBC material, but it was there. Outside the building, Peter Mansbridge, the host of *The National*, made his first and only appearance on the picket line. He wore a baseball cap, expressed vague words of solidarity, walked around the building and left. The rank and file were happy to see him.

The next morning, the lockout was front page news in the major newspapers. "Lockout ravages the CBC" was the lead article above the fold in the *Globe and Mail*. The *Toronto Star*'s media critic, Antonia Zerbisias, wrote, "CBC TV will never recover. You can already smell the dead air." John Doyle, writing in the arts section of the *Globe and Mail*, concluded tartly that "CBC management is committing political suicide." Indeed as the lockout progressed, his contempt for management became withering. On a number of occasions, he referred to us as "spineless rats" and the whole management team as "Fort Dork."

The coverage was similar across the country. The consensus seemed to be that whatever the issues, CBC management was a pack of idiots and that the lockout would irreparably damage the Corporation. There was no possibility that audiences would ever return. For reasons of vanity, pig-headedness or sheer venality, management was destroying Canada's greatest cultural institution.

Outside the Toronto Broadcast Centre, the silenced workers marched around the empty buildings, angry and confused. Their leaders demanded political intervention to save the beloved Corporation. Inside, management struggled with unfamiliar responsibilities, trying to produce television and radio. Many among their ranks feared that the papers were right and that the CBC would never recover. Television's audiences were the lowest in its history when the lockout began; we could not afford a further fall. The mood was grim.

MAINTAINING THE APS'S assistance in helping management run the Corporation during the CMG lockout was crucial—football was essential both to maintain our revenues and to show the CMG that we could continue without them.

To keep the APS members on-side, it was critical that we never ask them to perform "struck" work or put them in a position where they might appear as "scabs." We never did, but it was still very difficult for APS. Every day their members had to cross the CMG picket lines, past their locked-out brothers and sisters with their $300 a week of strike pay and into the arms of the wicked management.

These two unions represented 90 percent of the CBC workforce. The CMG alone was 85 percent of the employees and incorporated all sorts of skills and occupations, from electricians and clerks to archivists, cameramen, mechanics, producers, writers and hosts. It included everyone from obscure technicians and drivers to the Corporation's most famous and best-paid employees. Peter Mansbridge, Wendy Mesley, George Stroumboulopoulos, Anna Maria Tremonti, Ron MacLean, Don Cherry and Heather Hiscox all pay union dues. Indeed, the CMG represents all sorts of professions never normally seen within a union, including the sales force and many low-level managers.

Ninety percent is by any standard an extraordinarily high level of unionization. By way of contrast, only 45 percent of the BBC is unionized. At the rest of Canada's media companies, journalists and technicians are typically unionized but almost nobody else is. Media companies without news departments are often completely non-union shops. The high level of unionization at the CBC, combined with the multiplicity of rules and contractual arrangements, made for a rigid and complicated labour situation.

The CMG represents workers in a number of other Canadian broadcasters, including TVOntario and VisionTV (now ZoomerMedia). It is also affiliated with the Canadian Newspaper Guild, which represents journalists at all the big daily papers across the country. So the journalists covering the lockout were covering the travails of their brothers and sisters, cruelly silenced and impoverished.

It is odd that the CBC is unionized, let alone so heavily unionized. The CBC is Canada's largest cultural organization. It is supposed to search out and uphold the highest standards of creativity and imagination. It is about writing, composing, acting, directing, producing, talking and interviewing, all activities that place a premium on surprise, daring and originality. It needs to be able to recognize and nurture talent wherever it comes from.

Unions, on the other hand, are focused on ensuring that people keep their jobs. They are focused on tenure. They are about protecting employees from dismissal, and they are about ensuring that the longer a person has been employed, the greater the protection received. Security is the bedrock principle of trade unionism. If a senior person's job disappears, they can "bump" a junior and take the junior person's job.

Unions are also committed to establishing clear and rigid job descriptions. A writer cannot be a composer. A cameraman cannot be an editor. A host cannot be a producer. Unions like arrangements where everything is neatly categorized and defined. They do not like lines to be blurred, whether by imagination or technology. They do not like to see new ways of thinking and pursuing business.

What unions cherish is often the opposite of what creativity requires. One places emphasis on order, hierarchy, deference and age; the other prizes novelty, feeling, rebellion and youth. Trade unionism—despite its self-image—is inherently conservative. It works to advantage the old and exclude the young; it works to reward time served rather than ideas invented. It seeks order and predictability; it is uncomfortable with change.

Unions would, of course, dispute this characterization. They would argue that while they seek security for their members, it does not come at the expense of creativity. To the contrary, tenure is the very bedrock of freedom and imagination. How can one take chances if there is always the danger that in doing so one could lose one's job? How can journalists be bold if the price may be dismissal? How can artists, interviewers and producers challenge authority and break new ground if they can be arbitrarily disciplined? Tenure is the essential counterweight to the dead hand of management conservatism.

In fact, reality seems to be the exact opposite of theory. Those people who are most secure are typically the least daring; and those who are the least secure are often the most daring. Film producers, entrepreneurs, freelance journalists, politicians, musicians—none of them have guarantees of job security. They make their own way. If they fail, there is no one to catch them. To avoid failing, they must do new things, they must take chances to distinguish themselves and give people a compelling reason to come to their movies, companies, articles, platforms and songs. They certainly will not come if the same old, same old is all that they're offered.

This dispute about the value of tenure lay at the heart of much that separated the CMG's goals from those of management. The union believed that job security was the key to freedom of expression. Management, for its part, believed that creative renewal required an infusion of new blood and new ideas at the Corporation. Ultimately, the interweaving of the themes of creativity, job security and journalistic integrity served to politicize the debate. A dispute about contracts and labour relations was transformed into an ideological campaign that inevitably led to polarization and bitterness.

These differences in view were compounded by the pace of technological and competitive change. The union's traditional preferences for seniority, rigidity and job clarity were being challenged on every side. As the old world of analogue cameras, edit suites and production gave way to the new digital one, distinctions among technologies and jobs began to collapse. When everything is digitized and computerized, old occupational walls are removed. Not only is it easy to shoot, record, edit and report at the same time, it is increasingly desirable. More and more, the traditional team of cameraman, producer and journalist is giving way to a single person performing all three functions. The videographer—as the name suggests—supplants the team that came before.

Not only do these developments erode the old job classifications, they erode the hierarchy of traditional skills. Older workers who grew up in the analogue age often find themselves hard-pressed to keep up with the digital performance of their younger colleagues. Young people who grew up computer literate, as much at ease with the new media platforms as the old, challenge the assumptions of seniority. If their skills are greater than their elders', if the beginners look more like the masters, the ladder of age is compromised.

None of this, of course, was unique to the CBC. The digital shift affected every media organization. The private newspapers and television companies were equally overwhelmed by the speed of technological change. As well, the new technologies created whole new competitors offering news and entertainment on previously non-existent platforms. Websites had emerged to challenge the dominance of the old print and television companies. Great search engines—Google and Bing—found relevant stories and information without the time-consuming rustle of pages or the wait for the hourly newscast. Social networks—Facebook, Myspace, YouTube— called into question the power of the ancient commentariat. They flattened the hierarchies of authority, opening the conversation to everyone.

Ultimately these changes would require the CBC to re-conceive its very character. As it became increasingly possible for Canadians to find the shows and news that they wanted wherever and however they wanted them, it was necessary to rethink the nature of our business. We could no longer think of the CBC as a radio company or a television company; we had to begin to understand it as a "content" company. When we covered the news, we needed to produce it for all the ways Canadians might consume it, whether on TV, radio, Twitter, Facebook or YouTube. Similarly when we made a drama series, we had to envision from the outset how its associated website, interactive game or social media forum would work. Inevitably this transition to a "content" company would require more fluidity in job descriptions and a much higher level of skills.

For the CBC, these pressures were—if anything—even greater than they were for the private sector. The Corporation's audiences, which have always skewed old, were aging faster than the privates'. Management's inability to stop the precipitous collapse in television's audience share could only be compounded by the new platforms, which would inevitably steal more share. If the CBC could not strengthen its skill set, increase its flexibility and move more aggressively into the digital age, it could find itself falling even further behind. For its part, management felt that it had no option but to seek significant changes in its agreement with the CMG.

When I arrived at the CBC in 2004, negotiations with the union had been underway for almost six months. They had yielded very little. Discussions took place regularly, but nothing of substance was agreed. Instead, the parties met, recited their positions to each other, made little speeches and adjourned.

The negotiations were led on the management side by George Smith, the vice-president of Human Resources, who was an expert on labour relations. He had previously worked at Air Canada and Canadian Pacific, which like the CBC had histories of combustible tensions between management and labour. Despite working in a notoriously chippy and aggressive area, George Smith was himself calm and measured. He exuded an air of quiet thoughtfulness. Many described him as wise. His tranquility and wisdom would be put to a severe test by the lockout of 2005.

The negotiations were not about money or benefits. They were about workplace management, skills and employment status. They were about the arcana of operating a modern media company. It seemed to me—in my vast naïveté—poor ground for mounting a holy war.

The first and most important issue—and the one that became the basis for real bitterness—was management's desire to employ more contract workers. Management's reasoning was simple. Particular shows came and went, depending on their success. The same was true of hosts and anchors. Why not, therefore, simply hire the appropriate producers, directors and hosts for the life of the show? When the show was over, those people would depart. This seemed sensible enough, since the skills needed to make a cooking show were very different from those involved in mounting an investigative series on financial fraud or producing a dancing competition.

To ensure fairness, the contract workers would enjoy the same salaries and benefits as the CBC's permanent staff. They would also pay dues to the union in the usual fashion. This would prevent concerns that people were being hired on contract to save money, or disadvantage the union. They would be hired simply because their skills were the best match for the shows being made.

The second issue was management's wish to increase the level of cross-skilling and multi-skilling. In the era of digital technology, it was important that employees be able to handle multiple tasks and technologies. Management wanted to make sure that they could shoot, record and edit, that they could file reports for both television and radio, and that they were able to embrace new media as well as old. At the very least, the CBC had to be able to keep pace with teenagers producing content in their basements.

This set of requirements was essential if the Corporation was to navigate emerging new media and make the transition to a "content" company. It would need a much more skilled workforce with the flexibility to move easily and seamlessly from one platform to another. To accomplish this, we needed to create a common set of practices and standards, since it was impossible to imagine working in these new environments when the most elementary work rules differed significantly from one group of workers to another within the Corporation. Management wanted to harmonize the contracts so that the rules on everything from lunch breaks to bumping would be the same.

This was a particularly difficult set of demands for the CMG, since it had only recently been formed out of the merger of three separate unions: the original CMG, which had represented journalists; CEP (Communications, Energy and Paperworkers Union of Canada), which had represented technicians; and CUPE (Canadian Union of Public Employees), which had represented administrators. As a result of the merger, bruised egos and internal rivalries lingered.

Finally, management wanted to ensure that when senior workers "bumped" into jobs held by junior workers, they would have the skills to do them. In the past, significant problems had arisen because this was not necessarily the case. On one occasion, for example, an archivist was bumped into a producer's job on a daily radio show. It is hard to imagine more different skills and operating environments. The archivists are trained as librarians and conceive their work over time spans that sometimes cover decades. Radio producers, on the other hand, are trained typically as journalists and work within time spans of minutes. Asking an archivist to work as a radio producer is like asking a banker to work as a veterinarian. The jobs had nothing in common, save that they were represented by the same union.

The bumping standard that management wanted was "Demonstrated Occupational Qualifications." If a person was to bump into a job, they had to be able to demonstrate that they could do it. This becomes even more important with the transition to digital technology and advanced platforms. Younger workers often have more relevant digital skills than older ones, so it is essential that when they are bumped their skills not be lost at the same time. When the pace of change is slow, bumping is not an issue. When the pace of change is fast, it can become an enormous problem.

My impression after I first reviewed management's objectives for the labour negotiations was that nobody could seriously object to them. The CMG would never be able to convince the CBC employees to strike in order to avoid these objectives. How, I asked myself, could the union ask its members to strike on behalf of contract workers who had not yet been hired? How could it argue against higher skill levels or ensuring that the people bumping could actually do the jobs they were going into? Thoughtful CBC employees—many of whom were exceptionally gifted journalists and well-educated producers—would never vote for a strike over issues as sensible as these.

Besides, strikes at the CBC make no financial sense. In normal companies, strikes are designed to put pressure on the shareholders.

As the strike wears on, revenues decline and profits with them. As a result, less and less money is available to pay costs, meet banking covenants or pay dividends. As the shareholders see the value of their investments decline, they eventually throw in the towel and agree to enough of the union's demands to get their employees back to work. Strikes work by creating financial pressure on the struck company.

This could never be the case with the CBC. The Corporation does not have any dividends to erode or shares to depreciate. In fact, strikes at the CBC can work to the financial advantage of the Corporation, particularly in radio. When the radio employees strike, the CBC no longer has to pay their salaries, which are about 80 percent of the total costs of radio. At the same time, there are no revenues to lose if audiences decline, since CBC radio carries no advertising. Thus a strike at CBC radio will actually improve the financial position of the company. The same is also true to a lesser extent for CBC television.

But even if that were not the case, and the CBC faced significant revenue losses as a result of a strike, striking would still make no sense. Because the Corporation spends all the money it takes in, there are no profits or dividends. Losses cannot be covered from the pockets of the shareholders. Rather they must be paid for in job reductions. Looking again at radio, where the impact would be greater, if 80 percent of the cost base is salaries, then 80 percent of any losses must be recovered from salary reductions. The horrible dilemma for a CBC union is that if it strikes and succeeds in inflicting financial pain on the Corporation, its own members will ultimately pay the price.

I was confident that given the sheer silliness of a strike, the union could never get the CBC employees to vote for it. Robert Rabinovitch and George Smith disagreed. There had been a long history of strikes at the CBC. They fully expected the CMG to win a strike vote. The employees would happily provide the union an overwhelming mandate to strengthen its hand. Then, they doubtless hoped, the CMG would deliver an excellent contract at one minute to midnight, when management folded its hand. That had happened on a number of occasions in the past. They cautioned me that I was being naive. But I was optimistic in my ignorance and confident in the good sense of the employees—and I turned out to be utterly and completely wrong.

The union regarded much of management's position as nonsensical. They saw it as an attempt to roll back concessions that had been achieved through tough bargaining over the years and an effort to limit the union's power. If new skills were needed, the solution was obvious: retrain the workforce. If greater flexibility was required, hire more workers. If there was not enough money, go to Ottawa and get more. That surely was management's job: not to grind the employees, but to make the case compellingly to the federal government that the CBC needed a bigger budget. If management could not do that, then it simply showed—again—how inadequate they were.

By May 2005, negotiations had been going on for over a year. Regular meetings had accomplished nothing. The poisonous culture of the CBC made everything worse. The blistering contempt for management, the ideological overlays of self-righteousness, the sense of peril in the collapsing audiences, the vanity and self-regard of the institution—all made for a dangerous climate. As negotiations unfolded and gave way to the lockout, the two sides became more and more polarized. Compromise began to seem like weakness.

The talks ground on endlessly, with both sides making little speeches at each other, reciting lists of ancient grievances and slights, denouncing each other's honesty, impugning each other's motives and being rude about each other's mothers. Through it all, no real bargaining occurred.

The glacial pace of the talks confirmed for management that the CMG was playing for time. We assumed that it was dragging things out so that it could claim to its members that management was intransigent. It could say, in effect, "Look at this. A whole year and no progress. None. Management is utterly unresponsive!" It could then say that it needed a strike vote to give management an incentive to begin real bargaining.

If there was a strike, ideally it would be taken at the time when the union felt it could do most damage to the company. Everyone agreed that this would be with the launch of the fall season and the return of hockey. And the return of hockey in 2005 was the real return of hockey. The National Hockey League had locked out its players for the entirety of the previous season, and Canadians had been suffering serious hockey withdrawal pains for over a year. The prospect that hockey would come back, but not come back to the CBC, was too much to bear.

The timing was also politically attractive. The minority Martin government looked like it might fall at any time. Certainly nobody expected it to last for very long after the Gomery Report on financial shenanigans was delivered in October, charging the Liberals with much bad behaviour. This meant two good things for the union. First, the pressure on management to settle would become intolerable if an election was called. Could anyone—even the lunatics running the Corporation—imagine a federal election without the CBC to cover it? Impossible.

Second, and equally importantly, the mounting election fever meant that all the parties were ready to go. None of them would do or say anything to disadvantage themselves with the electorate. None of them would side with management. It would be political suicide. What sensible politician would contemplate coming out against the journalists who were to cover his campaign? It would hardly be a way to endear oneself or get a fair hearing. In fact, the opposite would be the wiser course. Attacking the stupidity and cruelty of management could work to one's advantage. The journalists would be grateful.

Timing a strike—even just a threatened strike—for the fall of 2005 seemed exceptionally promising. To get there, the union needed to conduct a strike vote in the summer. If they timed it for mid-July, they could strike anytime up to mid-September, which would coincide nicely with the return of Parliament, hockey and the fall shows. Besides, mid-July was a pleasant time to have a strike vote. Sunny weather and summer holidays would put the union members in a cheerful and optimistic mood, making it easier for them to say yes.

The idea of a strike was a terrible prospect for management. The audiences for CBC television were at an all-time low, and there was deep concern that if the audience share collapsed further, it might never recover, even to its current anaemic levels. If that happened, advertising revenues would dry up and the Corporation would fall into even greater financial difficulties.

We were also pretty certain that the CBC's competitors would try and take advantage of a strike. Our spies had told us that CTV was planning to relaunch their all-news network to make it a stronger competitor to Newsworld. The dreaded Ivan Fecan, the president of CTV, was taking a close personal interest in the matter—it was widely believed that he wanted to have the number one news network. He was apparently following the labour negotiations with enthusiasm, hoping that a strike might be called according to the CMG's ideal timing. If that happened, he would be able to relaunch his news network just as his most important competitor went dark.

The CBC board was also anxious. Two of its members were old CBC hands: Peter Herrndorf, who had been head of English services in the 1980s, and Trina McQueen, who had been head of news. Herrndorf and I had a relationship that went back many years. It was, unfortunately, an unhappy one. He had been distressed by my conduct on a number of occasions and, I believed, held a significant grudge. During the mid-1990s, I had attacked a report he had prepared on the future of Canada's cultural industries. We had clashed again a few years later when I had ousted him from the chairmanship of the Canadian Television Fund. As a result, he had stopped sending me Christmas cards. Although he would never say it, I assumed that he did not wish me well.

But the tensions were not only personal, they were also philosophical. Peter Herrndorf was of the old school. He believed that the CBC was fundamentally about news and information programming. To the extent that he thought about anything else, he was a proponent of the high arts on TV. His views had not changed over the years. If anything, they were reinforced by his position as head of the National Arts Centre. He was, as well, famously consensus-oriented. He did not like confrontations. We expected he would not support a tough line with the CMG.

Over lunch one day, Peter and I discussed the labour situation. He was blunt. "Your share is too low to take a strike," he said. "Besides, the whole thing is silly. There are not two sides at the CBC.

There is only one." I sensed that he felt we should concede and make a deal on the union's terms. The potential damage and strife within the family was not worth any gains management might make.

The board had been briefed extensively on the labour situation. Robert Rabinovitch, who had already had two strikes and a lock-out on the French side, made sure they understood exactly what was at issue in the negotiations. He and George Smith explained the necessity of creating common working conditions, greater flexibility and higher levels of cross-skilling and professional competence. The future of the CBC was at stake. If it was to succeed in the digital future, it had to change. The board was committed. The mood was grim but determined.

As the conversations with the board continued through early 2005, we pressed ahead with our contingency plans. Executives from all over the country were brought in and trained on operating the equipment. Sales executives were sent into edit suites, regional managers were put behind cameras, and financial whizzes were placed in the studios. Some had done these things before; some never had. The pressure on management was becoming great. Everyone had two jobs: the one they normally did and the one they were training to do.

The great focus was news and sports. Much of the airtime on radio and television could be filled with music and pre-recorded shows. News and sports, on the other hand, had to be live. They had to be shot, hosted, directed and produced by real people in real time.

The bigger of the two challenges was sports. Although we had worked out a method of getting our trucks to the football games, we could not figure out any way of providing play-by-play or colour commentary without using scabs, which would compromise our relationship with the APS. And if we lost its people, we lost our ability to cover the games at all.

At the time, Tom Wright was the commissioner of the Canadian Football League. For reasons that I did not understand, he was having difficulties with his bosses, the owners of the various teams. His contract was running out in the next six months and they refused to tell him whether they wanted to renew him. Instead, they forced him into a series of small humiliations that were the subject of cruel accounts in the press and considerable *schadenfreude* in the sports world.

From the little I had seen of Tom Wright, I liked him. He seemed a capable, straightforward, friendly sort of person. It was, therefore, with some reluctance that I phoned to tell him the bad news. It was going to be of no help to him with the owners.

I began by explaining what might happen if there was a strike or a lockout.

"No play-by-play or colour?" he asked incredulously.

"No," I confirmed.

"Is there absolutely nothing you can do about this? Could we have someone doing it remotely from the United States?"

"No. Not really. They would be seen as scabs."

"Well, what are you going to do then?"

"Nothing."

"Nothing? Will the games be silent?"

"No. We'll use the arena announcer. He calls the downs and penalties. It may be nicer, actually, without the endless blither blather of the commentators."

"Nicer?" he asked, his voice moving up a register. "Nicer? It will be a disaster."

"Well, there's nothing I can do about it. So let's make a virtue of necessity. Let's celebrate it as Arena Football. We'll tell the fans it will be great, just like being in the stands."

"Great? Just like being in the stands?"

As we finished our conversation, he moaned like a beast being conducted to the slaughterhouse.

At the board meeting in June, the board agreed that if no progress was made by the end of the mandatory conciliation period in August, we would lock the employees out. Nobody was happy with this decision, but the alternative would have been irresponsible. The damage would be much greater to the Corporation if the union struck in September.

For my part, I was pleased by the decision but I found the timing a little late. In my opinion, if we had to lock the employees out, it would be better to do so in July, since it would give us more time to resolve the issues with the CMG before the new season started and hockey returned. Robert Rabinovitch and George Smith felt that July would be too soon. We needed to show that we had gone the extra mile to avoid taking such drastic action.

As June gave way to July, the negotiations at the bargaining table ground to an almost complete halt. Nothing of any substance was resolved. The big issues about contracts, multi-skilling and bumping rules had not even been coherently broached, let alone advanced. Tempers were becoming short. Even calm and rational people were becoming frustrated. The hotheads in the union were becoming more dogmatic and fixed in their positions.

Early in July, the union began preparing a strike vote. In a series of detailed briefings, it explained to its members the inadequacy of management's position. It explained further that it needed a strong vote in favour of a strike to be able to strengthen its hand. It might not actually call a strike, but it needed the authority to do so.

The vote was held on July 13, a hot summer day. The result was overwhelming. Over 87 percent of the members voted for a strike. Now the union was in a position to put maximum pressure on management.

As if to aid the CMG further, the NHL settled with its players the same day. Gary Bettman and the League had won a crushing victory. It was nice for him, but it meant for certain that hockey would return in the fall. Calling a strike in September would now be ideal for the union.

I called Gary Bettman the next day to congratulate him and explain where we were with our own union. Unlike Tom Wright, he could not have been more genial. When I explained that we might have to lock the employees out and might not be able to broadcast the games, he laughed amiably.

"Well," he allowed, "I am hardly in a position to complain if you lock out your employees, am I?"

"No," I laughed with him.

"In fact," he said, "you may find it quite salubrious. I have done it twice and always feel much the better for it."

The principal officers of the CMG—the Central Committee, so to speak—were now in an excellent position. Arnold Amber, the president of the CBC branch of the CMG, was a news producer. He looks like what he is: tough and pugnacious. He had enjoyed a long career within the news department, chasing stories, making shows and defying management. His politics were of the libertarian left, expressed not just in his trade unionism but in his championing of journalists' rights. He was admired and feared for his cleverness and rigid determination. He had been elected by very large majorities of his colleagues.

His boss, the president of the CMG as a whole, Lise Lareau, was also a journalist. She was on leave from the CBC to the union, where she had been re-elected a number of times and in charge for a number of years. Although not as clever as Arnold, she was equally doctrinal. She deeply believed that the interests of the union and the CBC were one and the same. For her, management was an interloper, an uncalled-for and undesirable barrier to the realization of the Corporation's real mandate. The union struggle was a struggle for the soul of the CBC. As the lockout wore on, Lise Lareau began to claim that the CBC could only be saved if it was "taken back" from the management.

The final member of the Central Committee was Dan Oldfield, the unelected, permanent senior official of the CMG. He too had been a journalist, and quite a good one. He ran the office, managed grievances, worked out the practical details, papered over differences of view within the union and generally kept things working. Dan Oldfield had been around for a long time. He was noted for the profundity of his memory, the sharpness of his tongue and a taste for endless debate. He appeared to share Arnold and Lise's views on the appropriate role of the CBC. News and public affairs came first, and anything else broadcast by the CBC should be of the "higher" arts variety. That was the mandate.

As part of our efforts to facilitate a resolution, we had created a back door to the negotiating table. A couple of months earlier, I gave Arnold Amber my cell phone number. I explained that if he ever needed to speak to me privately, outside the confines of the formal process, he should call. We thought that unorthodox back channels might succeed where the more traditional methods did not.

On August 9, three weeks after the successful strike vote, Arnold Amber called asking to see me at his hotel room in downtown Toronto. He offered me a coffee. He looked confident, calm, a man in possession of himself and his circumstances. He advised me that there were two things he wanted to tell me.

"First," he said, "you are new here. Do not assume that because the CMG has not gone on strike before, that it will not do so."

"All right," I allowed.

"Second," he went on, "it is important for you to know that we have a substantial strike fund."

I told him that I already knew that.

He stared at me for a moment.

I asked if there was anything else he wanted to discuss. Did he, for example, want to review any of the issues between us at the bargaining table?

"No," he said. "That's all. It's important for you to know those two things." The whole meeting took maybe five minutes.

The message was simple. The CMG was perfectly able to go on strike. They had the will and the money. We should, therefore, stop our foolishness about contracts and demonstrated occupational qualifications. If we did not abandon our silly positions, he would pull the plug.

The next day, we gave the union seventy-two hours' notice that we would lock them out if we had not settled.

This seemed to come as a surprise to the Central Committee. They had misjudged the situation. They had apparently not learned anything from the experience on the French side, where the union had been locked out for a month. They must have thought that management and the board would never be tough enough to take such a step on the English side. Later, it became clear that certain board members may have encouraged them in this belief. We found out that there had been secret meetings, meetings that may well have left the CMG with the impression that the board was split. The union may have believed that they would have the upper hand and that the board would help them discipline the lunatics in management.

The CMG's rhetoric grew increasingly heated and intemperate. In press releases and communications to their members, they began referring to the management as "sociopaths." They started calling Robert Rabinovitch, George Smith and me "the Gang of Three." Sometimes they would extend this honour to Jane Chalmers, the head of radio, and call us "the Gang of Four." This was presumably a reference to Chairman Mao's mad wife and her associates, who had engineered many of the worst excesses of the Cultural Revolution. It seemed a little harsh to be lumped in with the people who had destroyed the Chinese educational system and economy, murdering millions in the process. But worse was to come. The vilification of management was just beginning.

THE FIRST FEW days of the lockout had a vaguely festive air. The weather was lovely. The employees circled the building in shorts and T-shirts, waving their signs at passersby. (In a clever piece of wording, signs opposing an increased number of contract workers decried a "disposable workforce.") Little kiosks were set up, providing cold drinks. Occasional songs and fragments of laughter ran through the crowd.

On the first day of the lockout, there were still over forty unresolved issues between the union and management. Rather than backing down and negotiating, however, the union took ten days off. The Central Committee had decided that the first order of business was to win the argument in the press and then with politicians in Ottawa.

The other media outlets were on board with the union from the start. If anything, their rhetoric was even angrier. The "spineless rats" and "sociopaths" had made a terrible blunder. The CBC's tiny audiences would be further eroded. The brand would be permanently damaged. The CBC's supporters—its "stakeholders"—would revolt. The other networks would eat the Corporation's lunch. The CBC would never recover. The chorus of expert opinion was deafening and unanimous.

Typical of the sneering quality of the coverage was Michael Posner's attack on management in the *Globe and Mail*. He started referring to Robert Rabinovitch, patronizingly, as "Little Bobby" (Rabinovitch is not tall). He called the lockout "Little Bobby's Brainstorm" and wrote, "And why, in a hopelessly fractured media universe, where audiences were as fickle as the fingers on the remote control and with CBC television floundering for an identity, had he decided to play Russian roulette with the future of the country's most important, tax-payer funded cultural institution?" It was, he went on, "typical of CBC management's unerring gift for mismanagement." There it was. CBC management had been measured and found wanting. We were obviously idiots.

In fact, the coverage seemed to me so lopsided that at a certain point, I phoned the editors of the *Globe and Mail* and the *Toronto Star*. "Did they," I gently inquired, "not think that there might be another side to the story?" Well, huffed the editors, you know how it is: our journalists hate management, and if we were to intervene it would only make things worse, and journalists are a difficult lot, and besides, you are overreacting, it's not as bad as you think; don't be so thin skinned, there are issues of freedom of expression involved, etc., etc. It was pretty clear that they would not do anything.

Expressions of support for the union cause poured in from all quarters. The National Union of Journalists in Britain picketed the BBC for allowing us to use their news feeds. Buzz Hargrove and the Canadian Labour Congress arrived to make speeches supporting the locked-out workers and denouncing the sociopaths. Passing cars honked in solidarity.

Meanwhile the Central Committee toured Ottawa, popping into MPs' offices, urging their support. They did not need to remind the politicians that the locked-out employees included many of Canada's most senior and influential journalists. Every night, on the rival newscasts, they could see the workers walking around the Toronto Broadcast Centre and the shuttered regional offices across the country. Many of the journalists themselves were actively distributing leaflets and organizing rallies. Brian Stewart and Hana Gartner sponsored an evening entitled CBC *Sings the Blues: An*

Evening of Celebration and Solidarity. The irrepressible Shelagh Rogers made her way across the country denouncing management. Andy Barrie broadcast from the university radio station at Ryerson. When the Central Committee visited the politicians, everyone knew who they represented.

As part of their Ottawa effort, they asked the government to withhold the public subsidy for the duration of the lockout. They phoned the Corporation's big advertisers, suggesting they should pull their money. Why, they urged, would anyone want to be associated with the degraded and villainous management? Just read the papers. Everyone acknowledges the lockout was a terrible mistake. Fortunately for the Central Committee and the members of the CMG, both the government and the big advertisers ignored their request. That averted significant job losses.

Meanwhile, inside the CBC's Toronto office, management went about the unfamiliar task of putting out the *National* newscast. The first night, they managed to produce a ten-minute program. As the weeks wore on, *The National* grew to a full thirty minutes. The management team settled into their new jobs. The newscast strengthened and became more compelling. The troubling and disturbing thing was that the audience numbers were not that much lower than those of the real *National* in all its majesty, with Peter Mansbridge in the chair. The show held almost two-thirds of its normal audience.

The newspaper journalists were particularly certain that football would fail. *Toronto Star* sports reporter Chris Zelcovich observed that our plan to cover the games was fraught with peril: "Whether this is arrogance or desperation, this could be a disaster waiting to happen . . . television people say that football is one of the last sports they would want to do with a skeleton crew comprised of management long removed from the production truck. It is also one of the last sports they would want to do without announcers. Why do they think the CFL has been fighting this all week?" He concluded that a fiasco was in the works.

The first game in the new format did well. We managed to sneak our trucks into the arena. We then took the play-by-play as it was called inside the stadium by the arena announcer. Just as I had promised CFL commissioner Tom Wright, we promoted the games as the real football experience. It was—we crowed—just as though you were sitting in the stands. Surprisingly the audience numbers for the first game were more or less the same as they would normally have been.

The following weekend, we did the same thing again; we actively promoted our Arena Football broadcasts, snuck our trucks into the arenas and picked up the stadium announcers calling the downs and the score. This time, the numbers were significantly better than normal. It appeared that Canadians preferred Arena Football to the intrusion of the play-by-play and colour commentators. This was helpful in strengthening our hand against the union.

Tom Wright, however, was another matter. He was almost apoplectic. His spokesperson would appear in the press, fulminating about the inadequacy of our efforts. I found this mystifying. The CFL knew that we really had no alternative. We were doing our best to make the proverbial silk purse from a sow's ear. What was the point of mocking our efforts and talking down their own product? When I asked Wright about it, he could not see that he was damaging himself. To the contrary, he was adamant that *we* needed to change. Later we would pay a heavy price for his unhappiness.

The commissioner's dismay was nothing, however, compared to the relentless drumbeat of attacks in the press. The newspapers poured it on. Our sanity was challenged; we were dismissed as "vandals." The union's references to us as the Gang of Four began to resonate in other places. As we continued our desecration of the CBC and its distinguished employees, we were characterized as hooligans and cultural looters. The Red Guards seemed moderate by comparison. Our communication strategy was not working.

We redoubled our efforts, but nobody was listening to us or wanted to listen to us. It was reported that the contract workers would receive no benefits. They would toil like indentured serfs under the cruel whip of the CBC overlords. The newly cross-skilled workers would be required to do everything, leading to inevitable exhaustion and burnout. Workers with seniority would not be able to bump into any job unless they possessed doctoral degrees from distinguished European universities.

We tried everything to clarify our views. We printed up pamphlets with accurate accounts of our proposals, but to no avail. The CBC's own journalists, notoriously sceptical of everything, declined to read them. In my son's political science class, the professor denounced the CBC management as "thugs." My son was obliged to ask whether the professor recognized his last name.

At one point, Jane Chalmers and I decided to write an "open letter" explaining management's position and what we were looking for in the new contract. It was not well received. Reviewing it in the *Globe and Mail*, Heather Mallick wrote: "The open letter was a giant splat of euphemisms, jargon, pointless repetition, self-congratulation and cliché, but, perhaps most important, incomprehensibility, as if someone had just thrown a cream pie at the newspaper page and let it drip."

It seemed that we were not getting our message out in a convincing way.

With the wind in their sail, the Central Committee became even more intemperate. They began to target individual members of management even more aggressively. They began to speak about "taking back" the public broadcaster. It seemed they were calling for the establishment of some sort of broadcasting collective run by the members of the union. Perhaps they hoped to see a series of CBC soviets established across the country.

Outside the CBC offices, the employees continued to circle the buildings with their placards and signs. Every day I had to cross their lines. Every day I felt their hostility and anger. Every day my heart went out to them as they wondered how they would survive on their meagre strike pay. A month into the lockout, and many of them would have exhausted their savings and have difficulty making ends meet. Every day I knew they would be worrying about their children and their mortgages.

Despite all the union's marches and the financial plight of the employees, nothing much was happening at the bargaining table. Then, on September 14, a month into the lockout, the CMG announced that great progress was being made and that a deal would be done within a week. The next day it tabled proposals for arrangements so retrograde that they had been rejected in the 1970s. It felt like the negotiations were going backwards.

The board of directors was also coming under significant pressure. The union had bombarded them with memos since the beginning of August, explaining the wickedness of management and asking for meetings to explain its own point of view. Our lawyers objected to these activities, arguing that it was a violation of the union's duty to bargain in good faith. Nevertheless, it was clear that some board members had been meeting with them.

The board itself had changed significantly during the lockout. The president, Robert Rabinovitch, had been acting as chair since the departure of Carole Taylor, the previous board chair, some months earlier. For reasons that were never clear, the government decided to appoint a new board chair at the most delicate possible moment: Guy Fournier, a well-known screenwriter. It was a bizarre appointment.

Fournier had no experience managing a large corporation. He knew nothing about labour relations. He was in fact widely regarded as a buffoon. This reputation would later be confirmed when he made a series of silly and intemperate remarks. Most notably, he observed in the course of an interview for *7 Jours*: "In Lebanon, the law makes it possible for men to have sexual intercourse with animals as long as they are females. To do the same thing with male animals could lead to the death penalty." The Lebanese community was not amused.

He compounded the problem when he was interviewed about the pleasures of the flesh on a French-language station in Toronto. He allowed that he liked nothing better than a good shit. It was superior to sex. This became known as the kaka interview. Eventually he would have to resign from the board when the Conservative minister of Canadian heritage, Bev Oda, indicated that she would stand up in the House of Commons and say she had no confidence in him.

On September 20, the board met in a state of some despair. The lockout was in its fifth week. Opinion was overwhelmingly on the side of the CMG. Somehow the union found out where the meeting was being held and showed up to urge the board members to discipline the Gang of Four. When we arrived at the Place d'Armes, a little hotel in Old Montreal, the whole of the Central Committee was there. They smiled and greeted us with ironic enthusiasm. Arnold Amber, Lise Lareau and Dan Oldfield looked cheerful. This worried me.

As the meeting wore on, it became clear that a number of board members had met with the union behind management's back. *On the Line*, the CMG's newsletter, speculated that Peter Herrndorf, Trina McQueen and Guy Fournier had met secretly with the union. Certainly the CMG was in a position to know who had met with it and who had not.

Peter Herrndorf was not much of a surprise. He had told me months earlier that he did not think a work stoppage was a good idea. He was also a guy with a reputation for wanting to be liked by everyone. Guy Fournier was also not much of a surprise. Trina McQueen was, however, a bit unexpected, at least to me. I had always liked and admired Trina, respecting her judgment even when we disagreed. We had worked together on the board of the Canadian Television Fund and when I was executive director of Telefilm. The idea that she had met with the union seemed implausible.

The board meeting began inauspiciously. It was clear that some members had met with the union and some had not. The room crackled with tension. The members who had not met with the union looked dark. The chairman asked the management to leave. Presumably he did not want us to see the board fracture.

We stepped into the little lobby adjacent to the boardroom. The Central Committee was still hanging around. It looked bad that management was not in the room. No doubt they assumed that the board was weighing our efforts and our judgment. No doubt they hoped that we would be found wanting and the board would discipline us.

As we sat outside, shouting could be heard behind the closed doors. It was impossible to make out what was being said, but it was clear that a violent disagreement was occurring. Raised voices and angry words were not normal board behaviour. The arguments went on for some time before we were invited back into the room.

When we returned, the members looked red faced and unhappy, but they had managed to get themselves under control. It would not look good to quarrel in front of the children.

Despite the tensions, they issued a strong statement of support for management. In fact, it may well be that the unauthorized meetings with the union solidified the board more firmly behind management.

The next day, the union made a series of new proposals that were even more backward-looking then those of a week earlier. They proposed a model that would have eliminated contracting and temporary employment altogether. As well, they significantly increased their financial demands, which had previously not been an issue at all, and which would have increased the costs to the Corporation by an extra $80 million.

Apparently the union had been emboldened by its meetings with the board members. It may even have believed that management's negotiating mandate had changed, allowing the CMG to drive a bargain on its own terms. There was no other explanation for the change in their tone and demands. They clearly felt that the momentum was all on their side.

Three days after the board meeting, the minister of labour summoned the president and Arnold Amber to a meeting. He berated them both and offered his good offices to assist the negotiating process. It was not clear how this gesture would assist the search for a resolution. In fact, it may have made the union even more confident. Why compromise when assistance from the government is not far behind?

The political climate was terrible, and speculation was rife that the Martin government would fall. As a result, Members of Parliament were endlessly jockeying for position. Many of them, fearful for their seats, now moved into overt support of the CMG. In return, members of the union organized fundraisers and promised logistical support.

The board was split and the employees were outraged. They had all been out of work for many weeks with no income but their strike pay. The best employees were quitting the company altogether and accepting jobs with rival broadcasters. The picket lines were becoming much more threatening. Acts of sabotage were rumoured. There was concern about violence.

Finally, on October 2, after the two negotiating teams were "locked in" at the offices of the minister of labour, real bargaining began. Almost seven weeks had passed without progress. But now, in the space of thirty-six hours, the two sides closed all the outstanding items. The contract employees' problem was concluded with the creation of a cap on the total number of employees that could be on contract. The multi-skilling issues were resolved. And the Demonstrated Occupational Qualifications test was accepted as the bumping standard. At 1:00 AM on October 3, George Smith phoned to tell me the deal was done.

Remarkably, management seemed to have won all of its key points. It was an unexpected and welcome victory. After all the endless abuse and misrepresentation, it was satisfying to have concluded a deal that would allow the CBC to move forward. At the same time, a fair amount of the final language had been left vague. In many cases, the vagueness had been intentional. It seemed wise, given the length and bitterness of the lockout, to pursue a policy of selective obscurity. The real meaning of the language could be sorted out later. For the time being, the key was to conclude and get everyone back to work.

For its part, the Central Committee claimed that it had won a great victory and management had backed down. This was more than a little annoying, since we could not contradict them publicly. It was essential to everyone that the agreement be ratified by the members of the union. For the CMG to achieve a positive vote, it would of course have to claim the deal was good for the workers. We had to leave their crowing uncontested. A bitter pill.

And the pill was doubly bitter because now the employees would believe that management had needlessly prolonged the lockout.

Why, they could reasonably ask themselves, would we not have thrown in the towel earlier if we were ultimately going to agree to the union's demands?

The return of the employees was uneventful. They got back to their jobs. The radio talk shows returned. Peter Mansbridge appeared at his desk on *The National*; play-by-play returned to the football games. Within a couple of weeks, the programming was back to where it had been before the lockout.

The shows were back, but the mood remained vicious. Walking into elevators, meeting employees in the cafeteria or talking to them at meetings was painful. They would look at me as though confronted by the Great Satan himself. The stench of sulphur and charred flesh seemed to follow me everywhere. Employees looked aside when I came into view. They averted their eyes, not wanting to compromise themselves by appearing in any way to treat me as possibly human. The chill was terrible.

Not for the first time, I wondered what I was doing at the CBC. My first year had been spent fighting a war I had not started. I had been insulted, abused and mocked. It was enormously disheartening. The prospect for the next few years was bleak. It would be no fun to manage an operation where I was seen as the incarnation of cruelty and bad judgment. I wondered whether I could stay.

THE FINAL HUMILIATION occurred when Jane Chalmers, Robert Rabinovitch, George Smith and myself, the Gang of Four, were called to appear before a parliamentary committee a few weeks after the end of the lockout. The committee's objective was ostensibly to look into the issues associated with the labour disruption.

The meeting began badly when Robert fell out of his chair and spilled water over himself. The lead photo in the papers the next morning was me reaching down to help him back up. From that excellent start, it degenerated into complete silliness. The committee members competed to see who could gong the management most effectively. They demanded recantations and apologies. They accused us of wasting money, misleading the government, acting without proper board authority, destroying the Corporation and being needlessly cruel to the workers. They repeated their outrage in shriller and shriller tones as the morning advanced.

Eventually they started demanding resignations. Charlie Angus of the NDP said the president had to go. "I think the taxpayers of Canada were ripped off by this lockout, and I think he gambled recklessly with not just the reputation of the CBC, but the audience of CBC." Bev Oda, who ultimately would become the Conservative heritage minister, grilled the president as though she were cross-examining a devious felon. The Liberals' Sam Bulte, the parliamentary secretary of the minister of heritage, insisted that we should all be ashamed of ourselves.

Thus the lockout of 2005 came to its public end. The Corporation itself was—according to the pundits and know-it-alls—hopelessly compromised. It would never recover its reputation, its audiences or its advertisers. Everywhere was wreckage as far as the eye could see.

Except. Except that on all of these points, the pundits were wrong.

Once the lockout was over, we could turn our attention to repairing English television's long slide into oblivion. We could begin the process of renewing our shows, rebuilding the news-casts and relaunching radio. The new contract with the union would prove enormously helpful in ensuring that we could move forward successfully. The CBC not only recovered, it went on to achieve the highest audience ratings in the history of Canadian radio and in some ways enjoyed even greater success in television. The Corporation's reputation had not been permanently compromised—rather, the public came to like and have more confidence in the CBC than ever before. Instead of abandoning the Corporation, its advertisers came to trust it more than they ever had in the past, with *Marketing Magazine* voting CBC Media Player of the Year for two years running, in 2009 and 2010.

BUT THE SUCCESSES were in the future. The next two years were terrible. The mood was extremely foul. Small efforts were made to try and repair the relationship, but with little success. In 2006, a third party was hired to see if they could help put things back on a friendlier and more workmanlike basis. It was to no avail.

The mood was so frightful that even management was bitterly discouraged. Internal polls showed that only 40 percent of management was "optimistic about the future of English services." Less than half thought English services a good place to work. Only a third believed that their staff was "on board with the direction of English services." What had been a difficult and unhappy work environment had become poisonous.

As 2007 came and went, both union and management looked forward in despair to 2008, when the negotiation process would have to begin again, since the new contract expired in 2009. It looked like 2008 would bring more fruitless arguments, a renewal of name calling, the resurrection of the politics of personal destruction and the inescapable unhappiness of more labour disruptions. Misery gripped everyone.

At some point you have to set aside snobbery and what you think is culture and recognize that any random episode of *Friends* is probably better, more uplifting for the human spirit, than ninety-nine percent of the poetry or drama or fiction or history ever published. Think of that. Of course yes, Tolstoy and of course yes Keats and blah blah and yes indeed of course yes. But we're living in an age that has a tremendous richness of invention. And some of the most inventive people get no recognition at all. They get tons of money but no recognition as artists. Which is probably much healthier for them and better for their art.

Nicholson Baker, *The Anthologist*

three
ENTERTAINMENT

ON SEPTEMBER 11, 2001, the World Trade Center was destroyed by al Qaeda, acting in the name of Islamic jihad. Osama bin Laden had struck a blow against what he believed was Western "crusaderism," the oppression of the Muslim world by infidel Christians and Jews. In the process, nearly three thousand people were killed in New York, at the Pentagon and in a field in Pennsylvania. The worldwide outrage was instantaneous. The front page of *Le Monde* read: "*Nous sommes tous Américains.*"

The United States responded by invading Afghanistan and throwing out the Taliban regime that had sheltered bin Laden. The Taliban practised a medieval version of Islam that involved public stoning and beheadings, the complete suppression of women's rights and the destruction of educational and cultural institutions. When the world saw the full horror of the Taliban regime and the ruin it had created in Afghanistan, it shrank back in revulsion.

It did not go unnoticed that many of the World Trade Center attackers were of Saudi Arabian origin, as was Osama bin Laden. The Saudis themselves practised a puritanical form of Islam known as Wahhabism, in which women have no rights, punishments for religious infractions are barbaric and civil liberties are limited. Saudi Arabia is a richer, more polished version of the Taliban's Afghanistan. This also came as something of a revelation to the Western world.

The resulting backlash against Muslims was widespread and troubling. Throughout Western Europe and North America, a significant reappraisal of the West's attitude to Islam was undertaken. Citizens throughout the big democracies were increasingly concerned about the possibility of domestic Muslim terrorists. Their fears seemed confirmed when four Madrid train stations were bombed in 2004, killing almost two hundred. The sense grew that there were Muslim enemies both within and without the borders of the West.

In North America, the atmosphere grew increasingly shrill. The United States instituted colour-coded alerts to advise their citizens of the likelihood of a terrorist attack. It passed the Patriot Act, suppressing civil liberties, and began to employ torture and extraordinary renditions as policies of the state. In 2006, eighteen Muslim men were arrested in Toronto with plans to seize the CBC and behead the prime minister. The fear of militant Islam and its jihadi terrorists began permeating civil discourse.

The Muslim citizens of North America found themselves in a difficult situation. Their neighbours began to eye them with suspicion. Their sons and grandsons were racially profiled. They were put on "no-fly" lists. Community opposition arose to the building of new mosques. Revelations began to appear about radical imams preaching hatred of Canada and the United States from their suburban mosques in Toronto and Washington.

In this cauldron of fear and anger, it seemed a good idea to make a comedy about Muslims. In 2006 we commissioned *Little Mosque on the Prairie*, a charming series about a diverse group of Muslims living in a fictional town called Mercy, Saskatchewan. The opening episode spoke directly to North Americans' anxieties about terrorists in their midst.

It shows an Anglican church, with Muslims walking through its doors. They are wearing their traditionally modest dress, long pants and sleeves on the men, head scarves on the women. As they come in the door, Baber, the interim imam, says, "Our own mosque?"

He is reassured in a surreptitious way that it is.

Inside the church/mosque, men and women are sitting in separated groups on the floor, listening to Baber preach an absurd sermon.

"As Muslims we must realize the enemy is not only out there. The enemy is much closer than you think."

There are whispered complaints about the idiocy of Baber's sermons.

"My point is," he goes on, "*wine* gums, *rye* bread . . . Western traps designed to get Muslims to drink."

Baber grows more impassioned. "*American Idol. Canadian Idol.* I say all idols must be smashed. *Desperate Housewives*? Why should they be desperate when they are only performing their natural womanly duties?"

The service is interrupted by a local man from Mercy who thinks he has stumbled on a nest of terrorists when he hears them praying in Arabic.

Cut to the next scene. The airport in Toronto.

A young imam, Amaar Rashid, is standing in line to board a plane. He has been called by Allah to abandon his law practice and move to Mercy to minister to its tiny congregation.

Amaar is talking on the phone to his mother. "Mom, stop it with the guilt. Don't put Dad on. I am not throwing my life away. I am moving to the prairies to run a mosque."

A woman standing in front of him in the line looks alarmed.

Amaar goes on, "I have been planning this for months. It's not like I dropped a bomb on him. If Dad thinks it's suicide, so be it. This is Allah's plan for me."

He is whisked out of the boarding line by a security guard, who advises him that he will not be going to heaven that afternoon. This conflation of Islam and terrorism is the basis for all the jokes in the first episode.

Little Mosque on the Prairie was the first show made under CBC television's new strategy for entertainment. The strategy was focused on making Canadian shows that would be popular with Canadian audiences. We would judge their success by the audiences they garnered. To increase the audiences, we had completely redesigned our development processes and renovated all of our publicity and promotion strategies.

Little Mosque was the first time the CBC had shot a pilot for a series. Pilots are expensive, and so were almost never made in Canada. But they are the only way to see whether something can work. A pilot is typically the first episode of a show, fully written, shot and edited. It is tested with audiences, who are asked to rate whether or not they would want to continue watching it.

The first pilot of *Little Mosque* was discouraging. Audiences reacted badly to the female lead. We advised the producers that it would have to be re-shot. They resisted ferociously. That had never happened before. It was not CBC management's job to make creative decisions. Who did the CBC think it was? A studio? The pilot was re-shot with a new female lead. This required throwing out 40 percent of the previous effort. The result was a significant improvement.

Our original plan was to have the series ready for the launch of the 2007 fall season. We felt, however, that given the fever pitch of the debate about the place of Muslims in North American life, we needed to accelerate its production. We decided to pull it forward by almost a year and launch it in January 2007. That was a very aggressive schedule.

Knowing that the Canadian media rarely believe Canadian television shows are any good, we decided to use a novel approach for the publicity for *Little Mosque*. We planted the story in the United States, where the level of hysteria about Muslims was even higher than it was in Canada. The *New York Times* carried an account of the show as a lead story in its entertainment section. CNN sent a crew to Canada to cover it. Once the Americans had validated the importance of *Little Mosque*, the Canadian press could not get enough of it.

As the time came to launch the show, we poured promotion money into it. We spent more than we ever had before. Then we doubled the budget. There were camels in Dundas Square in Toronto; falafels were handed out at the train station. We bought endless newspaper, television and radio ads. *Little Mosque on the Prairie* was everywhere.

It was essential that the show succeed, since it was the first real test of the new entertainment strategy for the CBC. If it failed, the strategy was done. We would have proved all the detractors and naysayers right. It launched January 9, 2007, and we desperately hoped it would make a million viewers.

TELEVISION IS THE biggest and most important cultural medium in the world. People spend more time watching television than doing anything else, except sleeping and working. Canadians watch an average of twenty-four to twenty-six hours per week of television, a number that has not changed significantly in the last thirty years. Despite many claims to the contrary, Google, Facebook, YouTube and other websites have not overtaken television. Indeed, new media are increasingly being used to watch traditional television shows.

Which shows consume so much time and attention? Overwhelmingly they are entertainments: drama, comedies, reality, quiz and sports shows. Of these, far and away the most important are drama, comedy and reality. On the big private networks in the United States and Canada (CBS, NBC, ABC, Fox, CTV, Global and Citytv), entertainment makes up 95 percent of the prime-time schedule. The same is true of the big public networks in the rest of the world. The BBC, France 2 and the Australian Broadcasting Corporation's prime-time schedules are overwhelmingly entertainment shows.

In English Canada, the most popular television shows are—with the exception of hockey broadcasts—all entertainment-based, just as they are everywhere else. They are police procedurals (like the *CSI* and *Law & Order* franchises), hospital dramas (*House, Grey's Anatomy*), reality shows (*Survivor, The Amazing Race, American Idol*) or comedies (*Frasier, Two and a Half Men*). They are also overwhelmingly American.

The surprising part about English Canada's cultural failure is that it is largely confined to film and television. English Canadians overwhelmingly prefer Canadian newspapers and magazines, and Canadian songwriters and novelists are iconic not only in their own country, but around the world. Simply listing their names evokes their celebrity and accomplishments: Leonard Cohen, Joni Mitchell, Gordon Lightfoot, Neil Young, Mordecai Richler, Margaret Atwood, Robertson Davies. It is impossible to name a single Canadian television show that would fall into this category.

"Surely," critics will say "you are too harsh. What about *Anne of Green Gables, Road to Avonlea, Street Legal, Due South, The Beachcombers*? What about them?"

What about them, indeed. While it is possible to point to occasional English-Canadian successes, they are few and far between, and the vast majority never succeeded internationally. They were— at best—local favourites. Every year, since the dawn of television in Canada, the entertainment shows that appealed most to English Canadians were foreign.

There had been occasional stabs at strengthening the CBC's entertainment offerings over the years, but with little real enthusiasm or success. Occasionally, great shows would flare and then go out. They were notable for their infrequency, and were usually replaced with less "commercial" shows that were more "distinctive" or "demanding." There had never been a concerted effort to try and make shows that would consistently attract enthusiastic Canadian audiences. The fact that the CBC had never addressed this problem was compounded by the fact that it was the only Canadian broadcaster in a position to do so. With the best will in the world, the great private broadcasters—CTV, Global, Citytv—are in no position to make the effort on a sustained basis. Among all the large English-language television networks, the CBC is the only one where prime time is available for Canadian shows.

In Canada, prime time is defined for *regulatory* purposes as being between 7:00 and 11:00 PM seven days a week. But *real* prime time is actually between 8:00 and 11:00 PM five days a week, Sunday to Thursday. Real prime time has 20 percent more households watching television than regulatory prime time. In English Canada, real prime time garners almost ten million households watching television, while regulatory prime time has just over eight million. That means that if one is to get big audiences for Canadian shows, they must be put on during real prime time. Only then are sufficient numbers of Canadians watching TV to give the shows any chance of breaking the Top Twenty or Top Thirty lists.

The big private networks, CTV, Global and Citytv, schedule their Canadian entertainment shows in the regulatory prime-time periods between 7:00 and 8:00 PM, or on Friday and Saturday nights. Their real prime time is not available for Canadian shows, because their business relies on scheduling U.S. shows at that time. This is what they have done since the beginning of private broadcasting in Canada.

Every spring, executives from the Canadian private networks go to Los Angeles to buy American shows. They try to buy the shows that will draw the largest possible audiences—the most beautiful and most expensive American shows. They spend hundreds of millions of dollars on them, substantially more than they spend on Canadian shows.

Having bought the shows, they schedule them at exactly the same time as their big U.S. counterparts. If CBS is running *CSI: Miami* at 9:00 PM on Tuesday night, CTV will schedule *CSI: Miami* at 9:00 PM on Tuesday night. The cable companies are obliged to replace the CBS ads with CTV ads. This practice—known as simultaneous substitution, or simulcasting—ensures that every Canadian watching *CSI: Miami* can only do so on CTV, which in turn ensures that CTV maximizes its advertising revenue. Simulcasting is fundamental to the financial success of the private broadcasters.

The most beautiful, popular and expensive U.S. shows are always scheduled by the big U.S. networks in real prime time. This obliges their Canadian counterparts to do the same thing if they want to enjoy the benefits of simulcasting.

The CBC is therefore the only big network in English Canada where real prime time is available for Canadian shows. It is the only network in a position to try and solve Canada's most important cultural challenge. The others could not attempt it, even if they wanted to, without destroying the very foundation of their business.

WHEN I ARRIVED in 2004, the CBC was pursuing its Transformation Plan to make CBC television more "distinctive." Executives of the period had rejected the idea of making Canadian shows within the mainstream conventions of North American television. They feared that such shows might feel too commercial. Instead, they sought to work in novel formats, emphasizing docudramas, miniseries and edgier storytelling. The centrepiece of the Transformation Plan was *Opening Night*, a two-hour commercial-free performing arts program on Thursday nights. The Transformation Plan was designed to ensure that CBC television looked unlike television anywhere else in the world. It was the Transformation Plan that had reduced the CBC to the lowest ratings in its history.

In drama, the result was a string of historical re-enactments by way of miniseries on Pierre Elliott Trudeau, René Lévesque and the War Measures Act, movies of the week on events like the Halifax Explosion, tough-minded co-productions on the international trade in sexual slavery (*Sex Traffic*), a challenging and dark series on the life of a coroner (*Da Vinci's Inquest*), an odd courtroom drama about an eccentric lawyer who shouts a lot and appears to have Tourette's Syndrome (*This Is Wonderland*) and a Canada–South Africa co-production set in a trauma ward in Johannesburg (*Jozi-H*). Many of the shows were well made, sometimes beautifully so, but they were not well received by the Canadian public. Indeed, given how many of them were based on history or explored documentary preoccupations, they reinforced the sense that the CBC was a fact-based network, concerned with news and current affairs rather than entertainment.

The same thing was true of the comedy offerings. The flagship shows were *This Hour Has 22 Minutes* (its name was a reference to the old current affairs show *This Hour Has Seven Days*), *Royal Canadian Air Farce* (which had started on radio in the 1970s) and the *Rick Mercer Report*. All of them featured sketch comedy, usually emphasizing political jokes or stories based on current events. Again the general impression they gave was that the CBC was about news, even when it was being funny.

The result was that CBC had fewer viewers than CTV for its Canadian entertainment shows. Despite the fact that there were almost no Canadian shows on CTV's *real* prime-time schedule, the rival network drew a bigger proportion of viewers of Canadian entertainment programs. Where the CBC had taken 47 percent of all viewing of Canadian entertainment shows in 1998–99 and CTV had 37 percent, by 2004–05 CBC was at 30 percent and CTV close to 60 percent. It was a scandal.

Very early on in my tenure, to gauge the size of the challenge involved in strengthening CBC's entertainment offer, we did a study to look at its "brand." By "brand," we meant what Canadians think the Corporation is about. As marketing professionals like to say, your brand is the "promise" you make to your customers. It defines what they expect from you.

The results of the study were discouraging. Canadians saw CBC television as basically about serious stuff. They saw it as a news organization, sober, dull and responsible. It was the last place they would think of going to be entertained. If they tuned in at all, they did so to be informed. It never occurred to them to tune in to be moved, charmed, amused or seduced. The CBC brand was a huge obstacle to building an entertainment strategy.

The other huge problem was the CBC's Constituency, the very people for whom the Transformation Plan and its "distinctiveness" strategy were designed. They included the mandarins of Ottawa, the editors of the *Globe and Mail* and the chattering classes more generally. They felt a proprietary interest in the CBC, and to the extent they watched television—which was little—they watched mostly news and current affairs. For them, the CBC brand was just fine. If they had their way, it would feature even more news and current affairs, leavened perhaps by some thoughtful performing arts or science shows. Certainly they had no interest in entertainment.

The CBC's Constituency of the good and the great was what determined its direction. The board was drawn from its members. The presidents had historically come from the same group. The Constituency determined the budgets and the size of the public subsidy.

They all moved in the same circles, and they all agreed that the CBC brand should be sober and a little dull. It should be like them. The CBC should certainly not be in "show business," strutting around all made up, cracking jokes, looking sexy and telling stories. That sort of thing would not do.

These were serious people. They were deputy ministers, important lawyers from big firms, executives from respectable businesses, publishers of thoughtful newspapers, bishops and moderators of established religions, judges and university professors. They liked to read and listen to classical music. They went to the ballet and attended plays. They bought wine and collected art. They played bridge and golf. They did not sit around watching TV. They were an odd group to be in charge of the county's greatest entertainment medium.

So there it was. The difficulty of building an entertainment strategy focused on making hit Canadian shows was absolutely clear. There had never been a consistent series of hit Canadian shows, the CBC was the least likely place for the public to go looking for them and the CBC's Constituency was actively hostile to them. The shows would, of course, also have to compete against the successful U.S. shows that dominated the private networks' schedules and had been loved by English Canadians for decades.

Whatever we did would require a massive overhaul of all aspects of the CBC. The shows in development when I arrived were outside the mainstream of the entertainment genre. The internal culture, the history of the place, the people in residence and the external producers would all have to change. We would have to reinvent our schedule, our development process, our standards, our targets, our approach and our relationships. And we would have to do this in the teeth of significant scepticism, doubt and outright hostility.

TO START THE process, it seemed sensible to explain the rationale for what I was going to attempt and why. Beginning in 2005 and throughout 2006, I explained the reasoning for the change in strategy to everyone who would listen. I began with the president, Robert Rabinovitch. By then, he had been president for five years.

Although we had discussed the issue at some length before he hired me, he had been a partisan of the "distinctiveness" strategy during his tenure and its manifestation in the Transformation Plan. My predecessor, Harold Redekopp, who had been at the CBC forever, had pursued it with vigour. They were both publicly and privately committed to the old view.

Robert knew when he hired me that I did not share the "distinctiveness" view. I believed that it was wrong-headed and destructive to the CBC's long-term interests. We discussed at length the alternative. We discussed the cultural issues at stake, the question of who the CBC was to serve, the nature of television, the positions of the various parties and the likelihood of succeeding at creating popular entertainment shows.

He is a remarkable person, Robert Rabinovitch. He sometimes seems free of ego. While he listened to my ravings and proposals, ideas that contradicted most of what he had been doing, he did so without rancour or fear of losing face. He challenged me and poked holes in my logic. He tested whether what I was saying made any sense. At no point did he mind that it would make him look bad to change direction. When we were done, he said okay and we went to the board.

The board approved the new direction, but without—I sensed— a clear idea of what it really meant. The problem is that the board members are mostly amateurs. They know very little about broadcasting or media, let alone the history of Canadian culture or how television works. They are appointed as a favour from the party in power to add a little lustre to their CVs. They feel good about the CBC in a general sort of way—they watch *The National*, admire CBC radio and are pleased to make the acquaintance of Peter Mansbridge. When the new strategy was explained, they nodded with enthusiasm, unclear what it was they were agreeing to. If they had fully grasped it, they would probably have said no.

To start to roll out the strategy publicly, I made a series of speeches. The first was in February 2005 at the Broadcast Executives Society, where I explained the rationale for what we were planning.

In a similar speech to the Economic Club of Toronto in 2006, I reiterated the nature of our new approach. Neither of these talks gained much traction. There was little coverage in the press and little talk in the industry. Either I was not being clear enough or I was not being taken seriously.

The whole matter finally came to a head at the annual meeting of the Canadian Film and Television Production Association in Ottawa in February 2006. I explained again the shift in strategy. I made clear that we were looking for projects very different from the ones that we had financed in the past. We no longer wanted miniseries or movies-of-the-week. We wanted series with episodes that resolved within their sixty-minute arc. We wanted situation comedies. We wanted to work within the television conventions that English Canadians were most familiar with. We wanted to have hit shows, not just artistic successes.

This was all fine, until we arrived at the definition of success. I knew it was coming and had thought about it at length. It was important to put out a number or it would—once again—simply be more blather and fudging. The question arose inevitably. "So, Mr. Smarty Pants, what is success?" I paused for a moment and said, "A million viewers."

Pandemonium broke out.

There was a general consensus that this was not only an irresponsible target, it was stupid and destructive. It could never be accomplished on a consistent basis and would provide fodder for the detractors of the Canadian television industry, who would lampoon us for not making it. They would say, "Well, there it is. You said yourselves that success was a million viewers, so your shows are failures. Why, then, should the Canadian public be expected to finance failure?"

This was an excellent point.

At the time of the speech, there was only one Canadian show making a million viewers, and that was not even a CBC show. It was *Corner Gas* on CTV. The CBC's top dramas were way below the target. *Wonderland* and *Da Vinci's Inquest* were rarely pulling in more than a third of the number, drawing between 300,000 and 350,000 viewers an episode. It was unimaginable that the Canadian television producers could consistently build shows that made a million viewers.

I went further and said that it would be nice to have some Canadian shows in the Top Thirty. There were fresh cries of outrage and disbelief. At that time there were no Canadian entertainment shows in the Top Thirty. It was dominated by American dramas and reality series, every one of which was making more than a million viewers. Indeed, the top shows—*Grey's Anatomy*, *House* and *Survivor*—were pulling in more than three million viewers, a staggering and unimaginable attainment. Only *Hockey Night in Canada* ever broke into the Top Thirty.

The establishment of a real target seemed to have the desired effect. Everybody now took the new strategy seriously. They hated it, but they paid attention. They knew that there was going to be a real measure of success and failure.

The next day brought extensive condemnations in the press. Various producers were quoted about how irresponsible the strategy was. Not only was it a silly goal, they argued, it would lead to the erosion of quality. Everyone knew that there was an important choice to be made between being popular and being good. The search for a million viewers could only serve to compromise artistic excellence. It would result in the "Americanization" of Canadian television. It was extremely unwise.

Typical of the reaction was an article by Mark Dillon in the industry magazine *Playback*. He argued that "by setting the bar as high as he has, Stursberg could be in store for a big fall." But apart from failing, the whole notion of trying to make Canadian entertainment shows that could compete with American ones was wrong-headed. Mark Dillon went on: "Our public broadcaster should not be run like CTV or Global, nor, ultimately, is it able to go head to head with them."

There was nothing new in any of this. It was the same old sad song. Do not hold us to an objective test. Do not make us compete against the Yanks. Do not force us to surrender quality to the vile gods of the marketplace. Do not commercialize us. Do not force us to do anything hard.

A couple of years earlier, Paul Gross and I had been on a panel about the future of the Canadian film industry. Paul Gross is one of Canada's pre-eminent movie stars. He is handsome, charming and funny. He also writes, directs, produces and composes music. He was the star and show runner for *Due South*, up to that point the only Canadian program ever to be picked up by a major American network. He wrote, produced and directed two of the most success-ful films in Canadian history, *Men with Brooms* and *Passchendaele*. And worst of all, he is a great nationalist. Despite endless offers, he lives in Toronto, not Los Angeles.

During the course of the panel discussion, I spoke as the head of Telefilm Canada, Canada's principal financier of feature films. I allowed that we needed popular success in our movie industry. At that time, I was promoting the idea that success should be measured in box office ticket sales. A million-dollar gate would separate the winners from the losers.

An aggrieved party in the audience denounced the whole idea. "What," he demanded to know, "do you want? That everyone should make *Dumb & Dumber*?" Before I could say a word, Paul Gross grabbed the microphone and shouted "Have you ever tried to make *Dumb & Dumber*? It is easy to make art-house crap. Try making a real movie, a movie that people want to see. That's hard. That is really hard."

He was right. The terrifying thing about establishing popular success as the key test for movies or TV shows is that it is very, very hard to accomplish. Public taste is fickle. There is no simple recipe to make a hit show or a big movie. Nothing guarantees it. Not stars, not money, not big-time directors, not promotion, not anything. As the screenplay writer and novelist William Goldman famously lamented in *Adventures in the Screen Trade*, "Nobody knows anything."

That was the real source of dismay about the million-viewers standard. The producers had little confidence they could actually accomplish it. The same, of course, was true for me. In setting the standard, I was putting myself in a very dangerous position. Failure would be absolutely clear and very public. It was far from certain that success at this level was possible. I was afraid of what I had done. But if not audiences, then what?

THE FIRST STEP in the new strategy was to clear the decks. We needed to get rid of the shows that were not performing or change them so that they would. We needed to get new shows into development as quickly as possible to replace the ones we would inevitably have to cancel.

The quickest way forward was to see if we could fix what we already had. An early candidate seemed to be a ten-episode series on the FLQ crisis of 1970 that had already been ordered. It seemed a perfect example of our problem. It was essentially a docu-drama, a dramatic restaging of the events. It felt news-like, fact-oriented and not very entertaining. Besides, the events had taken place almost thirty-five years earlier. The only people who could remember them were more than fifty-five years old, hardly the demographic that was going to renew the CBC.

In what I thought was a great brainwave, I decided we should keep the series, but move it forward in time. The idea was to reset all of the events in 2005. Events would unfold exactly as they really had: the British Consul is kidnapped, the Quebec minister of labour is murdered, weird manifestos are read on TV, the prime minister declares a state of emergency, people are rounded up in Montreal, troops patrol the streets of Ottawa. Everything would happen just as it happened, but it would be 2005. The events would be seen in the light of 9/11 and the War on Terror, making them immediately more relevant. The promise of the series would be that these things really happened, but now it's not just boring old history, it's of the moment.

The thought excited me. Perhaps this was a whole new genre: History Today. Everything you see happened, but in a way that would be accessible to contemporary Canadians. We could restage the War of 1812 in 2005. The United States invades Canada; we beat them back, march on Washington and burn down the White House. We could restage the Riel Rebellion. Manitoba rises against the government in Ottawa. Troops are dispatched. There are battles. The premier of Manitoba is tried for treason. Great stuff.

I phoned the producer to explain the brainwave.

"It will be even better," I said. "We just need to tweak the scripts and you won't have to rent any cars from 1970. It will be cheaper and better."

There was a long pause at the other end of the line. "Well," he opined, "that is certainly an original idea. But you know, we are already in production, so it's too late." Too late. He may also have felt that it was a little impertinent for management to intervene on creative decisions. Historically the CBC did not act as a studio. Once a show had been ordered, management typically left the producers alone until it was done.

I tried a similar tack with *Doctor Who*, the iconic British series. The BBC had decided to remake it and wanted to know if we wanted to buy it. I was doubtful. British shows never do well in Canada. In many cases, the accents are impenetrable, and rather than soldiering on, Canadians simply change the channel. If we were to buy it, we had to find a way of making it more accessible to Canadians.

We met the BBC people at the Spoke Club in Toronto, a hangout for people in the entertainment business. Hilary Read, the head of the BBC in Canada, was there, along with the top person in drama from London and some others. Over dinner, they explained what the new *Doctor Who* would be like. We listened politely. After they were done, I suggested that they make two versions: one for Britain and one for North America. In the North American version, we would make the Doctor a Canadian and re-voice him with a Canadian accent. That would make the series much more accessible, since it would involve fewer incomprehensible British accents and a lead character Canadians could feel kinship with.

The plummy woman from London made a strangled noise. "Re-voice the Doctor," she croaked, "as a Canadian?"

"Yes. Why not?" I replied, "After all, he isn't even English. He is alien. He has two hearts and three lungs."

"Re-voice the Doctor, as a Canadian?" she gargled again.

"Sure. And it would be seamless. It's already made in English, so there wouldn't be any lip-synching problems. We could have the same actor do it."

"Re-voice the Doctor?" She sounded weak, like she might pass out. "He is an iconic British figure."

"Why not?" I persisted. "We'll do it for the Canadian version and if it works here, it'll be easier to sell in the United States. And, not to be unfair, but you've never had a hit in the States."

The conversation deteriorated. The BBC people politely drew the evening to an early close. We paid the bill and left.

We concocted a number of similar schemes to see if we could find some quick fixes, but none of them worked. Sometimes the suggestions came too late, as with the FLQ crisis series, and sometimes they were seen as too radical. For my part, I did not care whether the ideas were too wild. We had to do something, ideally very soon, since all the shows were flopping. It would be hard to do worse.

Quick fixes were, of course, not the solution for the longer term. What would be required was wholesale change. We needed new approaches, new people and new strategies. We needed almost to begin from scratch.

IN 2005, AS the horrible labour negotiations were winding into the lockout, I started the process of restocking the Arts and Entertainment department. The head of the network, the charming and voluble Slawko Klymkiw, had already decided to leave. We had discussed at length the issues of the new strategy, and he did not disagree. In fact, he did some excellent work in developing a slot-based development process to ensure that the shows we developed would meet the requirements of their particular "time slots" (a family show at 7:00 PM on Sundays, an adult drama at 9:00 PM on Thursdays, etc.). He was also one of the key architects of an extensive audience segmentation study that we had undertaken to determine the kinds of audiences we wanted to reach.

Slawko decided that he would leave to become the head of the Canadian Film Centre, Canada's leading training school for mid-career filmmakers. His departure was a blow, but at the same time it created an opportunity to rethink and repopulate the whole of the CBC's entertainment group. The first thing was to find some new and like-minded executives to rebuild the schedule. The search took a while, but the results were worth the wait.

To rebuild drama and comedy, I hired the remarkable Fred Fuchs. I had known him since we worked together at Telefilm. Fred was an American from Long Island. He had previously been the head of Francis Coppola's company, American Zoetrope. There, he had produced *The Godfather, Part III*, *Dracula* and a series of other films written and directed by Coppola. He had also produced a considerable body of children's shows under the aegis of Zoetrope. He had moved up to Toronto in 2001 because he had promised his Canadian wife that they would live there at some point.

One day he and I were having lunch at the Spoke Club. We were there to discuss *The Tudors*, a Canada-Ireland co-production starring Jonathan Rhys Meyers as a young and randy King Henry VIII. On the Canadian side, Fred was producing for Peace Arch Entertainment. The financial structure he had put together was remarkable. By financing it in both Ireland and Canada and pre-selling it to the great American network Showtime, the CBC could obtain what was certain to be a beautiful, wildly expensive series for a knock-down price.

As the conversation progressed, I asked him if he had any ideas about who I could get to run the drama department. He asked if I would consider him. I was thrilled and amazed that he would suggest himself. "Of course," I said, "but you know it's the CBC, it doesn't pay any money." He allowed that he did not care, since he had already made some money and was much more interested in challenging work.

My only worry was the likely reaction from the cultural nationalists. "This is the end," they would doubtless gripe. "Now he hires an American to run the country's most important drama department." I explained to Fred that he should not take it personally. It was the simple knee-jerk anti-Americanism of the nationalists in the Little Canada camp. If he had been Brazilian or Australian or

Congolese with the same background, they would have been fine, thrilled in fact. But an American? Oh dear. Oh dear.

We prepared him for the inevitable hostile questioning from the press and the graceless observations of the guilds, but strangely these never came. The appointment was received with muted approval. Excitedly I began to think that Toronto might be growing up.

Next on my list was to find a head of documentaries. Documentary production and commissioning were scattered all over the Corporation. Documentaries were purchased by Newsworld, commissioned and purchased by the Arts and Entertainment department, commissioned by the Network Program Office and produced in the Documentary Unit. There was no overall supervision of all this to make sure that the work was effectively co-ordinated and financed.

I decided that the best approach would be to convince Canada's most distinguished documentarian to take on the job. Mark Starowicz had been at the CBC for many years. He had famously helped revitalize CBC radio in the 1970s, in the process reinventing the iconic *As It Happens*. He had then created *The Journal* as the back half of *The National*. He went on to make *Canada: A People's History* and when I arrived was running a small backwater called the Documentary Unit. He seemed the ideal person for the job.

We went to lunch. I knew his work, but he did not know much about me. All he knew was that I was a member of the Gang of Four and belonged to the unpleasant cult of the Satanical Lockout Enthusiasts. He himself had been locked out. We exchanged pleasantries. He is noted for his sardonic self-presentation.

"Well," I opened, "would you consider pulling together all the documentaries in one place and running a documentary department?"

"No," he said.

I was taken aback by how categorical he was. "No?"

"Not really. I like what I am doing. I don't want to have to manage anything like that. It's a recipe for political infighting and unpleasantness."

He knew, having been a victim of political infighting and unpleasantness, during his long and storied career at the CBC.

I banged on at some length about how important it was, how he was the best person available, what fun it would be, and so on and so forth.

"Nope," he said again, thanked me for lunch and we left.

This was going to be a tough nut to crack. I was dismayed but not discouraged. It seemed I would have to spend more on lunch than I had planned. I took up stalking Mark like a persistent suitor.

The next time, we got as far as his asking me what I wanted him to do if he agreed to take the job. I told him that I wanted our documentaries to be stylistically and thematically relevant again. "Take *The Nature of Things*," I said. "It is Canada's most important science series, with an extraordinarily admired host in David Suzuki. Yet it looks as though the most recent episodes were made in 1975. It is slow, boring and uninteresting. I need you to make it into what it should be, a modern, compelling science show with a great host. The same is true of the rest of the documentaries. Make *Doc Zone*, our great weekly auteur slot, relevant again. Make things people want to watch."

"Nope," he said again.

"Nope?"

"Too much political infighting and unpleasantness. Thanks again for lunch."

On my third try, he cracked a little.

"Maybe," he said, "but only for a year. I'm a field commander, not a member of the general staff. I like being out with the troops, not crapping about at head office."

He went on with his Patton-like military analogies and said a year, no more. I had to promise that he could go back and that during the course of the year he could make a production of his own while supervising the others. We had a glass of wine to seal the deal.

For the third new executive, I needed someone who could build a whole department from scratch. Not only were we going to do reality shows, we were going to do them with a vengeance. It seemed sad and weird that the CBC had missed the greatest wave of innovation in television in the last twenty years. Unlike the big European public broadcasters, it had never put much energy or enthusiasm into reality shows. To the contrary, it pooh-poohed them even when it did them, and it did them occasionally well.

The Corporation had, for example, mounted a serviceable version of *The Greatest Canadian*, a format it purchased from the BBC. Canadians nominated candidates to be considered as the Greatest Canadian, a shortlist was established, and various media personalities made the case for their particular candidate. Canadians voted and Tommy Douglas was declared the Greatest Canadian. There were dark rumours that this only happened because the school boards of Saskatchewan conspired to have their students vote for him en bloc. David Suzuki was named greatest living Canadian, and Don Cherry came second. Cherry claimed the final result was rigged. "I was robbed," he said.

The CBC had even invented a very good elimination show, *Canada's Next Great Prime Minister*. Young people would compete in front of a panel of old prime ministers to see who had the royal jelly. All the old prime ministers—Joe Clark, Kim Campbell, John Turner, Paul Martin and Brian Mulroney—would show up. Only Jean Chrétien refused to play. The most surprising presence was Brian Mulroney. *The Fifth Estate,* the venerable and much admired investigative reporting show, had a long history of being beastly to him, and we had just savaged him once more. Nevertheless, I went around to thank the old prime ministers for participating. Mulroney could not have been friendlier or more genial. He even asked after my father and reminisced in an affectionate way about him. Later, we sold the format extensively throughout the world under the title *Next Great Leader* (a little Kim Jong-Il-ish for my taste).

I asked Julie Bristow to build the reality division. She had been at the CBC for some time. She was intense, ambitious and clever. Most recently, she had been in charge of the current affairs section of the news department. While there, she had overhauled *The Fifth Estate*. Over the years, its magazine-style format had grown old and tired.

She changed it to an hour-long movie-of-the-week format. Every investigation was narrated like a film, with an organized plot, clear characters and fine production values. The change turned *The Fifth Estate* around and dramatically reversed its sagging numbers.

Julie did not need much convincing. All she wanted was a promise to let her fail a few times while we figured things out. That seemed more than sensible. We dropped all the unscripted shows into the new division, including *The Hour* with George Stroumboulopoulos and what few lifestyle shows we then had. We called the division "factual entertainment," rather than "reality," to avoid offending the CBC's Constituency.

Finally, we needed a conductor for our little orchestra. We needed someone who would manage the television schedule and define what was required from the drama, documentary and reality departments. This person would replace Slawko Klymkiw and lead the Network Program Office. This is in many ways the most difficult job in television. It requires someone with a deep knowledge of all the different genres, an excellent grasp of audience needs, a keen sense of flow within the schedule and brutal competitive instincts. We needed a programming thug.

The search was intense. We interviewed executives throughout Canada and others in New York and London. When I first met Kirstine Stewart, I was surprised at how young she was. She was only thirty-eight, but her kewpie-doll looks made her appear much younger, as though she had just graduated from high school as the head cheerleader. At the time, she was running all the Alliance Atlantis lifestyle channels, including Food Network Canada, the Life Network, HGTV Canada and about seven others. Prior to that, she had been in the United States running the Hallmark international channels. She had been exceptionally successful at a young age.

When we talked about the job, we talked about why Canadian shows were not successful, we talked about development and production, we talked about break structures and genre styles. Through it all, we talked about audiences. We never talked about the mandate of public broadcasting or the trade-off between quality and popularity. We focused exclusively on audiences.

She was well-informed, intense and intelligent. When she laughed it was breathless, herky-jerky. She exuded the calm, controlled self-confidence of someone who knows how clever they are but is more concerned with the work. I liked her but knew she would be a big gamble. She would be the youngest person ever to run the Network Program Office and had no experience at the CBC. After she arrived, she met with each of the top managers. One of the old bulls, Tony Burman, the head of news, a man in his late fifties and with a fearsome reputation, reported after their lunch—with a certain amount of surprise and bewilderment—that she seemed very smart.

With our little band in place, we set about reinventing CBC television. The centrepiece of the new strategy was to respect the medium itself. We did not want to produce university lectures, books or performing arts. We wanted to make *television* for Canadians, television that would reflect their lives, their preoccupations, their narrative sensibilities, their traditions, their sense of humour, their unique way of being in the world. And we wanted to make television that Canadians would love, that they would talk about on the bus and at the hairdresser's, that they would dream about at night and come to every evening in large numbers after dinner, when the day was done and they were ready to be entertained.

We wanted to work within the television conventions that English Canadians preferred. We would jettison "edgy," auteur-driven projects for season-long series working within understood narrative traditions. We would make police procedurals, situation comedies, reality eliminations, lifestyle shows and quiz contests.

We wanted to make TV for the largest possible audience. We wanted Mr. and Mrs. Canada and their children, the great middle class of people who pay the taxes that support the Corporation. We did not want to make TV for the CBC's Constituency of deputy ministers, editorialists, corporate lawyers and politicians. We wanted TV for teachers, nurses, middle managers, mechanics, farmers and salespeople. We wanted television for the great sweep of Canadians.

As part of the change in culture, we changed the vocabulary of the CBC. We banned certain words. Most controversially, we eliminated the word *mandate*, which had become hopelessly over-used, from discussions about any aspect of our programs or programming strategy. It seemed—at its best—to stand for nothing more than what the speaker liked. At its worst, it conjured the pompous, self-important CBC we wanted to end. We wanted, as well, to eliminate any linguistic safe havens for failure. With *mandate* gone, nobody could say, "Sure the show was a flop, but it reflected the *mandate* of the Corporation." Enough with a language that had validated failure.

Trina McQueen accused me of having a "tin ear for the language of public broadcasting." She did not seem to understand that I wanted a tin ear. The old ear, attuned to reverential talk about "quality" and "mandates," had served to distract and befuddle the CBC. Better to be simple and clear.

THE FIRST ORDER of business was to develop shows that would reflect the new strategy, and halt the ones that no longer fit. Telling the old "distinctive" shows that they were no longer required was an unpleasant business. The toughest was killing the great performing arts show *Opening Night*, the centrepiece of the distinctiveness strategy. Every Thursday evening, between 8:00 and 10:00, the CBC offered—without commercials—the high arts on TV. There were plays, ballet, one-person shows—beautiful performances. The shows were made to a high standard. The audiences were dismal.

Over lunch I met with a number of the producers involved in creating *Opening Night*. Veronica Tennant, the acclaimed ballerina and now TV producer, was there, along with Larry Weinstein, the co-founder of Rhombus Media, Canada's most important producer of high art films and documentaries. The mood was dark. They knew that we were changing gears and that *Opening Night* was not part of the future. They had committed their professional lives to making this kind of television and had done so with great panache, winning many important prizes. It was difficult to tell them that they were being cancelled.

The conversation veered around the usual subjects: What is TV? Why the overwhelming focus on audiences? I tried to explain as gently as possible that the CBC could not afford to give up the most important evening of the week to a show that generated no revenue and rarely made 200,000 viewers. Whether we liked it or not, and despite how beautiful the shows were, Canadians were saying no thank you.

They asked if this was the end of performing arts on TV. I said no, but we would have to approach them differently. We could not do a regular two hours a week. Rather, we would do occasional large, high-profile shows that could make a big splash. They looked puzzled.

"What do you have in mind?" Tennant asked.

"Something like *Jerry Springer,* the opera that the BBC did," I suggested. "It was big, loud and controversial. It probably did more to reach the non-opera-going public for an opera than anything else. Something like that."

Something like that. Something like that. The conversation wandered around a while longer. Something like that. Something like *Brian Mulroney: The Opera.* A perfect subject. An ambitious small boy, the son of an obscure family, grows up in a tiny town and rises to the greatest heights as Canada's most successful conservative prime minister since John A. Macdonald, only to be flung from power and vilified. The story has the great tragic arc of opera: the ascent to the godlike uplands and the dismal crash to the bottom of perdition. It would serve to introduce Canadians to opera, at least comic opera, as an art form.

Brian Mulroney: The Opera. A while later, Larry Weinstein asked if I was serious. I said yes, and the CBC commissioned an opera. In fact, we commissioned two, putting *Jean Chrétien: The Opera* into development as well. Same wonderful arc. An ambitious small boy, the son of an utterly obscure family, grows up in a tiny town and rises to the greatest heights as Canada's most successful Liberal prime minister since Mackenzie King, only to be flung from power by his great rival. Actually, this might feel more like *Othello,* with Chrétien as the tragic hero, Paul Martin as Iago and Canada as Desdemona. Whatever the result, it was also important to be even-handed. If the CBC was to commission *opéra bouffe,* it had to do so in a non-partisan way. It was important to mock both sides equally.

Cancelling *Opening Night* was followed by cancellations of the other under-performing shows. We went on to unload *Wonderland* and *Da Vinci's City Hall*. In the latter case, we had tried to rejuvenate *Da Vinci's Inquest*, which had become dark and complicated, by having the crusading coroner run for mayor. That had actually happened with Mayor Larry Campbell in Vancouver, where *Da Vinci* was set, so it provided a nice historical parallel. We hoped that by making Dominic Da Vinci into the mayor, we could open the show up a bit. We could get out of the endless strip clubs, back alleys and corpses to explore Vancouver and themes of broader interest. The mayor would surely have to be concerned with more than post-mortems and junkies on the Downtown East Side. We would see him dealing with the great business barons of Howe Street, the brilliant cinema crowd of Yaletown, the socialite lunching matrons of Shaughnessy. But he never did. The mayor kept wandering around back alleys and dark bars, exploring the seedy underbelly of the city.

Nevertheless, we believed in the creative team behind *Da Vinci*. We commissioned a pilot for a new series called *Intelligence*. The pilot was actually a two-hour movie. We figured that if it did not work out, we could still play it off as a movie-of-the-week. It was the first of our efforts to start making pilots and taking a much more disciplined approach to the commissioning process.

The reaction to the cancellation of the shows was swift and brutal. We were denounced as idiots. ACTRA (the Alliance of Canadian Cinema, Television and Radio Artists—the actors' union) excoriated us in a press release: "The cancellation of three CBC series is a startling display of incompetence by irresponsible CBC brass . . . One has to ask whether there can ever be responsible decision making with the current regime."

The *Globe and Mail*'s television critic, John Doyle, headed his denunciation "Attention Fort Dork: Tactical Error." Not to be outdone, *Toronto Star* columnist Antonia Zerbisias trashed us as witless amateurs and concluded: "Now this is not to say that by sheer dumb luck, this combination of people [myself and the new creative heads] can't pull off a miracle and yank CBC-TV out of the ratings black hole into which it has descended." It never ceased to amaze me how negative and hostile everyone was to changes in direction, even when it was clear that the old ways were not working.

At the same time that we cancelled these shows, we also resolved to end the coverage of awards ceremonies. We had been televising all sorts of things from the Governor General's Performing Arts Awards to the Gillers, the Genies, the Geminis, the Songwriters Hall of Fame and the Aboriginal Achievement Awards. They were very poor television. There were no stars, no plots, no real surprises of any interest. There were simply earnest speeches thanking various people's mothers and agents. Nobody watched these shows.

The original rationale for doing them was similar to that of the Transformation Plan: they would make the CBC more "distinctive," and the Constituency would approve. They were essentially political shows, designed to build a favourable impression of the Corporation among decision makers. But even in this, they failed. Decision makers yawned with indifference, and the CBC continued to watch its parliamentary appropriation shrink.

BEYOND CANCELLING SHOWS, we began the process of creating new ones. We were particularly concerned to start work in the area of factual entertainment and start to learn the ins-and-outs of reality TV. The easiest way to begin was to purchase a format for a show that had already proven itself elsewhere and then make it for a Canadian audience. That way, we could be confident that our first foray would succeed, thereby disarming our critics and entertaining Canadian audiences.

The first format was called *Star Academy*. It involved a singing competition, where young hopefuls are chosen from many aspirants, given training by professionals at the Academy and made into stars. Ultimately, one is selected as the best and typically moves on to a record deal and a bright future. The show originated in Spain and had been remade by all the great European public broadcasters. Most notably, it had been a huge hit for the BBC. It seemed a fine point of departure.

Shortly after we settled on *Star Academy*, ABC in the United States decided to make an American version called *The One*. This seemed not only a good omen, but an excellent opportunity to strengthen our version in Canada. ABC planned to put it on in the summer and see if it worked. We decided to buy the ABC version and simulcast it rather than let it go to one of our rivals. If CTV or Global bought the ABC show, viewers would have been confused when we released the Canadian one. As well, we liked the idea of being involved with ABC. We could learn from their mistakes and use the show as a way of educating ourselves about how best to make reality television work.

This stroke of good fortune was further enhanced when ABC started searching for a host for their show. We suggested George Stroumboulopoulos, the host of *The Hour*. ABC auditioned George, liked him and hired him. This was lovely. We could then use him for our show. He would be experienced, and the audience would come to associate him with what we assumed would be a very good show by ABC. Everything was falling into place.

We broadcast the first episode of *The One* on July 18, 2006. Unfortunately, for scheduling reasons of their own, ABC had to change the timing of the show. They moved it from 8:00 to 9:30. This meant that it would bump *The National*. This was unfortunate, but it happened all the time during the Stanley Cup playoffs. Canadians were used to it. If they really wanted to see *The National*, they could watch it on Newsworld, our all-news channel. Besides, it was the middle of the summer. There was no news.

The next day, the *Globe and Mail* had the story on the front page. *The National* bumped for an American singing show! Great consternation. Much fulmination. The CBC Constituency was duly outraged. Even Knowlton Nash, the former host of *The National*, rumbled out of retirement to condemn the whole business. The parliamentary committee weighed in, grumbling about the sheer inappropriateness of it all. *The National* moved for an American singing show! Harrumph. Harrumph. The *Toronto Star* took the controversy surrounding *The One* as an opportunity to attack me personally:

"Since he joined the CBC in the fall of 2004, Stursberg has been a one-man wrecking ball. Morale at the CBC is at an all-time low." The fact that practically every Canadian subscribed to Newsworld and could see *The National* at 9:00, 10:00 or 11:00 seemed to mollify nobody.

Sadly, *The One* was not very good. In fact, it was terrible. The American stars were lame, the participants weak, the production uncertain. ABC had flubbed the format. Where everyone else in the world had managed to produce compelling local versions, ABC had made a stinker. It looked like a half-baked cable show. It was widely derided, rightly, by both the Canadian and American press. After two episodes, ABC realized it was a turkey and cancelled the show.

The whole fiasco poisoned the waters. The format had been so badly damaged that there was no possibility we could move forward with it. The experience also made clear how difficult it would be to mount any sort of big entertainment strategy at the CBC. If it involved anything that appeared to be a lot of fun, was vaguely associated with the USA, or seemed to compromise even marginally CBC's news brand, we would be attacked. The wrath of the CBC Constituency would fall on our heads. Beware.

By early 2007, the new development process was sufficiently advanced that we could begin commissioning new shows, hopeful that some of them might succeed. We ordered a big slate of dramas and comedies.

We confirmed the purchase of *The Tudors* that Fred Fuchs had proposed at our lunch. We also commissioned *Intelligence*, the series based on the pilot-movie we had seen. In this case, we were fairly directive with the producers. The episodes had to be structured in such a way that the plots resolved within the forty-five minutes available. We could not have plots that took multiple episodes to resolve, as had been the case with *Da Vinci*. The problem is that if a viewer misses a single episode, it is difficult to get back into the whole series. We also insisted on much better summaries for the longer arcs, so that the viewer was never lost. Finally, we insisted that there had to be much less mumbling in dark alleys. Arty and compelling as dark alleys may be, people had to be able to see and understand what was occurring.

We also purchased five other series based on the positive test results we had received for the pilots that had been commissioned by Fred Fuchs.

The first of these was *jPod*, based on the novel by Douglas Coupland. It concerned the lives and work of some Generation X'ers who find themselves toiling in the same "pod" because their names all begin with J. Douglas Coupland is one of Canada's most prolific and creative artists. He is famously the author of *Generation X*, as well as *Microserfs* and a biography of Marshall McLuhan. He is also a well-known painter and sculptor.

Next was *Heartland*, based on the series of well-regarded novels by Lauren Brooke. This was to be our family show for the 7:00 PM time slot on Sundays. It is about teenage girls and boys, their families and horses. The producers originally wanted to set the show in the Eastern Townships of Quebec, but we insisted that they move it to southern Alberta. We wanted the romance, beauty and tradition of Alberta's ranch country. We also wanted the western sensibility of the province and the Rocky Mountains. *Heartland* became enormously successful, pulling over a million viewers every Sunday night and selling in dozens of countries. It became CBC's first hit family show since *Anne of Green Gables* and *Road to Avonlea*.

For something completely different, we purchased *The Border*, a procedural, set as the name implied on the Canada–U.S. border. It was a thriller, with smuggling, illegal immigrants, spies, political shenanigans, guns, tough but resolute agents and exploding cars. There was also much tension between the Canadian and U.S. authorities over methods, style and approach. There were upright border agents and sinister bad guys from the CIA and CSIS, all plotting and counter-plotting against each other. It was to be one of the feature 9:00 PM shows for a more adult, male-skewing demographic.

From there, we commissioned *Sophie*, based on a series called *Les hauts et les bas de Sophie Paquin* that appeared on Radio-Canada. It was about the life of a charming single woman in her early thirties, with a small child and a circle of goofy, clever friends. It describes—as the French title suggests—the ups and downs of her life. It was not a remake of the original; rather it was an adaptation. We cut it down from an hour to a half hour, and rewrote it for an English audience. The idea was also to start building some cultural bridges between English and French Canada. The show was a half-hour dramedy, designed for women and to be shown between 8:00 and 9:00 PM.

The next big show was another drama called MVP *(Most Valuable Player)*. It was a soap opera about hockey players, their girlfriends, their money and their stardom. There are young phenoms, established older players, wives, puck bunnies, owners, coaches and hangers-on, all mixed into a stew of sex, ambition, greed, love and treachery. It was inspired by *Footballers' Wives*, the wildly popular series on ITV in Britain. We figured a hockey drama was essential to the culture of Canada.

Finally, and to satisfy the performing arts crowd, we bought *Triple Sensation*, a talent elimination show that searched the country for the most gifted young triple sensations, kids who could sing, dance and act. They were selected for specialized training by an extraordinary bunch that included Marvin Hamlisch, Cynthia Dale, Sergio Trujillo and Adrian Noble. It was produced by Garth Drabinsky, the great mogul, who had been charged with various felonies, including fraud and malfeasance for bilking investors in his earlier ventures. Our principal concern was to make sure that Garth would be able to wrap the show. We worried that he might be convicted and have to finish the production from cell block B.

So there was our best shot at a lineup of new entertainment shows for the 2007–08 fall season. Fred Fuchs and his group had worked hard to pull together a large new slate. Now we had a family show (*Heartland*), a period bodice-ripper with sixteenth-century costumes (*The Tudors*), two thrillers (*The Border* and *Intelligence*), a female comedy (*Sophie*), a big soap opera (*MVP*), a quirky something-or-other for twenty- and thirtysomethings (*jPod*), and of course, *Little Mosque on the Prairie*. We also kept the successful sketch comedies that had been a staple of the CBC for some time: *Rick Mercer Report, This Hour Has 22 Minutes* and *Royal Canadian Air Farce.*

Meanwhile, Mark Starowicz had been busy rebuilding *The Nature of Things* and designing new shows for *Doc Zone.* He had jettisoned the languid pacing of *The Nature of Things* and refocused its content on the most burning scientific issues of the day. He had kicked its iconic host, David Suzuki, into high gear. By the time he was done, he had increased its viewership from just over 300,000 to more than 500,000.

He did the same thing with *Doc Zone* even more successfully, doubling its ratings in just over two years. Where it had often featured esoteric subjects or obscure auteur-driven efforts, he started to focus it on more mainstream fare and major documentary series. My favourite was six hours he produced on the Second World War to commemorate the seventieth anniversary of its beginning in 1939. Called *Love, Hate & Propaganda,* it was introduced by George Stroumboulopoulos, CBC's hipster in residence and late-night talk show host. The charming younger host, and the use of "propaganda" as a lens through which to view the issues, made the Second World War accessible to young people. It pulled in three-quarters of a million viewers. Astonishing for a documentary on the Second World War.

When we unveiled the new slate for the media and the public, the response was discouraging. Despite the fact that the shows were as Canadian as could be imagined, challenging in their premises and based in some cases on the work of our much admired sister network at Radio-Canada or on the books of widely admired Canadian novelists, there was little enthusiasm. In a not atypical response, Jim Bawden of the *Toronto Star* demanded to know "where is the high culture, one of the prerequisites of a public broadcaster?"

In a similar vein, Lorne Gunter dismissed the new season in the *Edmonton Journal*: "And Mother Corp has also picked up... *The Tudors,* a prime-time soap opera about the sex life of young Henry VIII... a new security drama, *The Border*; *Heartland*, about life in Alberta; and *Sophie*, about a single mom... To me, this all sounds dreadfully dull... Once again, CBC executives are trying to remake their network in a vain attempt to find a hipper, younger (and bigger) audience." Where, Gunter demanded, was *Opening Night*? "For seven seasons, ON [*Opening Night*] showcased Canadian productions of ballet, opera and symphony. With its cancellation, Mother Corp no longer has a regularly scheduled, prime-time Canadian culture show."

There was much hand-wringing that it all looked a little too "commercial" or too "American," not highbrow enough, etc., etc., blah, blah, blah.

Most of the new shows would not be available until the fall of 2007 and the winter of 2008, but we had rushed *Little Mosque on the Prairie* into production so that we could get it on air in January 2007. We felt it was important to have a show we could point to as soon as possible to demonstrate that we were serious about our new direction and provide a concrete example of what we were looking for. We desperately wanted to make a million viewers.

When *Little Mosque on the Prairie* aired, I was in Venice with my wife, Carole. My BlackBerry was working, so I was able to get the "overnights," the audience numbers that came out every afternoon measuring how many people had watched the different programs the night before. The overnights came out between 2:00 and 3:00 in the afternoon, or around 8:00 or 9:00 at night in Venice.

Venice is arresting in January. It is overcast and cool. Fog rolls through the canals. There are no tourists, only the Venetians. It rains in a drizzling grey mist. The great monuments of Piazza San Marco seem crouched and huddled. The days are short. It feels a little sinister. We were having dinner in an almost deserted restaurant. I was waiting for the overnights. The waiter looked bored and a little restless.

When the numbers finally arrived, I scrolled through looking for *Little Mosque*. Finally, it was there. There was a 2 and a 1. I almost passed out. 210,000. It was a disaster. *Little Mosque's* audiences were even lower than those of the shows we had been cancelling.

Wonderland and *Da Vinci's City Hall* had been axed after receiving much better results. Even *Opening Night* started to look respectable. I reached for the bottle of wine. After all the brave talk, we would look like complete idiots. In despair, I looked at the BlackBerry screen again. It almost winked at me. There was the 2 and the 1, as before, but this time I saw the decimal point between them. We had made 2.1 million viewers, the largest opening for a show in the contemporary history of the CBC.

After dinner, we walked through the shrouded and glistening streets of the dark and dampened city. Venice looked beautiful and calm. La Serenissima.

The success of *Little Mosque* continued into the fall and winter seasons of 2007 and 2008. The new shows also did well, some better than others. *The Tudors* was solid, as were *The Border*, *Heartland* and *Sophie*. They were not posting U.S. show numbers, but they were substantially stronger than the programs we had cancelled. The 2007–08 season turned into a great success. We closed with an 8.0 share in prime time, which meant that 8 percent of all Canadian viewing in prime time was to the CBC.

We were coming off the all-time low of a 6.7 share, the result of thirty years of continuous descent. We were, as well, coming off the damage of the lockout, which most commentators claimed would destroy us forever. In fact, we had managed for the first time in thirty years to grow the CBC's share.

Even more satisfying was the fact that we beat Global in prime time, with their overwhelmingly U.S. schedule. An all-Canadian prime-time schedule had never beaten Global's or CTV's all-American version. Admittedly we did not beat them by much that year, but we did beat them. An historic moment.

By the end of the season, CBC had fifteen of the Top Twenty Canadian shows. CTV had three and Global had two. The season's success showed that it was, in fact, possible to make Canadian programs that Canadians wanted to watch. It was possible to reverse the descent into oblivion and irrelevance. It was possible to address the number one cultural challenge in English Canada. We all breathed a sigh of relief.

TRUE TO OUR mantra that if shows did not perform well we would cancel them, we axed *jPod*, MVP and *Intelligence*. After the cancellations, there was moaning about our failures. We were numbskulls because the shows had not all been successful, we were too precipitous with *Intelligence* (despite the fact its audience shrank every week), we would have nothing to replace them with—there was failure at the CBC on all fronts. What was surprising—and what continued to surprise me the entire time I was there—was that nobody gave us any credit for having turned around the audience share collapse or for beating Global in prime time. The Jeremiahs who had claimed we would never recover from the lockout seemed to have forgotten their prophecies.

The shows were all, of course, replaced with new shows, three of which would go on to be monsters. The first, *Being Erica*, is a dramedy that focuses on the life of Erica Strange, a thirtysomething who cannot get her life together. She is clever, pretty, charming, but alas nothing goes well at work or in love. Then she meets the mysterious Dr. Tom, who has a remarkable power. He can take her back to the key moments in her life when something went horribly wrong, so that she can relive them as her older, thirtysomething self. The concept was fresh, the scripts well done, and the acting—notably from the luminous female lead, Erin Karpluk—terrific.

With *Being Erica* we had added another show focused on a younger, more female demographic. The reviews for *Being Erica* were strong. It was much admired, not just in Canada, but in the United States and the rest of the world. It was sold to the Soap Network in the U.S., which promoted it with giant posters in Times Square.

The work that Julie Bristow had been doing on factual entertainment also began to bear fruit. The first show was *Dragons' Den*. The premise is simple: entrepreneurs come and pitch the Dragons on their business schemes. The Dragons poke away at their plans, asking them questions and assessing their merit, sometimes cruelly, sometimes positively and sometimes to hilarious effect. If the Dragons like the plan, some or all of them will make a deal on the spot to invest in it.

The show is based on a Japanese format that was picked up internationally and had a successful run in many European countries. Most notably, the BBC has featured the show for a number of seasons. The key to making the format work is the Dragons themselves. They have to be rich enough to venture their own money on the start-ups that are presented to them. They must also be funny, clever, interesting and at ease on their feet. The best of the Dragons was Kevin O'Leary, an extraordinary character who had made a great deal of money in a number of different ventures. He had also had some significant television experience on the Business News Network, where he was Amanda Lang's partner on *Squeezeplay*. He was important not just to *Dragons' Den*, but also to our efforts to make the CBC more business friendly and business savvy. He became our crusading right-winger.

The show started slowly and grew as the season wore on and people began to hear about it. Every week, the numbers improved. Over the next couple of seasons, as the flow and quality of proposed deals increased and as the Dragons themselves got stronger, the audiences would become very large indeed. It would consistently pull more than 1.5 million viewers and sometimes over 2 million. It was rumoured to be Prime Minister Stephen Harper's favourite show.

For some time, Julie Bristow's best idea had been to do a homegrown reality show called *Battle of the Blades*. The idea was to pair hockey players with figure skaters and have an ice dance competition. We would recruit retired hockey players who had had successful careers and pair them with our world champion female figure skaters. The best part was that the men would have to adapt to the women's world. They would have to learn to do pirouettes, lifts and toe loops. The big, bad hockey players would inevitably be shown up by the female skaters and would have to be prepared to be mocked. After the couples were established, there would be an elimination, where one of the couples was voted down each week until a winner was established.

We had originally wanted to produce *Battle of the Blades* in 2007–08, but it was too expensive and too complicated to mount quickly. When we finally managed to produce it in 2008–09, it featured some of the biggest names in professional hockey and figure skating.

We had paired Tie Domi, the Albanian Assassin (third in NHL history in penalty minutes), with the Olympian Christine Hough-Sweeney; Bob Probert, the enforcer and tough guy from the Chicago Blackhawks with Kristina Lenko; and Ken Daneyko, another hard case, with Jodeyne Higgins. The entire effort was designed to have everyone play against type. Three-time Stanley Cup champion Ken Daneyko said, "The tough guys are forming a pact that one of us has to be the upset and win. Unless we get frustrated and want to beat the crap out of each other on the ice."

The show was a staggering success. The results were featured on the front pages of newspapers' entertainment sections and sometimes on the front pages themselves. Even the CBC news department began covering the show. They did so, however, without the compulsory sneering. They covered it for what it was, a genuinely unique popular Canadian cultural event. It was the subject of cheerful conversation and enjoyment everywhere. Like *Dragons' Den*, it made sensational numbers.

None of this, however, cut much ice with the Constituency. Jeffrey Simpson, the distinguished columnist for the *Globe and Mail* pooh-poohed the whole effort to make CBC television more popular. He attacked us for producing stupid programs: "So just when you think English television can't get dumber—that is, more like the private networks—it does. A deep disdain for intellectualism pervades English-language television—or what CBC executive Richard Stursberg, quoting a British government white paper, called 'worthy' programming."

In a similar vein, we were pilloried by the *Globe*'s John Doyle. "There's the rub—CBC TV really wants to be a big shot broadcaster... and boast about audience success. And there's the problem—CBC doesn't know what it wants to be. A shrink would ask, 'Do you want to be popular or do you want to be smart?'... Then the shrink would tell the CBC to make a decision..."

So there it was, as it always was. If the shows are popular, they must be stupid. The CBC should eschew entertaining Canadians; it should make "smart" shows, "intellectual" shows.

At the same time that we were producing better programs, we moved to strengthen the schedule. Kirstine Stewart, the head of the Network Program Office, had asked me whether we should try and obtain the great American game shows *Jeopardy!* and *Wheel of Fortune.* CTV owned them but they would shortly become available, and we thought we could use them to strengthen our Canadian properties. The plan was to put *Wheel of Fortune* on at 5:30, as a lead-in to the revitalized local supper-hour newscasts at 6:00. We would then use *Jeopardy!* at 7:30 to give us a flow into the heart of prime time and the new Canadian shows.

Jeopardy! and *Wheel of Fortune* are venerable properties. They are the longest-running and most successful game shows in North America. We were confident that they would give us lead-ins to the local newscasts and prime time of a million viewers five nights a week. No other shows consistently delivered those kinds of numbers. Certainly no Canadian show comes remotely close five times a week. *Jeopardy!* had the added benefit that its host, Alex Trebek, had started his career at the CBC. He loved the organization and would do whatever he could to help make *Jeopardy!* work for the schedule.

We went to the board and explained the strategy. In television, a strong lead-in can be even more valuable than brilliant promotion. The audience does not need to do anything. It just needs to sit still and not change the channel. The two shows also had the distinct advantage over our Canadian shows of being profitable. Not only would they help drive audiences to the news and prime time, they would contribute positive earnings to finance more Canadian shows. The board approved the deal enthusiastically.

When we announced the acquisition of *Jeopardy!* and *Wheel of Fortune*, the predictable complaint arose. We were "dumbing down" the CBC with stupid American game shows. Clearly the critics had never seen or played *Jeopardy!* The show is difficult and clever. When people audition to be on the show, they have to pass demanding tests. The winner of *Jeopardy!* is often referred to as the "smartest" or "best-informed" person in North America. When IBM decided to explore the difficulties of building game-playing computers, it started with chess. Only when their computer Deep Blue had mastered chess to the point where it could consistently beat the world champion, Garry Kasparov, did they turn their attention to *Jeopardy!* After the expenditure of millions of dollars and four years of effort, they challenged the *Jeopardy!* champions in 2011.

The hue and cry in Ottawa and the *Globe and Mail* about *Jeopardy!* was breathtaking. One would have thought we were putting on insect-eating contests or plastic surgery competitions.

The complaints were formulated in the same way: it was a stupid "American" game show. It is hard not to believe that if the BBC had made the show, we would never have faced the same level of criticism. We never heard complaints about *Coronation Street*, for example, which has been running on CBC for many years. It is a cheesy daily British soap opera and significantly less intellectually demanding than *Jeopardy!*

Fresh outrages were to follow. As part of the schedule strengthening, we decided to move *The Fifth Estate* and *Marketplace* from Wednesdays to Fridays. The decision was driven in large measure by the fact that Wednesday night is one of the most competitive of the week. CTV and Global aired many of their best shows that night. Friday is less demanding. Kirstine and I discussed whether the two iconic current affairs programs might do better on Friday. We looked at the numbers, the nature of the competition and the demographics of the shows, and moved them.

Another round of wailing began. We cared only for entertainment shows. We were diminishing the CBC's commitment to public broadcasting. We were trying to strangle the shows, knowing they would die ignominiously on Friday nights, uncared for and unseen. The usual suspects suggested their audiences would collapse. The *Walrus,* the Constituency's preferred magazine, noted that: "*The Fifth Estate* ... was wrenched from its traditional slot on Wednesday nights at nine and moved to Friday, which everyone knew to be the graveyard of television. And it was moved—look, you see?—to accommodate a frothy new comedy, *Being Erica*." The distinguished host of *The Fifth Estate*, Linden MacIntyre, moaned that it was darkness, darkness: "Here you get an image of CBC collectively sunk to its knees, holding its head in its hands, keening in memory of its lost golden age . . . Gone, all gone."

In fact, from the first week of the change, their numbers improved. No longer confronted by the juggernaut U.S. hits of Wednesday night, they prospered. *The Fifth Estate*'s audience increased immediately from 525,000 to over 630,000.

By the end of the 2008–09 season, the audiences had increased again. The new shows and the new schedule strategies had taken us to an 8.6 share. Once more, we had managed to grow the CBC, a previously unimaginable accomplishment. Even more satisfying, that year our all-Canadian prime time clobbered Global, which had a 6.8 share. We put out press releases explaining what had happened, but they were met with yawning and indifference.

The 2009–10 schedule changed little from the previous year. The stalwarts all returned: *Heartland, The Tudors, Being Erica, The Border, Battle of the Blades, Dragons' Den, Rick Mercer Report, This Hour Has 22 Minutes, The Fifth Estate, Doc Zone, Marketplace, The National, Hockey Night in Canada* and *Little Mosque on the Prairie*. We added only one new show, *Republic of Doyle*, a father-son cop show set in St. John's, Newfoundland. The sophisticated older cop, played by Sean McGinley, and his knockabout wild son, played by the brilliant Allan Hawco, solve crimes, get into trouble, get out of trouble, then get into more trouble. Through it all, St. John's appears as a separate character. The extraordinary setting, the harbour, the beautiful downtown, the immense appetite for life, the laughter, the musical scene, are woven into the fabric of the show. It too did very well and went on to become a big success.

Ultimately, the 2009–10 season closed even higher than 2008–09, finishing with a 9.3 share. The overall share had improved every year from its lowest point in 2004. As we came through the lockout and developed the new shows, we had managed to increase the CBC's share by almost 50 percent. No other major network in North America had grown during that period, let alone by anything like that amount. Global, CTV, CBS, ABC and NBC all lost share. We were confident that we had laid the basis for going further, and we began to consider how to extend the strategy.

AS WE LOOKED beyond the upcoming 2010–11 season, we knew we would have to be more daring if we wanted to hold the gains we had made, let alone strengthen the performance of the CBC further. Global had recently been bought by Shaw, CTV by Bell and Citytv by Rogers. All of them now had significantly wealthier owners, who would doubtless be prepared to spend more money to recover the share they had lost. If we were to succeed, we would have to push even harder. We settled, then, on a two-part Plan to Extend Dramatically the Entertainment Strategy. The first part of the plan was to strengthen Sunday evening; the second was to open up the schedule to make room for more drama and entertainment. Together, these two thrusts would allow us to build on the momentum that had been established.

To strengthen Sunday evenings, we would search out spectacular new Canadian properties for the two-hour block between 8:00 and 10:00 PM. They would be "tent-poles" that would follow *Heartland*, which was consistently delivering a million viewers. The idea was that every Sunday evening there would be a major television event, something unprecedented, something so novel, so funny, so beautiful, so iconic, so exciting that everyone would have to watch it. Some of the tent-poles might be stunts, some might be wildly controversial departures, some might be celebrations of major Canadian events, some might be the most glamorous of all properties, original feature films.

We already had a project in hand that would start to fill the bill: *Mulroney: The Opera*. It would attract controversy and cause buzz among a host of commentators. It was, as well, the first comic opera the CBC commissioned, and as such a novel departure in genre and format. We had also made sure that it was shot like a feature film, rather than a staged piece. The plan was to release it in cinemas and then leverage the resulting prom otion to give it even greater visibility. It was hard to imagine that it would not be scorned, loved, loathed and denounced, even before it was seen. An excellent recipe for success.

We put the wheels in motion to make a dramatic re-enactment of the life of Sir John A. Macdonald. Strangely, it had never been done before. Unlike the Americans, who ransack their history endlessly with bio-pics of their important historical figures, we almost never do. The Trudeau miniseries aside, there is nothing on Macdonald, Laurier or Mackenzie King, the most important prime ministers of the first one hundred years of Confederation. We wanted to breathe life into Sir John A. in a four-hour, two-movie dramatic re-enactment of his life and career. Although there were no lurid sexual scandals, there was certainly enough material to make it entertaining. He was a fop, a drunkard, a brilliant political tactician, a dreamer, a wit and a spellbinding talker. He also had a great rival in George Brown, the cranky, anti-French editor of the *Globe*, who despised Macdonald. The story between them was the struggle to create the country we are. The first movie would take us to the creation of the United Canadas and the establishment of Ottawa as the capital. The second would bring us to Confederation. Through it all, there would be the strains with Britain, the Civil War in the United States, the falls from grace and power. Essential material.

Then we wanted to do something really big to improve Sunday nights: we wanted the CBC to begin commissioning feature films. For years, the Corporation had been criticized for not doing enough in this area. It was felt in many quarters that the CBC had a special responsibility to help English Canada's anaemic movie industry. The problem was that the Canadian industry made no structural sense. It was organized to fail.

Feature films are released through what the industry calls "windows." The first window is the cinema. The second is home video at the rental store or, increasingly, video-on-demand, whether on TV or on a computer. The third is pay-television, or premium television as it is sometimes called (Movie Central and The Movie Network). Then it appears on conventional television. Depending on how successful the movie is (that is, how long it stays in the movie house), up to three years can pass before the film is allowed to be shown on conventional television. The "windows" structure is designed to squeeze the maximum revenue out of a particular movie.

In recent times, with the advent of home video rentals and video-on-demand, by the time a film arrives on TV, almost everyone who wants to see it will have already done so. In the case of an English-Canadian movie, which typically fails at the cinema in the first instance, there is almost no value at all in it by the time it comes to TV. Since it made no splash when it was first released, little promotion is put behind the other windows, and by the time the movie can be scheduled for TV everyone has forgotten it, if they knew anything about it in the first place.

We made a radical proposal to the industry, one which would be far and away the most difficult, daunting and exciting part of the new Sunday night strategy. We said we would participate if we could have the third window after the movie houses and home video, but before pay-TV. If we could have the third window, we would make it our business to promote the movie and drive up the box office. We would put the network behind it, advertising it on our top shows and having the actors, writers and directors featured on all the big talk shows (*The Hour*, the morning radio shows, *Q*, etc.). We would dramatically increase the distributors' ability to market the film, and we might build some real success.

The problem was that the pay-television operators said that if we had the third window ahead of them, they would not participate in the financing of the film or buy it from the distributors. In effect, this would make the film un-financeable. This became clear when it came to the making of *Barney's Version*, Robert Lantos's wonderful movie of the great Mordecai Richler novel. When Lantos was putting the financing together, we agreed that we would see if it could be structured using the new windows model.

We went to see the presidents of the pay-television companies, John Cassidy at Movie Central and Ian Greenberg at the Movie Network. I explained that the CBC would promote the movie and that we wanted only one showing before them. They could then have it and run it as many times as they wanted. Besides, I noted, Canadian movies were hardly the bread and butter of their operations. The reason people subscribed to Movie Central and The Movie Network was to watch U.S. movies. The new structure would have no effect whatsoever on their business but might give the Canadian feature film industry a shot in the arm.

"No thanks," said Ian Greenberg.

"No thanks?"

"Nope. It's not for us. It would erode our exclusivity claim."

"But all your U.S. movies, your bread and butter, would still be exclusive."

"Nope."

We went round it a few more times to no effect. Eventually Lantos managed to negotiate a slightly better window, but it was still not enough.

Over the next few years, we struggled to figure out a way to finance films so that the CBC could participate. A eureka moment occurred when Fred Fuchs realized that we could combine the money that was available to finance feature films from Telefilm with the money available in the Canadian Television Fund to finance television drama. Without going into the technicalities of the problem, we ended up agreeing with Telefilm that the new model would work, since it would allow us to take out the pay-television operators without compromising the financing of the movie. On November 12, 2009, the CBC and Telefilm announced the new program. We were excited by the possibility that we might have created a huge structural improvement in the Canadian feature film industry.

The first major film that was financed under the new initiative was *Midnight's Children*, based on Salman Rushdie's Booker Prize-winning novel. The screenplay was written by Salman Rushdie and Deepa Mehta. It was financed as an international co-production, using the new arrangements to draw money from both the Canadian Television Fund and Telefilm. It seemed hard to imagine a more promising debut. We had one of the post-war period's greatest novels, one of the most gifted Canadian writers and directors and perhaps the best-known author in the world.

The second part of our plan to compete against Global and CTV was to open up the 10:00–11:00 PM weeknight time slot, where *The National* currently resides. This is in many ways the most important slot in television. It is where the adult dramas appear, the ones that are too grown up to be aired earlier. This is where shows like *Castle*, *CSI*, *The Mentalist*, *Blue Bloods* and *Unforgettable* appear. It is the place where the most serious and challenging fare can be found. Opening up 10:00–11:00 would not only provide new creative possibilities, it would also give us another four hours per week of space to pursue the entertainment strategy, during the primest of the real prime-time hours.

The idea that *The National* would move to 11:00 PM was political dynamite. The fact that it had originally been at 11:00 would cut no ice. The fact that it could be watched at 10:00 PM on CBC News Network, which is available to over 90 percent of all English-Canadian households, would cut no ice. The fact that the time slot would be better for *The National*, which we could infer from the positive results of shifting *The Fifth Estate* and *Marketplace*, would cut no ice. Nope. If we moved it, the controversy surrounding *The One* would be in comparison a minor contretemps.

There would be anger in the Constituency. The political classes, the opinion makers, the chattering classes, Knowlton Nash, everyone would attack the CBC with a vengeance. They would prophesy doom. Doom for *The National*. Doom for the new 10:00 shows. Doom for the network. The front page of the *Globe and Mail* would challenge our sanity. They would be wrong, as they had been about pretty much everything, from the effects of the lockout to our ability to make popular shows to the moving of *The Fifth Estate*. But it would make no difference. Despite the track record, we would be attacked.

So there it was. Our plan was to commission giant Canadian projects and make Sunday night the most important viewing night of the week. We would fill it with *Mulroney: The Opera* (maybe *Chrétien: The Opera* too), *The Life of Sir John A. Macdonald* and *Midnight's Children*. Spectacular. Then we would open a new block of the schedule for adult drama and comedy. We would meet the private networks' brilliant 10:00 PM U.S. shows with our brilliant 10:00 PM Canadian shows.

In the process, we knew that we would also accomplish something remarkable for Canadian culture. We would create major new opportunities for the feature film industry. If it worked even remotely the way we hoped, it would dramatically influence the production and distribution of Canadian movies. And with the opening of 10:00 PM we would create a major increase in the amount of Canadian drama produced, and allow Canadian talent to work in the most creative, daring and demanding part of prime time.

We knew that all of this would be challenging and controversial. We knew that it would cost more money, although we believed we already knew how to find it. We knew, as well, that it would take two to three years to put it in place. We needed to find the new properties, the new movies and drama series that would make it work. Then we had to develop and produce them. If we began work in 2010, we would be ready to launch the new schedule in 2012–13.

We were very excited at the prospect of taking these steps. They would amount to the second phase of the entertainment revolution we had been pursuing over the last four years. They would be ambitious and risky, but we were confident that given our success to date, they could be done. We also thought that they would cement the CBC as the cornerstone of the Canadian film and television production industries, and confirm its centrality as the most important cultural organization in the country.

If the president and the board approved, we were ready to begin immediately building on the extraordinary results of the 2009–10 season. We saw no reason why we could not grow our share even further and make the CBC even more central to the lives of Canadians. Alas, it was never to be. The whole venture was a bridge too far.

Je me souviens.
Eugène Taché

four
THE FRENCH

DANIEL GOURD'S FIRST question was, "When will you fire Don Cherry?"

We were standing in the boardroom of the CBC headquarters in Montreal, the Maison de Radio-Canada. He looked grim. I knew Daniel very well. He had been vice-chair of the Canadian Television Fund when I was chair. He never joked.

"When will you fire Don Cherry?" he repeated.

The year before I arrived at the CBC, Don Cherry had committed an outrage. In discussing the use of visors in hockey, he said, "Most of the guys that wear them are European or French guys." Real men were happy to take a puck or a stick in the face. The Europeans and the French were apparently not real men.

French Canada had reacted to this slight with ferocious anger. The papers worked themselves into a rage of editorial denunciations. Once again the wretched English had mocked them. Once again they had been insulted.

Worst of all, this was not some minor constitutional point. This was not a humiliation of fiscal federalism. This was not an unacceptable intrusion into provincial jurisdiction. No. This was an attack on the very soul of French Canada. This was an attack on Hockey. This was an attack on Les Glorieux. The Rocket, a wimp? Boom Boom? The Flower? The Immortals? Wimps?

And to make matters worse, the charge had been made on *Hockey Night in Canada*, the holiest shrine of all, by the High Priest himself. Don Cherry—the preposterous Don Cherry in his absurd collars and idiotic jackets—had called down the masculinity of Quebec. A million-and-a-half English-Canadian hockey fanatics had heard the charge. A million-and-a-half *maudits anglais* had nodded their heads in unison. Yes. Sad but true. The French are a bunch of pussies.

Daniel Gourd, the saviour of French television at Radio-Canada, the inventor of *Les Bougon*, the most politically incorrect show ever seen, was angry. Gourd weighed nearly three hundred pounds. He was known as "the warrior" for his take-no-prisoners approach. He was a Quebec nationalist. He pulled himself upright, and glaring, red in the face, asked again, "When are you going to fire Don Cherry?"

How could he not? *La Presse* described Don Cherry's remarks as insufferable. *Le Devoir* had been blunter still. Stiff speeches had been made in the National Assembly, blistering with indignation about this newest slur.

Montreal is a small place. A year after Cherry's attack, Daniel still had to go to cocktails and lunch and be asked what he was doing about Don Cherry. After all, Daniel was the most senior French Canadian at CBC. If he could not put an end to these humiliations, then it showed he was impotent, and that only compounded the humiliation. It was ruining Daniel's social life. It was ruining his lunch. It was ruining his credibility.

Of course, dumping Don Cherry was inconceivable. Cherry, the icon of English-Canadian hockey, could no more be dumped than Peter Mansbridge or Rick Mercer. He *was* the CBC. He was in fact the most important representative of that part of English Canada that normally felt ignored and patronized by the CBC.

From the pulpit at "Coach's Corner," he came out every Saturday night for the little guy. He came out for the police officers and firefighters and soldiers. He came out for the kids just learning to play hockey on frigid ponds and in tiny arenas. He came out for the country, expressing his great potato love for it, his old-fashioned nationalism, his celebration of the small-town virtues that underpinned English Canada's sense of itself.

Don Cherry loved Canada and he was loved in return. Wherever he went, he was mobbed. Everyone wanted to talk to him, get his autograph, touch the hem of his sacred jackets. He was bigger in English Canada than anyone else, bigger even than the hockey gods, bigger than Wayne Gretzky, bigger than Sidney Crosby.

"Fire Don Cherry?" I asked incredulously. Did Daniel understand the nature of his request?

"If you want to be accepted and respected by your French colleagues, he has to go," he explained. It felt like joining the Mob. To prove my bona fides and my loyalty, to be accepted by Radio-Canada, I was being asked—in effect—to murder a family member.

The truth was that I very much wanted to be accepted and respected by my French colleagues. I was the first senior executive at the CBC who could not only speak French, but who liked and admired French-Canadian culture. Over the course of many years, I had had the pleasure of watching French television and movies, reading French novels and newspapers, following the extraordinary complexities of Quebec politics and becoming immersed in the hopes and fears of the other Solitude.

Just before coming to the CBC, I had been the head of Telefilm Canada, the crown corporation that is the most important financier of feature films in the country. Its headquarters are on the rue Saint-Jacques in Old Montreal. Much of the English-Canadian filmmaking community bridles somewhat at the culture of Telefilm. They feel it is somehow too French. Most of the top officials are French; most of the conversation is in French; most of the preoccupation seems to be with French films. All of which is true and was part of the pleasure of the job.

On arriving, I decided that since I was the first English head of the agency in almost a generation, I would focus on reassuring Quebec that I admired French films and that I was not going to spend all of my time on the English side. To that end, it seemed a good idea for my first interviews to be with the French press, as a sort of gesture. I had anodyne conversations with *Le Devoir*, the nationalist morning paper, and *La Presse*, the federalist paper. In the course of the interviews I said that it appeared that films could be successful in Quebec with smaller budgets than in English Canada. ("*Au Québec, c'est possible d'avoir un budget moins élevé.*")

Immediately various influential figures in the French film community took my words out of context. Most notably, Serge Losique, the perennial president of the Montreal film festival, the *Festival des films du monde,* wrote an angry letter excoriating my views. He blustered that he was surprised at the new policies of Telefilm ("*C'est avec surprise que j'ai vu dans* La Presse *la nouvelle politique de Téléfilm Canada.*"). Of course, there was no new policy; it was a simple observation about the relative competitiveness of the two markets. Losique demanded that the French film community be properly respected and championed.

This precipitated a further series of misunderstandings, with the result that a lot of effort had to be spent disabusing people of the idea that I was unsympathetic or uninterested in the French film industry. In fact, it took another week of interviews to straighten things out and make clear that there was no new policy involved. What surprised me the most was that instead of phoning to ask my views, people like Serge Losique seemed to think it was better to begin our relationship with an attack.

Puzzled by the whole debacle, I phoned Denise Robert for advice. Denise is one of Quebec's most influential film producers. She has made many of the most successful films in the last twenty years, including *Ma vie en cinémascope*, *The Rocket*, and perhaps most importantly, *Les invasions barbares*, with her husband, the distinguished writer and director Denys Arcand. If anyone knew how to navigate these weird waters, it was Denise. "What's going on?" I asked. She laughed. "Welcome to Quebec," she replied.

Eventually things settled down. The French film community accepted me. The Académie canadienne du cinéma et de la télévision invited me to co-chair (with the distributor Guy Gagnon) their annual fundraiser and golf tournament. In 2003, *La Presse* rated me the fourth-most influential person in Quebec culture (amazingly ahead of Denys Arcand), and *Le Devoir* voted me the seventh-least influential person in Quebec culture. Enormous success came to the films we financed. By the end of 2003–04, Quebec films were taking more than 40 percent of the domestic box office (compared to 2 percent in English). *La grande séduction* and *Les invasions barbares* were playing to packed houses in France as well as Canada. As one commentator noted, "*Tous nos rêves étaient permis.*"

The high point of the period came with *Les invasions barbares*. It was the first film in a long time that Denys Arcand had written and directed in French. The script was widely admired, and hopes were high that he would redeem himself after a series of not very well received attempts in English. Much was riding on the success of the film, both for Arcand and for the reputation of Telefilm and the Quebec film industry.

When it was almost finished, I was invited to see it at the editing house, where Arcand was still working on the music. The screening room was small. Only one other person was there, Mitsou Gélinas, the actress, singer, writer and personality, who plays the young wife of one of the major characters. Mitsou has been famous since she was sixteen, when she released the crossover-hit song "Bye Bye Mon Cowboy." Her pouty beauty and sexy singing vaulted her into superstardom in Quebec (and for a while in English Canada as well) and laid the basis for a formidable career. This was aided by the fact that she comes from cultural royalty. Her grandfather was Gratien Gélinas, the playwright and actor widely regarded as the founder of modern theatre in Quebec.

I introduced myself, made a few banal remarks and sat beside her on the sofa. She smiled—her breathtaking smile—and made some friendly small talk, and the film began. It was like watching a rough cut of *Some Like It Hot* with Marilyn Monroe. Mitsou has many of the same qualities: beauty, intelligence and remarkable performing gifts. We spoke a little at the end, with me babbling inanities about the film and her performance.

Outside the editing facility, snow fell in the dark Montreal winter. The film is the second in a loose pair that begins with the seminal

Le déclin de l'empire américain. In *Les invasions*, the central character of the original film is dying of cancer. The friends from *Le déclin* assemble for the first time in many years, now with careers, marriages (some failed) and adult children. They surround their friend, reminisce, talk, tell jokes, eat and wait for him to die. The film is remarkable, funny and very moving.

My cell phone rang. It was Denise.

"So," she asked. "What did you think?"

I pondered for a moment, still overwhelmed by the movie. "I think," I said, surprising myself, "that it's the best film ever made in Canada."

"No, really?"

"Really."

"Let me get Denys on the phone."

Denys came on the phone. I said the same thing. He laughed and demurred, in his funny, ironic way.

"Really," I said again. "You will see."

And as it turned out, I was right. The film went on to be named one of the best of the year and won an Academy Award as best foreign language film of 2003. The night of the Academy Awards, we all sat together, Denys, Denise and her producing partner, just in front of Harvey Weinstein, the head of Miramax. For a little English guy from Toronto, Ontario, this was big fun indeed.

My hope, then, when I arrived at the CBC was to win the confidence and respect of my French colleagues at Radio-Canada by building bridges—show-business bridges—between the solitudes, by figuring out ways to draw the two cultures together, by making shows that would reveal for English Canadians just how clever and interesting French Canada was. It was my fervent hope that if we approached the issues of linking the Solitudes intelligently—and given the resources of CBC/Radio-Canada, why could we not?—we would accomplish something culturally historic. Little did I know that the whole venture was doomed to indifference and failure.

SHORTLY AFTER ARRIVING at the CBC, I was having drinks with Moses Znaimer, the ex-wunderkind widely credited with inventing a series of successful television innovations. He was the first to understand music videos and the creation of music television channels. He created Citytv's high-impact, low-cost, on-the-streets news format. He was also the father of "flow," his mystical theory of programming and scheduling, that, whatever it meant, he claimed was at the root of his remarkable success. Znaimer is regarded in many circles as a sort of Svengali-like Marshall McLuhan hipster of mass media. In others, he is regarded as a charlatan.

We were sitting in the Spoke Club. He was dressed completely in black, drinking a manhattan. Recently departed from his old job, he was busy reinventing himself. As part of his reinvention, he had made an interesting set of deals to buy the English "remake" rights to some of the most popular shows in French Canada. He figured that he could remake them with English actors, using the same script, sets and costumes. That way he could save money on the production and development costs, while being confident in their appeal, since they already had a track record of success. Broadcasters would be fools not to buy these shows from him.

"So what do you say to *Rumeurs*?" he asked.

Rumeurs was an hour-long situation dramedy set in a celebrity/gossip magazine. It had been running successfully on Radio-Canada for some time. It concerns the funny, sad encounters in love and ambition of the twentysomething, thirtysomething employees who work there. It includes the usual: a fish-out-of-water sports journalist who would never normally work for a woman's magazine; a predatory, man-killing, sexy vamp; an aging but still sexy publisher; plus an assortment of gay art directors, aspiring writers and ambitious editors, all falling in love, chasing stories and stabbing each other in the back.

"You can have it at a knock-down price. Since you will be the first to buy a show from me using this formula, and since I need a first buyer, you can get it cheap. In fact, I will give you a two-for-one. If you buy *Vices cachés (Hidden Vices)* as well, I'll throw it in for the same price."

Vices cachés was a Quebec show, a bit like *Desperate Housewives*, except it was a sort of Desperate Househusbands.

"It's in the zeitgeist." He went on, "Everyone will get it."

"Perhaps," I allowed.

"You know, Richard, if you were a real TV mogul, you would just green-light them now, and we could seal the deal with a couple more manhattans."

Moses has a remarkable capacity to make you feel inadequate when you are not doing what he wants.

Eventually we moved ahead with *Rumeurs*—now *Rumours*—but not at the speed Moses wanted. We carefully screen-tested the actors and actresses for the English version. We wanted to make sure not only that they were good but also that audiences would like them. As well—although we would never say it—we knew they had to be better looking than their Quebec counterparts. A sad truth of English TV is that, generally speaking, it's important for actors—and even newsreaders and journalists—to be physically attractive.

We tested the actors and shot the series according to Moses's method, using the same scripts and sets as the French version. We had Sphere Media, the original producer of *Rumeurs*, produce *Rumours*. The principal of Sphere, Jocelyne Deschenes, is one of Quebec's most respected television producers.

We finished the show and put it on air, and it flopped. Moses was beside himself. He claimed it was badly scheduled and promoted. (This is, indeed, something of a leitmotif of producers' claims. Their shows never fail because they are bad; they only fail because they are poorly scheduled and promoted). In this case, Moses was wrong. The show failed for much subtler and more interesting cultural reasons.

When we did a post-mortem, a number of things became clear. The style, pacing and shot structure of French television are very different from English. Where the French are happy to let characters develop slowly over a long narrative arc, English viewers need things to happen more quickly. In the original *Rumeurs*, one of the female leads starts as an unpleasant harridan in the early episodes and then develops into a much more complex and likeable character later in the series. An arc of this length across multiple episodes is unacceptable to most English viewers. If the characters are unattractive in the first episode, it's hard to move them to the second.

As well, the visual style is different. Where English shows have fluid and unobtrusive shots and edits, the French prefer a style that is much livelier, more herky-jerky. This gives their shows a slightly breathless quality, as though one is rushing through an exciting and unpredictable experience. It makes most English viewers feel tired and anxious.

With this in mind, we went back to try again. This time we chose *Les hauts et les bas de Sophie Paquin*, another intelligent, funny show on Radio-Canada. To accommodate what we had learned, we cut it down from an hour to half an hour, restructured the lead character's development and smoothed out the visual style. We even shortened the name to appeal more to the attention-challenged English audience. It was called, simply, *Sophie*.

This time the development process was even more rigorous. We screen-tested all the major actors, shot a pilot and tested it, left Moses out of the equation, got a punch-up writer to work on the jokes and generally tried to make it as compelling as possible to an English audience, without losing the flavour and charm of the original. It launched to positive critical notices and then slowly sank in the sea of American shows competing against it. We kept it on life support for a couple of seasons, but it never gained any traction in English Canada and ultimately had to be scrapped.

These failures were sobering. It seemed that drama and comedy might be too hard to adapt. The cultural differences were too large. Jokes did not translate well, the attitudes of the audiences were too different, the visual and narrative styles were often in conflict, and maybe the truth was that English audiences were not going to assign value to a show just because it had been a success in Quebec. This was probably something the French had already concluded, since they never bothered to try and adapt English shows for their audiences.

In a final attempt to build cultural bridges, we thought it might be better to do a nonfiction cultural affairs show, something that would open up Quebec to English Canada. For this purpose, we hired Mitsou. She was magical on television. The screen loved her, ate her up. The top people in the province came to her show, even people who would never otherwise give interviews, such as Guy

Laliberté, the founder of the Cirque du Soleil. But all to no avail. The hostess was fabulous, the guests were excellent, but nobody in English Canada cared. The ratings were anaemic and the show was ultimately cancelled.

These essentially one-way efforts by the CBC to reflect Quebec back to English Canada have been supplemented over the years by attempts to create shows that would work in both languages. When Robert Rabinovitch was president, he created a $10-million Cross-Cultural Fund. Its purpose was to help finance the development and production of shows that were jointly commissioned to be run on both the CBC and Radio-Canada.

The most ambitious of these ventures were a multi-part drama about motorcycle gangs, called *The Last Chapter* (*Le dernier chapitre*), and *Trudeau*, a miniseries. *The Last Chapter*—despite its lurid and promising subject matter—was a flop. It opened with much fanfare and heavy promotion, only to watch its audiences leach away as the weeks went by. Various reasons were adduced for its failure: it was not well done, the English did not like reading the occasional French subtitle, the plot and character arcs were too long or too short, it seemed awkward and cheesy. Whatever the reasons, it flopped.

The same was true of *Trudeau*. Although the first episode was considered a great success, reaching an audience in English Canada of well over two million people, it lost viewers rapidly as the weeks went by. In this case, the reason was easier to find. After the initial thrill and charm of Pierre Trudeau the glamorous bachelor meeting Margaret the beautiful flower child, the whole thing ground to a turgid halt. Love and sex gave way to abstruse constitutional arguments and elaborate dissections of the British North America Act. All across the country brave viewers soldiered on—more, one supposes, out of a sense of public duty than anything else—until, unable to stand it any longer, they switched over to real entertainment shows.

On arriving at the CBC, I inherited a number of these docudramas masquerading as entertainment that had been commissioned out of the Cross-Cultural Fund. There were six hours of the young *Trudeau*, and—unbelievably—six hours of the young *René Lévesque*.

This latter seemed an enormous stretch. By the time of its making, the average English Canadian would not have heard much of René Lévesque since the 1980 Referendum, some thirty years earlier. This meant that people had to be at least fifty years old to remember who he was, let alone to be interested in his early life as a war correspondent or as a Quebec cabinet minister in the 1960s. Knowing this, we were terrified that if we ran it in prime time during the regular season, it would sink like a stone in the ratings, inciting more mockery and opprobrium from our critics. Instead, we ran it—at significant expense—in the summer and vowed to make no more shows about recently dead politicians.

I discussed what to do with the fund with Sylvain Lafrance, the charming and clever head of French services, who had—with the recent departure of Daniel Gourd—taken over the management of the whole operation. He had spent his entire career at Radio-Canada and was widely liked and admired. France has made him a Chevalier des Arts et des Lettres (which means he can wear a red thread in his lapel). No matter what disasters befall the French network—or him personally—he is relentlessly sunny and cheerful. He is known affectionately as Monsieur Tout Va Bien.

We agreed that there was not much point in trying to make any more drama or comedy jointly, and certainly no more docudramas. Instead, we agreed to focus on documentaries and kids' shows. This seemed more sensible and—I thought—gave us an elegant way out of making any more shows about recently dead politicians. As I was leaving the meeting, however, Sylvain slowed me down.

"Whoa. Whoa," he said. "Not quite so fast on *René Lévesque Part II: The Mature Years*."

"Excuse me." I hesitated. "I thought we agreed no more."

"Yes indeed, but after *The Mature Years*."

"I thought you hated the young *René Lévesque*. Why go on?"

"Richard, think about this for a second. We agree to make René Lévesque's life while he is a federalist and then refuse to finance a show on his life as a separatist? There would be no more lunch for me in Montreal."

He was right, and to the dismay of the English side, we financed six more hours of Mr. Lévesque.

CBC/RADIO-CANADA IS A microcosm of Canada. The tensions, suspicion, mutual ignorance, indifference and envy that characterize French-English relations generally are found in even higher relief at the Corporation. They are in higher relief because the CBC is not a real mirror of the country; it is a distorted one. Where French Canada makes up less than 25 percent of the real Canada, at the CBC it receives 40 percent of the money granted by the government. Where the real Canada has a population of 33 million people, 8 million of whom speak French, the CBC is a Canada in which more than 12 million of its citizens appear to be French. It is a Canada where the *revanche du berceau* was actually achieved, where the dreams of the most ardent nationalists of the Saint-Jean-Baptiste Society have been realized. It is a fantasy Canada created by a disproportionate allocation of the public subsidy that is given to the Corporation.

This is unique among the major cultural agencies of the country. At Telefilm, the Canada Media Fund (the television financing agency), the National Film Board and the Canada Council, the split has historically been one-third of government funds to French cultural production and two-thirds to English. While this split overstates the relative size of the French population and fails to reflect its continuing decline as a percentage of the total country, it is nowhere as egregious as at the CBC.

The result is that the French Canada of the CBC is very different from the real world French Canada. While still principally located in Quebec with Montreal as its epicentre, it extends across the country in a manner unknown to demography. It features French television and radio stations not only in the traditional pockets of francophones outside Quebec, in Eastern Ontario and New Brunswick, but right across the country.

In Vancouver, Calgary, Edmonton, Regina and Winnipeg, radio and television broadcasts are available in French. They provide local and regional weather, information, news and sports just as though there were real French audiences in those places. But, in fact, the audiences are so small that they cannot be counted. In the language of audience measurement, they are "hashmarks," viewership so tiny that it is invisible to the system. The joke in Vancouver or Regina is that the number of CBC French employees is larger than the French population they serve.

These tiny audiences can be accommodated because of the disproportionate allocation of the public subsidy. But it also leads to deeply inequitable arrangements. For example, where it costs $15 to provide service to an English speaker in Saskatchewan, it costs over $700 for every French speaker. This is almost three times as much as it costs to service Northern Canadians throughout Yukon, Nunavut and the Northwest Territories, the most remote and inhospitable parts of the country. This pattern repeats itself in every major market outside Quebec.

The problem of greater resources being available to French speakers leads to difficult situations. During the downsizing of 2009, when four hundred positions were eliminated in English services, staff was being reduced in the English side of the Vancouver office while it was being increased on the French side. Vancouver is, of course, the second-largest English-speaking city in Canada. It is culturally, economically and socially the most important city in Western Canada, and one where the CBC must be profoundly present. It is also English. French is not the second language of Vancouver; it is not even the third or fifteenth. If the citizens of Vancouver speak languages other than English, they are Punjabi, Cantonese, Mandarin, Urdu, Vietnamese and Greek, not French.

It is difficult for the English side of the CBC to understand how these arrangements can be right. Not surprisingly, when the English side is forced to reduce staff while the French side grows to service a population that does not exist, they take offence. More broadly, the English side cannot understand the overall logic of the situation. English Canada is—and has been since the emergence of mass media—in the cultural fight of its life against the overwhelming sea of American television shows. French-Canadian culture has already won. French Canadians prefer Canadian shows to foreign ones.

Quebec is in many ways a normal place culturally, like Britain or the United States. The top shows are all locally made and produced. The most popular musicians and actors are all local. A serious star system flourishes, with endless small magazines covering their comings and goings. Quebecers, like Americans, are fascinated with their own celebrities. They follow their successes and failures, their love affairs, their plastic surgeries and their scandals. Women in hair salons do not talk about going to bed with Brad Pitt or George Clooney, they fantasize about Roy Dupuis.

English Canada is not the same. There are no stars. There is no gossip. There are no magazines to follow the stars' doings, because there are no stars to follow. The popular imagination is filled with American stars. The checkout counters at grocery stores feature the latest on Angelina and Brad, Jennifer Aniston's newest boyfriend, on Scarlett Johansson, Catherine Zeta-Jones, Julia Roberts and Robert Downey Jr., plus innumerable inconsequential reality TV stars such as the Kardashians, none of whom are Canadian.

English-Canadian TV exists in the most competitive television market in the world and labours under crushing economic disadvantages compared to its U.S. competitors. It's the only place in the industrialized world where—over many decades—its own citizens have preferred foreign television shows to their own. In this sense, English-Canadian TV has been an historic flop, while French-Canadian TV has been—within its own market—a success on a par with American TV in the United States.

Given the challenges confronting the CBC compared to Radio-Canada, the disproportionate split of resources becomes all the more difficult for the English side to understand. Why, as a matter of policy, would the successful side be advantaged while the unsuccessful side is disadvantaged? It seems a strange logic to put the bulk of the resources where they are least needed.

If the resources were to be properly rebalanced, there would be a massive movement of dollars. Simply bringing the CBC in line with other cultural institutions would require moving $50 million of the public subsidy from the French side to the English (reducing the French take from about $300 million to $250 million and increasing the English from $450 million to $500 million). To make the split reflect the relative size of the two populations would involve moving almost $150 million from the French to the English side (leaving $160 million for the French and $570 million for the English). No president of the CBC has been prepared to contemplate such a restructuring.

This fraught relationship is compounded by problems of mutual ignorance. With almost no exceptions, the senior management on the English side cannot speak French. As a result, they have no idea what the French shows are about. They cannot watch any of the iconic and brilliant French programs. *Les Bougon, Grande Ourse, Les hauts et les bas de Sophie Paquin, Rumeurs, Une heure sur terre* might as well be produced in Mongolia. And with ignorance of the shows goes ignorance of the narrative and comedic preoccupations they explore, the producers, writers and directors who make them and the stars who drive them forward. To the English side of the CBC, the French side is all but invisible.

The situation is not much better when the French look at the English. Though in many cases their mastery of both languages is superior, they have little interest in what is happening on the English side. Their understanding of the English shows, stars, directors and preoccupations is just as limp. They do not know—nor do they much care—what is on English TV or radio. To the French side of the CBC, the English are equally invisible.

This compound of mutual ignorance and resentment—writ large in the country as a whole and writ small in the microcosm of the CBC—occasionally breaks out in public incidents that illuminate the underlying problems. In recent years one of the silliest of them revolved around the Claude Dubois affair, which reflected both the cultural tensions between English and French Canada in the society at large and their translation inside the Corporation. Like the Don Cherry fiasco, it sheds light on the tectonic structure of Canada's cultural and social geography.

Claude Dubois is one of French Canada's most gifted, celebrated and iconic songwriters and singers. He has been described as the last great chansonnier and Quebec's first punk. Since he was seventeen, he has been writing masterpieces that have become enormous hits. Now in his early sixties, he has a vast catalogue of important compositions beginning with "Ma petite vie" in the 1960s, through "Comme un million de gens"—his greatest hit—and "Femmes de rêve." He is Quebec's best-known living songwriter, with the possible exception of Gilles Vigneault. Nobody in English Canada has ever heard of him.

In 2008 Dubois, along with Paul Anka, was inducted into the Canadian Songwriters Hall of Fame, along with five of his songs. The Hall of Fame is one of those worthy Canadian institutions that attempt to bridge the Two Solitudes. Every year it has a big gala where the inductees are announced, celebratory speeches are made and the featured songs are sung. It is a lovely evening, although often a little long, where everyone has a good time.

During the previous two years, the CBC had broadcast all three hours of the event on radio and produced an hour-long special for TV. Nobody watched the show. In 2008, when the producers cut the gala down for television, they focused on Paul Anka and Oscar Peterson, who had recently died and for whom a tribute was made at the event. They did not include Claude Dubois, on the grounds that there was little time available and the show was for English Canadians.

The next morning in Montreal, Dubois expressed his reservations about not being on the TV show. Among other things, he denounced the CBC as "a pack of racists and anti-francophones" and indicated that Toronto could fuck itself. While this seemed a pretty strong reaction to not being on TV, his theme was picked up with enthusiasm by the French press and Quebec politicians. The fact that none of the Songwriters Hall of Fame was aired on Radio-Canada seemed to mollify nobody.

The morning after Dubois's outburst, the papers in Quebec all weighed in on the matter. They agreed that he had been unforgivably slighted, that the English had once again behaved in a high-handed and insulting fashion, and that Quebec itself had been humiliated. At the National Assembly, the same theme was re-explored, with an even greater degree of indignation and alarm. Like the Don Cherry affair, it seemed that the *maudits anglais* had gone out of their way to perpetrate another outrage.

As the controversy unfolded, the CBC's head of communications, Bill Chambers, phoned to see what might be done. Chambers is perfectly bilingual. He comes from one of Quebec's most distinguished English families. His mother is Gretta Chambers, the celebrated journalist and former chancellor of McGill University, and his uncle is Charles Taylor, one of Canada's most eminent political philosophers.

"I think we may need an apology," he opined.

"An apology?" I replied, somewhat startled.

"Yes," he advanced. "Things are pretty hot here in Montreal. We need to pour a little cold water on this."

"But why should we apologize?" I asked. I was genuinely baffled. "Surely the apology should come from Dubois. He has just called us a bunch of racists and told us to go fuck ourselves."

Bill sighed a little sigh, the little sigh that one sighs when trying to bridge the unbridgeable gulf that separates the English and French sensibilities in Canada. "Perhaps you are right," he went on, "but we need to nip this thing before it gets completely out of control."

"Well, I think it's absurd," I retorted. "Imagine if the French decided not to put Neil Young on TV because nobody in Quebec had heard of him, and then he called Quebecers a pack of racists and said Montreal should fuck itself. People in English Canada would not defend him. They would call him an idiot."

Again the little sigh, before he came at it once more. We went back and forth with me feeling indignant about having to kowtow to vanity, while not wanting to be wholly unhelpful. Finally I agreed to apologize. Bill produced a statement saying something to the effect that we recognized that we could have done a better job reflecting the full diversity of the participants in the gala. Of course, it satisfied nobody.

A couple of days later, the parliamentary Standing Committee on Official Languages called me to appear to explain the inadequacy of CBC's efforts in the Claude Dubois affair. It was clear from the outset that the plan was not to engage in a disinterested examination of the pros and cons of putting Dubois on TV. No, the plan was to organize a gong show and give Quebec nationalist MPs a chance to gong a big English media executive from the dreaded Toronto.

Knowing this, it seemed a good idea to do all my statements in French, to answer all their questions in French and not to let a word of English slip from my lips. "How," I reasoned with myself, "could the members of the parliamentary committee accuse me of being an anti-francophone racist if I spoke only in French?" Of course, I was wrong.

Denis Coderre, the Liberal MP for Bourassa in Montreal, chaired the committee. He is not known for understatement.

"Well, Mr. Stursberg," he began, "are you prepared to apologize to Mr. Dubois?"

"Apologize?" I replied.

"Yes. He has been done a great wrong."

"Apologize? I think it is Claude Dubois who owes the CBC an apology."

"What?"

"He called us a pack of racists."

"We aren't looking into Mr. Dubois's conduct here, we are looking into yours."

"I hardly think we need apologize for not putting someone on TV. But surely he needs to apologize for calling us racists."

There were cries of disbelief and outrage.

Various Quebec members of Parliament asked how we could bridge the two cultures if we did not show Quebec artists to English audiences. I explained—as gently as I could—that putting people on TV that the audience had never heard of, singing songs in a language they do not understand, is simply an invitation to change channels. Nothing is accomplished by that. Fresh cries of disbelief and outrage followed.

Further attempts to describe the Cross-Cultural Fund and the other methods we were using to explain the Two Solitudes to each other fell on deaf ears. Not surprisingly. It was never, of course, the committee's purpose to thoughtfully consider these questions. It was to show the good citizens of Matane and Rimouski that their members of Parliament were righteously smiting the Anglo Beast. The low point arrived when a member of the Parti Québécois pointed his finger at me and shaking with indignation said, *"C'est à cause de vous, monsieur, qu'on a des séparatistes au Canada."*

Beyond the silliness of it all, the parliamentarians' consternation reflected the thrust of many attacks on the CBC. They believed—like Canadians generally—that somehow if things or people were not on TV, they did not really exist. It was not enough that Claude Dubois was inducted into the Hall of Fame and covered by CBC radio. If he was not on TV—and Quebec with him—his existential status was eroded, he was not fully real.

The committee members declared my appearance a fiasco. They decided to call the new president, Hubert Lacroix, and have him make the appropriate apologies. A few weeks later, he showed up and took a more conciliatory tack. He allowed that we could have been more sensitive and more inclusive, that Dubois was a fine fellow, that Stursberg did not really mean what he said, that the Corporation believed in inclusiveness, etc., etc. The committee members were warmed by his remarks, and the matter was concluded.

Some time later, I happened upon one of the editors of *La Presse* and asked him what he thought. I asked him specifically whether he thought it appropriate that Claude Dubois had called us a pack of racists and that nobody in Quebec had said he was an intemperate fool. "Well," he replied, "we are a minority and sometimes a little prickly as a result."

"So," I replied, "that means what? That we should hold you to lower standards of civility? Surely that would be patronizing and even more humiliating and insulting."

"An excellent point," he allowed.

THIS TWO-STEP OF mutual ignorance and longing pervades the governance of the CBC as well. In 2010, there was only one French board member. None of the others could speak French. As a result, they had no idea what was going on at Radio-Canada but wanted to appear enthusiastic all the same. They were impressed by what they had never seen or heard, and eager to be viewed as supportive and enthusiastic about French culture. This schizophrenia creates complications for the English network.

Sylvain Lafrance had pursued a strategy in the Quebec market that is different from the English strategy but appropriate to French Canada. Since all the top shows in French are Canadian, he does not need to repatriate the market from foreigners. Rather, he needs to distinguish Radio-Canada's offerings from those of its great rival, TVA. He cannot simply focus on ratings for Canadian shows; he needs to demonstrate that he is doing something different from the private sector.

The approach he had taken—like his predecessors—was to claim to emphasize "quality." He pursued what are called "*séries lourdes*"—more expensive shows with greater production values—in contrast to the vulgar "*téléromans*" of his competitors. He also put more emphasis on public affairs and documentaries in prime time, something his competitors never did. The notion was that where TVA appeals to a larger audience with more popular fare, Radio-Canada speaks to a higher standard.

The whole strategy is encapsulated in the broad claim that Radio-Canada is about Culture and Democracy. Culture here is meant to be taken with a capital *C*. Sylvain would explain regally that it was about providing more demanding shows that strive to attain the highest possible standards. It was about setting the cultural and intellectual bar for French Canada.

The fact that this was at best a half-truth in no way diminished the power of the claim. The shows on Radio-Canada, while occasionally focused on the high arts, are by and large indistinguishable from those of the CBC. In fact, the prime-time schedule of Radio-Canada is almost identical to that of the CBC. It is pretty much the same mix of genres in about the same proportions. There are dramas, comedies and reality shows between 8:00 and 10:00 PM, five days a week, with public affairs and documentaries on the other two nights. Every evening, *Le Téléjournal* comes on reliably at 10:00 PM, the same time as *The National*.

Unfortunately, claims are often more compelling than reality. The notion that Radio-Canada is really about Culture and Quality, compared to the vulgar striving for ratings at the CBC, becomes a stick with which to beat the English side of the Corporation. The board members never really asked the French any questions, since it's hard to ask about things you have never seen or heard. Rather, they would listen to the simultaneous translation of the French presentation and smile happily as Sylvain explained the Culture–with–a–big-C strategy, knowing that none of them had seen any of the shows. Once the French are done, the board members then turn with despair to the English side and ask why its efforts cannot be as lofty, why they cannot be as noble and, well—gosh—why they cannot be as superior as the French.

They look sadly at the English schedule, demanding to know why it's so vulgar. They search in vain for the big-C shows, the monuments to taste and sophistication that are being produced with regularity by the French. They shake their heads in despair at the situation comedies, family dramas, reality shows and police procedurals on the English-Canadian side. Sad, very sad. They collectively agree that the English are just not as cultured as their French counterparts.

This amalgam of disproportionate financing, differential challenges and patronizing sneering from the board is difficult for the English side. It is a game that can never be won. Excited by the French claim that their shows are culturally important, the board imagines these programs to be an amalgam of classical ballet, high opera and the most demanding twentieth-century playwrights (all Ionesco and Beckett, all the time). And that, remarkably, the French have managed to foist this extraordinarily difficult and sophisticated set of programs on an audience that laps them up. Radio-Canada enjoys a 20 share of the Quebec market, more than twice as many viewers as the sad-sack English team.

TO DATE, NOTHING much has worked to help bridge the enormous cultural divide between the French and English sides of CBC/Radio-Canada. The difficulties of remaking French shows in English, the disinterest of each audience in the artistic and cultural achievements of the other, the ongoing English discomfort about the allocation of resources, the utter inability of the English executives to watch French TV, and the linguistic limitations of the board members make it very hard to build bridges.

In this sense, CBC/Radio-Canada is again a microcosm of the country. Earnest members of the chattering classes—journalists, politicians, senior civil servants—all think it's important to build bridges between the Two Solitudes. They talk enthusiastically about both groups getting to know each other better, without any appreciation of the practical difficulties involved. And meanwhile, the vast majority of Canadians sigh their great sighs of indifference and go about their business.

Over the course of my time at the CBC, I suggested on a number of occasions that we might want to make a big effort to examine the issue of how to bridge the Solitudes. We had been fiddling at the margins. Perhaps we should go to the core of the matter. What was required was an in-depth investiga tion of the needs, styles and preoccupations of each side by the other. And who better to carry it out than Sylvain and me?

I suggested we switch jobs for a few months. He would run the English services and live in Toronto, and I would run French services and live in Montreal. He would get to know all the shows and top executives in real depth; he would learn our work methods and procedures; he would understand CBC better than any head of French services ever had. And the reverse, of course, would be true for me. By the time the Switch was over, I would know Radio-Canada better than anyone in English services ever had. Once we were finished, we would be in a position to have a real conversation about how to bridge the Solitudes.

The circumstances for making the Switch could not have been better. I spoke French and admired Quebec culture. Sylvain Lafrance spoke English and was widely liked at the CBC. We also liked each other. There might never be another opportunity to make such a move.

I thought the Switch would send a powerful message. It would attract wide attention in both the French and English press. Certainly it would precipitate a debate about how CBC/Radio-Canada could more effectively showcase the two great cultures of Canada. It would also underline the fact that CBC/Radio-Canada is the only large media company that straddles the linguistic divide. It would remind everyone why the Corporation is unique and why it matters.

I put the proposal to Sylvain on a number of occasions. He demurred. I could understand why. Toronto is not Montreal. It would be a lot less fun for him than for me. I discussed the idea with Robert Rabinovitch and then his successor, Hubert Lacroix. They both thought it might be interesting and valuable. I pressed Sylvain, joking with him about the possibility at dinners and lunches, in front of others. I promised to borrow his language and talk his talk. It would be Culture and Democracy all the way.

Finally, I thought a propitious moment had arrived. Radio-Canada had been under relentless attack by Pierre Karl Péladeau, the combative head of Quebecor, which owns TVA. He had been savaging Sylvain and company for inflated expenses, poor management, unfair reliance on government subsidies, not buying ads in his newspapers—anything he could think of to damage the Corporation and impair its ability to compete with him. At one point in 2007, as a way of reducing the money available to Radio-Canada, Péladeau decided to stop contributing to the Canadian Television Fund. In a famous interview in *Le Devoir,* Sylvain said of Péladeau, "*Ce gars-là se promène comme un voyou*" (he walks around like a thug).

Pierre Karl Péladeau sued Sylvain and Radio-Canada for $700,000 for calling him a "*voyou.*" The case became a *cause célèbre* in Québec. Everyone talked about it. It wound its way slowly through the courts. I figured that Sylvain might like a little break from the relentless drumbeat of bad feeling and attacks coming from Quebecor. Perhaps Toronto would be a pleasant change. Nobody there knew who Pierre Karl Péladeau was or what the word *voyou* meant.

"The timing might be good," I said.

Sylvain considered with wistful longing the relative tranquility of southern Ontario, far away from the cruel reach of the French press.

"Maybe," he said.

AFTER THE END of the NHL lockout, Don Cherry and I met to sort out his contract for the new season. We talked about not making any negative generalizations about particular groups. No comments about the French as a whole, or the Swedes, or the Catholics, or the Gays, or the Whomever.

"I never said anything about the Gays or the Catholics," Don observed.

"No. I know. But you understand what I mean, Don. We need to sort this out because I need to stop this foolish talk that you should be fired."

"You know, Richard, it was Ron [MacLean] that started me up on the Iraq War and whether we should be there. I never started it."

"I really don't care what you say about the Iraq War. I don't care what you say about anything, except when you make remarks about the French."

"Okay. Okay. What do you want?"

"How about we put in the contract that you cannot do that."

"Sure."

"Sure?"

"Sure. But you know, Richard, the French actually do control everything. You know that, right?"

We put a clause in his contract, and Don was as good as his word. There was never another outburst to humiliate and anger my colleagues at Radio-Canada.

In fact, as the seasons wore on, he became something of a champion of tolerance, almost to the point of political correctness. During the winter of 2010, a conversation took place on *Hockey Night in Canada* about whether the game was becoming too genteel. One of the commentators expressed anxieties that the Great National Game was being taken over by "pansies," that it was becoming "pansified."

Rage gripped the gay community. They were as offended as the French had been about visors. Rick Mercer phoned me to complain and urge that I put an end to the matter. The gay community in Canada—like the French—took strong exception not only to the use of the word *pansification* but also to the idea that they might be wimps. It was a double outrage, a slur within a slur.

In this case, however, Don had nothing to do with it. The pansification controversy was initiated by the pugnacious Mike Milbury. Indeed, as the controversy escalated, with gay rights activists across the country demanding various forms of satisfaction, Don was asked to help cool everyone down. On one notable "Coach's Corner" he released a series of sallies that put an end to further discussion of "pansies." He pronounced with solemnity that he supported gay rights.

Don's apparent conversion to political correctness seemed to shock some of his more traditional enthusiasts. "First," they muttered, "he's for the gays. Before you know it, he'll be coming out for the French. Yikes."

five
SPORTS

SALT LAKE CITY, February 2002. The Winter Olympic Games. Wayne Gretzky, the Great One, had assembled the best players in the country. The incomparable Mario Lemieux, the unbeatable Martin Brodeur, the terrifying Eric Lindros and the wonderful Steve Yzerman were on the Team, along with Jarome Iginla, Joe Sakic, Chris Pronger, Theoren Fleury, Curtis Joseph. All of the players on the roster were likely future Hall of Famers. It was a spectacular team. Canada had not won a gold medal at the Olympic Games in fifty years. The dreams of the entire country rested with the Great One and his team.

The opening game was a disaster. The Team was beaten by Sweden, 5–2. Sweden! Worse was to come. The Team barely beat Germany. Germany! Barely beating the Germans was like barely beating the squad from Nigeria or Venezuela. And then the Czechs: nothing more than a tie! A tie! The first three games and the Team was 1–1–1. It appeared that they might not win any medals at all. The media was in a lather.

Second-guessing and hand-wringing were everywhere. The hockey writers seized on the smallest mistakes. They trashed the spirit of the team, the selection of the players, the strategy used in games, everything. Finally the Great One could take it no longer. At a press conference after the tie with the Czechs, he denounced the officiating and the media. He accused them of a double standard, of failing to penalize Europeans for actions that would have drawn game misconducts for Canadians. He said that everyone wanted the Canadians to lose. It was us against the world. His speech appeared to have a galvanizing effect. The Team pulled itself together. It started to win.

Meanwhile, the women's team had been winning. Unlike the men's team, they had had a fairly easy time of it, not allowing a single goal in the preliminary rounds of play. The astonishing Hayley Wickenheiser, who would ultimately be named the MVP and become the top scorer, led the women into the finals against the U.S. Despite lopsided officiating, with the American referee calling substantially more penalties against the Canadians, Wickenheiser and company prevailed, defeating the dreaded ones 3–2. It was the most widely watched female hockey game in Canadian history.

The women's victory gave the Team a further lift. They entered the finals against the United States. The whole country held its breath. Every television set in every bar, house, restaurant, airport, barn, doghouse, store and bus station was tuned to the game. Every Canadian watched: the street sweepers and bank presidents, the university professors and dog-catchers, the lumberjacks and society queens. Everyone. When it ended, with the Canadians defeating the Yanks, bedlam broke out. More than 10.5 million Canadians had watched the game, the largest television audience in Canadian history, and the largest television audience in the CBC's history.

When I arrived at the CBC, it had all the most important sports properties in Canada. Apart from the Olympics, it had *Hockey Night in Canada*. With its irrepressible hosts Ron MacLean and Don Cherry, it was the most watched and most profitable show the Corporation owned. The CBC was also the principal broadcaster of the Canadian Football League. Every Saturday afternoon, it offered one major match. It controlled the eastern and western playoffs and the Grey Cup, the most important event in Canadian sport other than the Stanley Cup. The CBC was the rights holder for the biggest curling competitions, including the Brier. It owned the World Figure Skating Championships and innumerable other winter events. It covered the major transnational games, including the Common-wealth Games and the Pan American Games. It was overwhelmingly the most important amateur-sport broadcaster in the country.

But all was not well in the sports department, and it became clear that one of my first jobs would be to secure the future of CBC sports. The National Hockey League and the Players Association were at odds. Contract negotiations were not going well. There was a serious possibility the players would be locked out by the League. Ultimately this happened, and the entire 2004–05 season was cancelled. CBC lost its biggest show and biggest money earner.

The Canadian Football League contracts were two seasons away from expiring. The CBC's arrangements were based on a sub-licencing deal with the Sports Network (TSN), a CTV affiliate. There were rumours that CTV and TSN would try and take football away from the CBC.

The Olympics were safe for the next few Games, but the International Olympic Committee had indicated that it would open the bidding early for the 2010 and 2012 games. The 2010 Olympics were to be held in Vancouver, the first time an Olympics had been held in Canada in a generation. CTV had indicated it would be bidding on the Games. Even if they lost, they would drive up the price.

Canada is the only country in the world where the Winter Olympic Games are bigger than the summer ones. More people watch them on TV, more advertisers spend more money on them, more journalists spill more ink on them and more Canadians agonize more deeply over them. *Mon pays ce n'est pas un pays, c'est l'hiver.*

Canadians are pleased if their athletes run fast, jump high, dive gracefully, box cunningly or row well. They are happy to celebrate the triumphs of their summer athletes. But the Winter Games are something else again. They are woven into the soul of the country. If the athletes do not do well, despair grips the land. When the hockey teams falter, when they do not sweep all the other countries before them, Canada falls into an existential crisis. Beaten by the Swedes, by the Russians, by the Czechs? Oh, no! It cannot be! But worse still: to be beaten by the Americans. The Americans!

Every time it happens, there are endless learned discussions of what went wrong. The state of the national game is examined by the great boffins of the hockey commentariat, each trying to outdo the others in parsing our national humiliation. Team selection was poor. Not enough speed and too much checking. Too much speed and not enough checking. Why was the phenom from Winnipeg put on the third line and not the second? What idiot passed over the hooligan brothers from Upper Wabush? Why did they play the trap against the Finns? And on and on. Weeks of hand-wringing, finger-pointing and questions in Parliament.

But when they win. Oh joy is it then to be alive! The sun shines more brightly on the crisp winter days. The children behave better in their schoolrooms. The beer is stronger. The women more beautiful. The men more charming. The country relaxes into an easy grace. All is well with the world.

There is nothing bigger than the Winter Games, except the Winter Games when they are held in Canada. Lillehammer, Salt Lake City, Torino—these are all fine places to show up the wretches from Sweden and the United States. But the place to really show them up is at home. Only once had the Winter Games been held in Canada—in Calgary, in 1988—and the Canadians failed to win the gold for hockey. Worse still, the TV rights had gone to CTV.

But now, in 2010, the Winter Games would be at home again, for the first time in a generation.

In the 1990s the CBC had purchased the previous five Games: Sydney, Salt Lake City, Athens, Torino and Beijing. It had made the Olympics and the lead-up to them a pillar of its programming strategy. Every Saturday afternoon, winter and summer, the CBC featured Canada's greatest amateur athletes. It covered ski racing, speed skating, pole vaulting, shot putting, swimming, high jumping, race walking. It went to the world championships, the national championships, the Commonwealth Games, the Pan American Games, everywhere, covering Canadian athletes. The promise it made, both to Canadians and the International Olympic Committee, was that the athletes would already be known when they participated in the games. No other Canadian sports broadcaster covered amateur sport.

As the time arrived to begin preparing bids for the next round of Games, it became clear that CTV would participate. Because the 2010 Games would be held in Vancouver, they would be enormous.

Knowing this, and knowing that CTV had much deeper pockets than the CBC, Robert Rabinovitch approached Ivan Fecan, the CEO of CTV. Fecan had been CBC's head of entertainment programming in the early 1990s. During his tenure, he had commissioned some of the CBC's best and most iconic shows, including *Degrassi*, *The Kids in the Hall*, *Road to Avonlea* and *This Hour Has 22 Minutes*. When he left the CBC, he went to CTV, which he famously transformed from a creaking co-op of loosely connected stations into a real television network. Then, through a series of transactions in 2000, CTV acquired control over TSN, Canada's most important sports cable property, along with Discovery and a host of other attractive channels. The resulting group was much richer and more broadly based than CBC. Robert feared that between CTV and TSN, they would be able to outbid us.

At the same time, many people wondered if Fecan harboured some strange grudge against the CBC. Rumours circulated that he wanted to damage us. He had apparently been heard cackling in dark corners of expensive boardrooms as he laid out his plans for domination of the Canadian broadcasting industry.

Certainly he seemed to enjoy sticking his finger in the CBC's eye. When I first arrived, it was hard not to notice that he had rented all the billboards immediately across the street from the Toronto headquarters. They were of little commercial value for attracting audiences, but they confronted the CBC employees every day with ads for CTV's hit shows. They seemed to say, "Here we are: big and bad with our great U.S. shows. And there you are with your sad little Canadian ones. Have a terrible day!"

It was, then, with some trepidation that Robert approached Ivan Fecan. To bid together, he argued, would make sense for both companies. If we combined forces, nobody else in Canada would be able to bid against us, and we would be able to obtain the rights at a lower price. As well, CTV's presence in French Canada was weak. They would be hard-pressed to compete with the breadth and depth of Radio-Canada's network. For our part, we would also be happy to throw our extensive amateur experience into the mix, along with the best-known Olympic sports broadcasting personalities. Together we would be able to mount a much better and more compelling bid.

I was not at the meeting, since I had not yet joined the CBC. It did not, however, go well. No agreement was reached. I heard two quite different stories about what had happened. According to CTV, the CBC had been arrogant and high-handed. They had proposed to take all the best properties and treat CTV as a junior partner. For its part, the CBC said CTV had been arrogant and high-handed. They dismissed the CBC's much more extensive experience and knowledge of the Games and wanted to have a preferential position. Whatever the truth of the matter, each side left the discussions annoyed with the other.

Some time later, CTV ended up making an agreement with Rogers Sportsnet to bid on the games together. Why this happened was hard to say. Sportsnet and TSN are normally competitors, not co-operators. Rumour had it that Ted Rogers wanted to be nice to Ivan Fecan for other reasons. Some thought he wanted a good relationship because CTV controlled the block of specialty channels that was most important to his cable business. Some thought he wanted to buy the CTV group. Some thought he just liked Fecan because they shared a mutual interest in world domination. Whatever the reason, the Rogers-CTV marriage was a dark development for CBC.

To prepare our bid, I sat down with Nancy Lee, the head of sports, and Neil McEneaney, the CFO for English services. Nancy had been running the CBC sports department for a number of years. She had maintained its historic glory and had concluded an extremely advantageous deal with the NHL for the most recent round of hockey rights. She was the most senior female executive in Canadian sports. She hated losing.

McEneaney had come to the CBC from the Southam newspaper chain. Ferociously hard-working and clever, he had gone prematurely grey from the sheer weirdness of working at the Corporation. He was relentlessly sunny and optimistic. He hated losing.

We decided to build two business cases: one to see what we could pay and one to see what CTV could pay. Our business case was pretty straightforward. Given our extensive experience with the Olympic Games, we knew exactly what they would cost to produce and how much revenue they would generate. To calculate what we could afford to pay the International Olympic Committee for the rights was simply a function of subtracting our costs from the revenues. Presto, the amount appeared that we could pay and break even. If we wanted to make some money, we would simply offer less. How much less money we offered would determine how much we made.

To decide how much less we could offer, we had to understand what CTV could afford to pay. We wanted to understand it from two points of view. First, we wanted to know what they could bid if they bid *rationally*. How much could they afford to pay and not be worse off than they would otherwise be? If they were making a profit of x million with their normal schedule of U.S. shows in the middle of the winter, how much could they afford to pay and still make x million. This is what we meant by a rational bid.

We also wanted to know how much they could afford to bid if they were prepared to bid *irrationally*. How much cash did they actually have? How much could they spend without impairing the financial performance of the group as a whole? How much could they spend to slake Ivan Fecan's desire to dominate the CBC?

To answer both of these questions, we built a model of CTV's business. They had until a few years earlier been a public company, so we pulled out their previous financial reports and filings. We then updated them to take account of the changing costs and revenues of the industry in the years that had passed. It is surprising how much data is publicly available in Canada. We used reports from consulting companies, the information filed by CTV with the Canadian Radio-television and Telecommunications Commission

(CRTC) and our own internal information on changes in the advertising markets. The results were discouraging. It appeared that CTV could spend almost any amount of money if they wanted to bid irrationally. The group generated so much free cash that even an outlandish bid would have little impact on its multi-year performance.

When it came to a rational bid, the answer was a little more encouraging. They had two disadvantages that we did not have. First, a normal private broadcaster will typically make a gross margin of about 25 percent. CTV at that time made more. The CBC makes no margin. Thus, all things being equal, they would either have to forgo their margin or bid 25 percent below us. As well, they would have double costs. Since the Olympic Games go on for two weeks, they would also have to pay the costs of the U.S. shows that they had bought for that time period but could not show. Either they ate the losses or had to lower their bid further.

Our only hope was that CTV would bid rationally. If they bid irrationally, we could never keep up. It would, in fact, be wrong for us to keep up. If we did and took a big loss on the games, we would rightly be accused of competing against the private broadcasters using public money. Besides, if we took a loss we would have to make it up by cancelling shows, whether on radio or TV. It would be crazy to compromise the main schedules for four weeks of games.

We met the International Olympic Committee (IOC) on a number of occasions to understand the bidding process. They explained to us the rules and timing. Most importantly, they explained the criteria they would use to judge the bids. They said that money was not everything. Far from it. They were not a vulgar professional sports league. They were a movement, the international Olympic Movement. A dream of youth and health. They stood for peace and excellence. Higher. Faster. Stronger.

Money was important, they explained, but what really counted was the quality and reach of the productions. They wanted to know that the games would be beautifully showcased, that they would contribute to amateur sport, that they would be seen by everyone in the country, that they would be covered in both languages, that they would celebrate youth and the Olympic spirit. Money, yes, but it was secondary. What really mattered was the promotion of the Movement.

We took much heart from this. If it was true that it was not ultimately about money, we were confident we could win. We had the experience. We had complete coverage of the country in French and English. We had our long history of supporting amateur sport. We had the best production facilities. We had the most experienced announcers and analysts. We had Brian Williams, for God's sake. On every conceivable dimension, we were stronger than CTV and Sportsnet.

Our only concern was that CTV might be able to argue that they had more shelf space. After all, their bid included English Canada's two biggest all-sports networks. We reached out to Canada's second-largest private network, Global, and the sports news specialty channel, the Score. They joined our bid, as later did Telus, the country's second-largest telecommunications company. We now had a group that was easily as big as theirs.

On January 19, 2005, we went to the board. We showed them the presentation, explained the financials and asked them to approve an upper limit on the amount we could bid. It was a not inconsequential sum. We assured them that we would go no further than we had to, and under no circumstances would the games result in a loss to the Corporation. The board approved the bid and we went off to Lausanne confident that if CTV bid rationally, we would win.

Lausanne in early February is a dark and dreary place. I had never been there before but had a certain sentimental interest in it. My mother had been sent there as a teenager to go to school. Her parents thought it important for her to speak French, as all good Scottish girls of the period did. This meant, of course, that you went to Switzerland. Paris would never do. It was too interesting and cosmopolitan. Switzerland was much better. Like Scotland it was cold, dour, cautious and gloomy. There was little to choose between Inverness and Lausanne.

As we prepared for our meeting with the International Olympic Committee, we had one last discussion about the bid price. I was comfortable with where we were.

"Let's raise our bid a little," Robert said.

"We don't need to," I replied.

"We have room in the business case approved by the board," he said. "Let's put our best foot forward."

"We really don't need to," I went on. "If they bid rationally, we will win where we are; and if they don't, we can't match them anyhow."

"It's not just about money," Robert went on. "If we are close financially, we should win. Let's not lose for a few million dollars."

We tussled a while longer. Robert, of course, prevailed. We raised our offer a little, wrote it on to the bid paper and signed it.

There had been sightings of Ivan Fecan around town. Although we had not seen him ourselves, he had apparently been spotted in various expensive bars and restaurants meeting with his confederates and plotting to outbid us. We were worried that his lust for domination might push him into the irrational bid camp. What greater prize could there be than the Vancouver Olympics? They would make Salt Lake City look like small beer. And what greater monument could there be to Ivan Fecan's creation of the modern CTV-TSN group than the biggest sports property in the world?

The day of the presentation, we arrived at the IOC headquarters early. The walls are clad in white marble. Trophies of past triumphs hang from them. A quiet hush permeates the building, the same hush one encounters in private banks, corner offices and vaults: the hush of money. They gave us a little tour, showing off the choicest morsels of their environment.

Robert Rabinovitch, Nancy Lee, Daniel Gourd and I had practised our presentation over and over. It was very polished. We began with a highlight reel of the great moments in CBC's past coverage of the Games. We reminded the IOC of our long relationship, emphasized our commitment to amateur sport, showed off the size and extent of our networks in French and English, introduced our partners, explained our plans for outreach and engagement by the Canadian public and concluded with a rousing commitment to extend the Games on the emerging digital platforms. We spoke half in French and half in English. While we spoke, dazzling images of past triumphs were projected on the walls. Twenty minutes later, it was over. We waited for their questions.

We wanted to be closely examined on our presentation and the piles of supporting materials we had filed with them well in advance of our meeting. There were production plans, program strategies, financial details, technical arrangements, hundreds of pages of carefully reasoned diagrams and explanations. We waited patiently for their questions. A minute passed. Nothing. After all our work, they had no questions.

They thanked us for coming to Lausanne and asked us to provide our financial bid. The number itself had not been mentioned during the course of the presentation because they had asked us instead to deliver it in a sealed envelope. They produced a sort of urn and Robert dropped in our offer. They thanked us again and promised to get back to us shortly.

We went back to the hotel to await the results. We were very discouraged by the meeting. Not a single question. It could only mean that the proposal and the details did not matter. Only money would talk. The clock ticked. Outside, the grey winter day gave way to a black winter night. We could only hope that Ivan Fecan would bid rationally. It seemed a faint hope.

The phone rang shortly after we returned to the hotel. We had lost. CTV had bid a colossal $153 million. It was an unbelievable amount of money. Our models of their business estimated that they might lose $50 million at that price, and if one factored in the forgone profits, $100 million. This was breathtaking.

We saw Fecan and his coven out walking later in the evening. His long white hair curled up from his shoulders. He was wearing a black wool coat that fell below his knees. He has a strangely youthful appearance. There are very few lines on his face. We congratulated him on his winning bid. He smiled the smile of the satisfied. He may even have licked his lips.

We returned to the hotel for dinner. It was weirdly deserted. We were the only guests at the restaurant. The conversation turned to what we would say the next day when our loss was announced publicly. I felt we had done the right thing, but it was disappointing to have my first big outing at the CBC result in failure. Nobody would understand that the CTV bid was irrational. People would just think we were not very good at business. People at CBC television would doubtless conclude that the new vice-president was an idiot. How could he lose the Olympic Games? How could he lose Vancouver?

The next day we took calls from journalists in Toronto who wanted to know how we could have screwed up the bid for the Olympics. We explained carefully that we had not wanted to overpay, that the games had to make money, that CTV would lose its shirt. We knew, of course, that our account would convince nobody. CTV would dismiss it as nonsense. They would claim that they were going to make a fortune. The journalists would inevitably assume that CTV was right because they were a private business and knew much more about these things than the sad sacks at the CBC.

The fact that we ultimately proved to be right was no comfort at all. Rogers and CTV lost money on the Vancouver Games. They also anticipate losing money on the London Summer Games in 2012. So bad was the bruising that Rogers broke its partnership with CTV and announced in September 2011 that they would no longer bid on the Games. All this was in the future. Sitting on the shores of Lake Geneva in 2005, we just looked like dopes.

This would not be the last loss of a major sports property. More were to come in the months ahead. They would be so severe as to imperil the foundation of CBC sports.

Across Lake Geneva, snow-capped mountains rose behind the town of Evian in France. I looked at them wistfully, wanting to be spirited away to a happier place. They had a particular shape. I could not recognize it at first. What was it? Then slowly, it became clear. They were the same mountains that appear on the label of Evian water: clear, distant, promising and out of reach.

Strike one.

TWO WEEKS AFTER we lost the Olympic bid, the roof fell in on curling. We owned many of the most important properties, including the Brier and the Scott Tournament of Hearts. Unfortunately we could not put all the games on the main channel. There were simply too many scheduling conflicts. In a brainwave of negligible proportions, we thought it might be a good idea to put the games that were being played during the week on Country Canada, a small digital specialty channel we owned.

At that time, Country Canada had only about a million subscribers and was located on a part of the cable dial so remote that finding it required a compass and orienteering equipment. Our plan was to use the curling properties to help sell Country Canada. We would start advertising well in advance of the tournament that if viewers wanted to watch the matches, they needed to phone their cable provider and order Country Canada. The cable companies loved the idea, and we organized a sales and marketing campaign to support it.

We started three months ahead of the tournament. The cable companies promoted it. Their sales representatives in the call centres were briefed. We put bill stuffers in the mail. We promoted its availability on our sports shows. We advertised in rinks around the country. Everyone worked hard to make sure that all the curling fans knew that they had to subscribe to Country Canada. After three months, it was clear the campaign was a flop. Not nearly enough people signed up. There was no possibility that the hardcore curling fans would be able to see all the Brier matches.

With some trepidation, in late February 2005 we launched our coverage. No sooner did people discover that the games were inaccessible except on Country Canada than the shouting and moaning began. Nobody knew where Country Canada was on their dial. Nobody knew that they had to pay for it. Nobody even knew what it was. A torrent of angry letters, emails and phone calls began pouring into the CBC.

The problem was compounded by the fact that the regulations governing Country Canada limited the amount of sports we could broadcast on any particular day. As a result, we sometimes switched away from the game before it was over. Thus, even those who managed to find Country Canada and subscribe to it were badly treated. Nobody could believe that we would leave the match before it ended, but we did.

The papers had a field day with the CBC's bizarre incompetence. There was much laughing at our expense. Even CBC radio covered the controversy in an aggressive and unpleasant way.

The principal flak-catchers for all the discontent that comes the CBC's way are a group known as Audience Relations. They inhabit a windowless set of offices in one of the more obscure parts of the Toronto Broadcast Centre. The work is unenviable and their lives brutish. All day, aggrieved viewers and listeners bombard them with complaints. A certain show is too sexy. Peter Mansbridge's tie is hideous. The correspondent in London is a communist. They hate the music on Radio 2. Whatever. All day long, they sit there being lambasted by tidal waves of grievance and invective.

As the curling controversy mounted, it became clear that the Audience Relations department was imploding. Shell-shocked employees could be seen, trembling and glassy-eyed, stumbling out of their warren. They twitched and spooked like veterans of too many firefights. Even their leader, normally proud and fearless, seemed tentative and jumpy, uncertain which way to direct his broken troops.

Nancy Lee and I decided to visit the wretches and buck them up with donuts and encouragement. They welcomed us with desperate enthusiasm. We listened to their tales. Some were near tears. The enraged curling fans, it turned out, were the most abusive and unpleasant complainers they had ever had to deal with. One hardened veteran said she could not believe the invective.

"I could tell from her voice that she was old. It croaked and creaked. She called me 'dearie' and then described the CBC as a bunch of 'poisonous toads' and 'shit bags.' Another old lady screamed at me for five minutes. She told me to do terrible things to myself with a toilet brush. I have never been so abused by anyone."

They showed me emails that consisted of strings of curses and maledictions, one expletive after another, brutal and angry. The viewers seemed sometimes in such a rage that they fell into utter incoherence.

"You are a pack of shit brained idiots. You cut away before the last end!! What a collection of ignorant, stupid, ugly, demented, moronic pieces of crap. Death to the CBC. Death!"

The effect was startling. I had no idea that people could be so rude.

"Is this typical?" I asked. "Is this what happens if we have an outage during a hockey game?"

"Oh, no," they said, "the curling fans are the worst. Far and away the worst. Hockey fans are never as bad. And the old ladies are the worst, far and away."

As the firestorm progressed, the advertisers were also getting clobbered by the unhappy fans. Some seemed to feel that Scott paper was responsible—it was, after all, the Scott Tournament of Hearts. They threatened not to buy any more Scott paper. For its part, Scott was, not surprisingly, quite upset with the whole sorry business. As the fiasco unfolded, they were being towed under with us.

I called the head of Scott's marketing department to apologize and engage in some mea culpa. Scott was a big and important customer of the CBC. I explained that we were blitzing the country with ads explaining where to find the games, that we would never again leave a game before it is over, that all the really big matches, the finals, would be on the main network, etc., etc., woof, woof. His response was not warm. He clearly agreed with the curling fans that we were a collection of idiots, although he was too polite to put it that bluntly. Doubtless we would pay for our stupidity in the future.

The Canadian Curling Association, which owns the curling championships, was equally unhappy. They demanded that we turn the property over to TSN. We refused. They announced that they would unilaterally abrogate our contract with them. We threatened to sue them. They said rude things to us. We turned the whole mess over to the lawyers. Eventually we realized that the relationship was beyond repair and released them. They signed almost immediately with TSN.

Strike two.

THEN THERE WAS football. In late 2007, we got wind of the fact that the Canadian Football League (CFL) was negotiating with TSN for a renewal of the television rights. The CFL had had the rights for the previous five years, but they had sub-licenced many of the games to the CBC. We put on the Saturday afternoon matches, as well as the Eastern and Western finals and the Grey Cup. This suited everyone well, since the biggest games were available to all Canadians free on the CBC, while the diehard fans could watch everything else on TSN.

The problem with the new negotiation was that it was going on exclusively with TSN. We had told the CFL that we were interested in bidding, but they had not offered us any opportunity to do so. This seemed strange, since it's always better to have more than one suitor.

My mind returned to our unhappy experience with Tom Wright, the commissioner of the CFL, during the CBC lockout. We had covered the games without play-by-play or colour commentators. He had been very troubled by it and complained bitterly to the press at every opportunity. He had demanded that we release the games to TSN so that they could be broadcast properly. We had refused. Now, apparently, it was time for payback.

Writing in the *Globe and Mail*, William Houston had come to the same conclusion: "Another reason for the CFL not requesting a CBC bid might have been a deteriorating relationship between the two sides. Club owners were angered when the CBC aired games without play-by-play audio during its lockout of employees in 2005."

Undeterred, we sent our spies to find out where the negotiations stood. We learned that Keith Pelley, the president of the Toronto Argonauts, was dealing with TSN on behalf of the league. TSN had offered to take all the games. The negotiations had been going on as Tom Wright's contract as commissioner was expiring. Perhaps he hoped to conclude a deal and save his job. I did not know.

To mount an offer for all the games to counter TSN, we needed a partner. I phoned Leonard Asper, the CEO of CanWest, the company that controlled Global. Asper is a lovely guy. Although he ultimately lost control of CanWest when it was driven into bankruptcy, in 2007 he was still a man very much in possession of the organization. We had joined forces a couple of years earlier for the unsuccessful Olympic bid. He was CTV's principal competitor and like us could not bear the thought of the dreaded Ivan Fecan obtaining another great property.

I explained the situation. "Would you mount a bid with us?" I asked. "We would produce the games and then share them with you."

"Do we have enough room on our schedules to carry all of them?" he asked.

Global had never produced any sports properties. They owned the rights to the NFL and the Super Bowl but did not produce them. They simply bought the productions from the rights holders in the United States and inserted their own commercials.

"I don't know. Let's find out."

We got our scheduling people together. We sat down and looked at the CFL's plans for the upcoming season. It was clear that between us we could show every CFL game. This should be fantastic for the league. Instead of having their games on TSN, which was only available to the cable and satellite customers who subscribed to it, we could make them available to all Canadians for free. This would dramatically enhance the league's reach and brand. We also worked out an arrangement to show the Eastern and Western finals, along with the Grey Cup.

At the same time, our spies had determined what TSN was prepared to pay for the rights. We did our business cases and concluded that we could easily handle the price. We assumed that if the league could get the same amount of money from us as from TSN, and get the games on the much bigger networks, it would be thrilled. We phoned and said we wanted to make a joint bid. Nothing.

We concluded that something odd, very odd, was happening at the CFL headquarters. Not entertain another bid? Hmm. We started to phone round to the owners of the teams. Leonard Asper called the Blue Bombers, and Robert Rabinovitch called the Alouettes and said we were ready to bid. There was considerable back-and-forth. Word came back that the TSN bid was very advanced, time was short and the league needed certainty. None of it made any sense. It appeared that even the owners were being blocked by the CFL management.

And then, in November 2006, without our being able even to present a bid, the CFL announced their deal with TSN. It seemed incomprehensible. Tom Wright was ultimately not renewed as commissioner, and his successor was now bound to a deal that he had had no part in negotiating. And Wright had done this without entertaining any bids from the two other largest broadcasters in the country.

I could only assume that the incoming commissioner would be troubled by what he inherited. But it got worse. Later, CTV announced that it had stolen the NFL's rights away from Global early in 2007 (probably at the Super Bowl, maybe even at Global's Super Bowl party). Ivan Fecan's lust for domination struck again. It was a great blow to Global, but even more to the CFL. The deal provided that the NFL games, including the Super Bowl, would appear on CTV, while CFL games, including the Grey Cup, would appear on TSN, CTV's much smaller network.

When we lost the CFL, we were in the middle of negotiating a new contract with the NHL. Everyone knew we were working on the NHL, but nothing had been concluded. Rumours were rife in the press that Fecan was stalking the *Hockey Night in Canada* rights as well. There was considerable worry within the CBC. The new management of television had now lost the Olympics, curling and football.

When the loss of the CFL contract was revealed, greater gloom fell over the sports department and the rest of the Corporation. The potential loss of the NHL plunged the place into anxiety. There was nothing I could say to offset it, since I had no idea whether or when we would land the NHL deal. Strong men from the sports department could be seen weeping quietly in corners of the building. Even precious programmers from radio looked depressed. Tense uncertainty fell over all parts of the CBC. The book shows sounded tentative, the news more gloomy than usual, and even the irrepressible George Stroumboulopoulos seemed twitchy and slightly worried in his late-night talk show.

Strike three.

HOCKEY NIGHT IN CANADA is the Shrine where the Game is worshipped. Every Saturday night for over eighty years, Canadians have gathered in front of their radios and televisions to hear the scripture intoned. All across the frozen country—in tiny hamlets and on farms, in taverns and homes, in the mighty downtown of Toronto itself—they have come through the darkness of winter to share the belief that is cast and recast across generations. The ancient relics are produced and venerated, the incense is burned, the glories and disappointments of the past are remembered, and prayers are lifted for the hopes of the future.

Just to name the names of the high priests is to recall the power and wonder of the Shrine: the sainted Foster Hewitt, the venerable Danny Gallivan, the beatified Ward Cornell, all of them and the rest—Dick Irvin, Ted Darling, Ron MacLean. Through the Depression, the Second World War, the Korean War, Flower Power, Stagflation, Greed, the Free Trade deal and the Referenda, the Shrine has been there, steadfast, comforting, filled with mystery.

The Shrine stitches the country's discordant fragments together: the plutocrats of Bay Street, the Inuit hunters, the wily Quebec separatists, the dreary Ottawa civil servants and the rugged loggers of British Columbia. Every Saturday night the worshippers can cast out the apostates of the Maple Leafs, lift their hearts in celebration of the Original Six, chant their jeremiahs of longing at the loss of the Nordiques and the Jets, and perform their ritual denunciations of the Fallen One, Gary Bettman, destroyer of Canadian hockey and wickedness personified. All of these things can be agreed every week in the dead of winter from Halifax and St. John's to Vancouver and Tuktoyaktuk.

There is no question that *Hockey Night in Canada* is the oldest electronic media property in North America. It may in fact be the oldest in the world. No other show has endured since the earliest days of radio. It began in 1931, over the Canadian National Railway network, at the height of the Great Depression. In 1936 it moved to the newly created CBC radio, then transferred to television in the early 1950s and onto the Internet in the twenty-first century, with play-by-play and colour commentary in Punjabi and Mandarin. And since the creation of the CBC seventy-five years ago, it has belonged to the CBC.

As the Shrine is the country, it is also the Corporation. It preceded the creation of the news service and to this day enjoys significantly larger audiences than *The National*. When Radio-Canada lost its counterpart, the equally iconic and revered *Soirée du hockey*, the president of the CBC was called before a parliamentary committee to explain the unconscionable loss. When Robert Rabinovitch explained that the television rights had been sold by the League to the Réseau des sports, charges of apostasy began. Did he not understand that the Shrine and the CBC were indivisible?

When we began to think about negotiating a new contract with the NHL, we started by commissioning an extensive study. Its purpose was to understand how Canadians felt about the show and to explore what they felt about the brand. We wanted to understand the emotional, social and psychological attributes of *Hockey Night in Canada*, so that we could value it properly. The results were remarkable. It was clear that *Hockey Night in Canada's* brand was not only more valuable than that of any other television show in the country, it was in fact more valuable than any other sports brand, more valuable even than the NHL's own brand. Canadians believe that the show is not only the apotheosis of hockey, it must also be its protector. They believe that it has a responsibility to support the game in all its aspects—amateur as well as professional—and ensure its quality and survival.

As we looked through the data, we began to understand that *Hockey Night in Canada* is deeply ingrained in Canada's sense of itself. Whether Canadians watch it regularly or not does not seem to matter. The name itself, or the sounding of its purloined theme— Dum-da-dum-da-dum—was enough to evoke the mythic Canada. As the three stars are called, the train whistle blows across the darkened prairie night, the fiddlers break into their next jig at the Cape Breton house party, the bears rumble and dream in their hibernating sleep and the first maple sap rises in the mid-March thaw.

When Don Cherry and Ron MacLean battle over their conflicting views of the Game, their conversation spills into the national conversation, animating the newspapers and setting the focus of dialogue for all the other sports talk. Rock-em sock-em, wimps in visors, the Iraq War, firefighters and soldiers, the quality of European hockey, head shots, the removal of the red line, the meaning of life, the mysteries of the Trinity (Orr, Crosby and Gretzky), a citizen's duty to the state—it's all there, every Saturday night. And every Sunday morning there is the inevitable chorus of complaints from the politically correct chatterati denouncing the unspeakable stupidity, the positively Neanderthal quality of it all.

Hockey Night in Canada is also central to the CBC's financing. Without *Hockey Night in Canada*, the CBC would fall into a grave financial crisis that would imperil its survival. Every year, it contributes 400 to 450 hours of prime-time Canadian content to the CBC schedule, more than even *The National*. If it were lost, it would have to be replaced by other Canadian shows. The problem is that all Canadian shows—whether documentaries, current affairs, drama, comedy or reality—lose money, whereas *Hockey Night in Canada* has historically made money. Indeed, over the course of the "old" contract with the NHL (that is, the one that ended in 2007-08), the Shrine was overwhelmingly the CBC's most profitable property. Each year it generated tens of millions of dollars for the Corporation.

But even if *Hockey Night in Canada* were to break even or lose moderate amounts of money, it would be better to keep it than replace it with other Canadian shows. The economics of the problem are simple and brutal. An average one-hour drama costs the CBC between $400,000 and $450,000 per hour to commission on a total budget of $1.2-1.4 million (the rest being made up from the Canadian Media Fund and tax credits). Given their normal audiences, Canadian dramas rarely make $200,000 in advertising revenue. This means that each hour of drama commissioned by the CBC produces a loss of at least $200,000.

It can be seen, then, that if four hundred hours of hockey were replaced with four hundred hours of drama, the CBC would need to find an additional $80-100 million. At the same time, the Canada Media Fund would have to be supplemented with another $80-100 million, and the government's television production tax credits would be further drawn by a comparable amount. In other words, if the government wanted the CBC to eliminate hockey and replace it with original Canadian drama, the costs would be somewhere between $240 million and $300 million.

The likelihood that the government would want to inject this amount of money into the CBC is nonexistent. The problem for the CBC, then, is that if it lost hockey, it would be unable to finance another four hundred hours of original Canadian programming to replace it. Under these circumstances, the CBC would have to contemplate two options: break the Canadian-content quotas (now 80 percent on CBC prime time) by replacing *Hockey Night in Canada* with foreign shows, or replace it with repeats of shows that are already available on the prime-time schedule. Apart from making Saturday nights unspeakably boring, this latter course would also ensure a significant collapse of CBC's share of the Canadian audience, with further consequences for its reputation and relevance.

In 2006 we found ourselves contemplating how best to move forward with *Hockey Night in Canada*. The final season of the old contract with the NHL was 2007–08. If we did not successfully negotiate a new deal, we would be without hockey in 2008-09. We would find ourselves—like our French counterparts in Radio-Canada—bereft of our most important property, facing a financial crisis and more charges of apostasy. The problem was further compounded by the loss of the Olympic Games, the CFL contracts and curling. If we did not renew our arrangements with the NHL, we would have to contemplate exiting sports altogether and losing one of the oldest and most admired parts of the CBC.

In April 2006, Robert Rabinovitch and I flew to New York to have dinner with Gary Bettman, the NHL commissioner. Bettman is a small, intense, extremely clever businessman. During his tenure at the NHL, he had managed to enrage most Canadian hockey fans by pursuing a U.S.-based growth strategy. Franchises were awarded in Georgia, Arizona, Tennessee, North Carolina and Texas, places that had never seen ice outside a mixed drink, let alone a game of hockey. Meanwhile, he had not only refrained from expansion in Canada, he had allowed two Canadian teams—the Nordiques of Quebec City and the Winnipeg Jets—to pack their bags and move to the United States. And when efforts were made to bring failing franchises to Canada— the Nashville Predators and the old Jets, now the Phoenix Coyotes— he had blocked their removal back to the Holy Land. So disliked had he become in Canada that he was lampooned in one of the country's most successful films, *Bon Cop, Bad Cop*, where he appears as a malevolent midget named Harry Buttman.

We first met Gary Bettman at Nobu, an overpriced sushi restaurant in New York. Bettman was with Bill Daly, the deputy commissioner of the NHL. They were sitting in the middle of the loud room, stargazing. As we sat down, Bettman pointed out Sugar Ray Leonard, the world champion boxer, and Barry Diller, the media mogul. Last week, he assured us, Bruce Willis had been there, along with some other people whose names elude me now.

Bill Daly is the physical opposite of Bettman. He is large and completely bald. He looks like a menacing professional wrestler. His background is in competition law. Like Bettman, he likes to negotiate, indeed lives to negotiate. When they are together alone, I assume they spend their time practising their negotiating skills: Who will pick up lunch? Who will go first into the elevator? Who will be meaner to the public broadcaster? Bill Daly is often described in the press as the kinder and gentler of the two.

We were concerned that CTV might attempt to outbid us for the NHL rights. A month earlier, I had approached Rick Brace, the head of TSN, about bidding together to avoid being whipsawed by the league, thereby keeping his parent, CTV, out of the bidding. He declined, which made little sense unless CTV was going to try and outbid us.

Indeed, there were rumours in the press that CTV was after the rights. The *Globe and Mail* reported that "two well placed sources say Bell Globemedia, which owns CTV and TSN... is likely to proffer a bid that the CBC would find impossible to match—$140 million a year for ten years." This was a colossal amount of money, but not completely unimaginable in light of what they had paid for the Olympics.

Robert Rabinovitch and I wanted to negotiate a new contract earlier than would be usual, because we feared that mounting pressures in Ottawa to get the CBC out of sports might bear fruit. The private broadcasters—CTV and TSN in particular—had been going around town for some time, whispering in politicians' ears that it was absurd and unfair for the CBC to be in sports. Why, they asked, should the public broadcaster do what the privates were prepared to do without any government support? Besides, how was it right for the CBC to use public money to compete against the privates when bidding for sports rights?

The fact that we were not using public money to subsidize *Hockey Night in Canada*, that in fact the Shrine was subsidizing the rest of the CBC, seemed to make little difference. Politicians of most stripes would listen to the privates sympathetically and then nod their heads and wag their tails. We feared that if the privates got much more traction, we would be ordered not to bid again. That, of course, would be a disaster for the Corporation, since no government was ever going to cough up the hundreds of millions of dollars required to replace the Shrine.

Shortly before Robert and I flew to New York to meet with Bettman and Daly, our fears had been confirmed when the Senate Committee on Transport and Communications issued a report on broadcasting. Embracing the private broadcasters with unseemly enthusiasm, the committee recommended that the CBC get "Back to Basics." Among other things, this meant dropping professional sports and getting out of advertising. How this amounted to "Back to Basics" was anyone's guess, since the CBC had been involved with professional sports and advertising since its founding in the 1930s. How we were to finance the shift was also unknown. Apparently the committee had neither the time nor inclination to address the details.

Given all this, Robert and I hoped we could use the possible forced withdrawal of the CBC as a negotiating lever with Gary Bettman. We would argue that if he didn't settle with us now, we might not be available to buy the rights in future. If that happened, either he would have nobody to sell to, or CTV and TSN would force a knock-down price on him.

That evening we laid out our concerns about being excluded from bidding and proposed that we pursue an accelerated timetable to a new contract.

"The danger," Robert explained, "is that the government will order us not to bid. They could just say don't do it. We don't know if they will, but as time goes by, it grows more likely."

"Hmm," Bettman replied noncommittally. "Hmm," he said again, his voice almost lost in the cacophony of the celebrity crowd.

"If that happens," Robert continued, "you will of course have only one bidder. So we think it's better to renegotiate the contract earlier to ensure that neither of us is disadvantaged."

Bill Daly passed us more sushi. He stared at me balefully. Sugar Ray Leonard wandered by, shadow boxing, throwing little lefts and rights into the expensive restaurant air.

"Hmmm," Bettman said once more. He ordered the cheque, smiled menacingly and promised to get back to us.

So what is a contract with the league for *Hockey Night in Canada* worth? How much should we offer? We knew that wherever we landed, the contract would be the largest in Canadian history. This was no surprise, since the contract would cover the most valuable games for the most valuable sport on the most valuable sports show in the country.

At the same time, we needed to maintain many of the contractual arrangements we already had. For example, the current contract focused on the Canadian teams, particularly the Toronto Maple Leafs. The contract stated that the Shrine's games would all involve Canadian teams, the CBC would have exclusivity on Saturdays and there would be a guaranteed minimum number (a large one) of Leafs games. The CBC also had first pick over TSN on all playoff games—always taking the Canadian teams—and complete exclusivity for the Stanley Cup final. The reason for this was simple: Canadians overwhelmingly prefer Canadian teams. No matter how many Canadians are playing on the Phoenix Coyotes, nobody in Canada cares about them. And no matter how few Canadians are playing on the Montreal Canadiens, they are still followed with obsessive interest. The Toronto Maple Leafs are something else again; regardless of their dismal performance over the last forty years, they attract bigger Canadian television audiences than any other team.

The challenge going into the discussions with Bettman, then, was to preserve as much as possible both the conditions and the price of the old contract. For its part, TSN would want more access to the Canadian teams in the playoffs and a reduction of the Saturday exclusivities. In particular, they would want more Maple Leafs games. If CTV were part of the mix, the situation would become more complicated. They would presumably try to take out the CBC altogether, in partnership with TSN. Even if CTV were uninterested, Bettman would try and draw them in, or at the very least give the impression that they were possible bidders.

Our strategy going into the talks was to try and keep them focused on the business case. That, we figured, would bring discipline to the process and ensure that everyone had to behave rationally. Besides, we were confident that we knew much more than the NHL about advertising revenue and sports production costs. This was, after all, our business, not theirs. If we could not win on our own turf, we should hang up our skates and retire from the rink forever.

At our first negotiating session, a couple months after the dinner at Nobu, Nancy Lee, Neil McEneaney and I suggested we build a joint business model. "If you are prepared to do this, I will share our most sensitive business secrets with you," I offered. "We will show you everything: total revenues, revenues by game, the lot."

Gary Bettman looked startled. We knew it had never been done like that before. "You will show us your revenues?" he asked.

"Yup. We are partners. We should be open with each other," I said.

"Open with each other?" Bettman repeated, as though considering an incomprehensible mathematical formula. Open was not something Bettman did.

"Sure. That way we can work with real numbers and make sure the models are accurate," I went on.

Bettman and Daly looked puzzled. They sniffed the air, unclear what trap was being laid for them.

For my part, I hoped that if they agreed, it would force them to show us their numbers and models. I hoped, as well, that pursuing this approach would compel both sides to negotiate as long-term partners, imbued with a spirit of candour and mutual trust.

"Let us think about it," Bettman said. He pushed back from the table, stood and looked out the window into the canyons of Manhattan. Only Bill Daly was left at the table with us. He glowered menacingly. Perhaps they had a bon cop, bad cop routine.

Eventually Bettman assigned Bill Daly the job of working out the terms for the negotiation. He was to sort out with me the issues of timing, access to data, overall approach, whether we sat at separate tables, or the same table, whether a round table or a square one. It was worrying that Bettman left these issues to Daly, since it suggested that he wanted to be in a position to repudiate—if necessary—whatever came out of the preliminary talks.

Weeks drifted by. The league dithered. Meanwhile the CBC sports department was becoming restive. They were worried about the rumours circulating in the press that CTV was making a play for the NHL rights. At one point, I went to talk to the members of the sports department. They crowded into a gloomy boardroom.

"Are we winning?" one asked.

"I don't know," I said candidly.

"We've lost everything so far," he continued, referring to the recent losses of the Olympics and curling.

"Yes, but we're working hard to tie up the hockey rights well before the contract expires," I replied.

There was a strangled quality to the conversation. Nobody really knew what to say. A mood of impending doom hung over the burly men—they were almost all men—in the room. Almost no one looked at me directly. The place had a final-days feel to it.

In June, Brian Williams announced that he was leaving for CTV to work on the Olympic Games they had taken from us. Williams had been with the CBC since 1974. He had been the lead sportscaster on many of CBC's most important properties, including the CFL and the Olympics. Famous for his vanity, he was also notable for his naïveté. When he advised us that he was thinking of going to CTV, Nancy Lee called me.

"I presume that if he leaves he is in breach of his contract," I said.

"Yes," she replied.

"Well, tell him if he goes, he's fired."

She did. According to Nancy, he moaned a little. He asked her somewhat plaintively if that meant he would no longer be able to call the football games for the CBC.

Nancy fired him on June 8, 2006.

Brian Williams's dismissal received a mixed reaction from the sports department. Although he was widely disliked—indeed, a cheer went up when his firing was announced—it still felt like another twist of the knife. It felt as though CTV had scored another coup at the expense of the CBC.

As spring gave way to summer, nothing much happened. Our brilliant strategy of trying to stampede Gary Bettman and Bill Daly into signing an early deal at a reasonable cost seemed to be getting little traction. If they were worried, they were not showing it. There were some conversations, with expressions of good wishes and enthusiasm for the great and historic relationship. But there were no actual negotiations.

Finally, in July, I called Bettman and said we would make him an offer to get the ball rolling. We had actually had an offer ready for some time that we thought would be attractive and fair. We also had a pretty good idea where we might end up and the steps we would need to follow to get there. We were in fact itching to move ahead. No doubt he knew this, and knew that the best thing for him was to continue to give us the slow roll and try to reverse the pressure. If we believed what we said, he probably reasoned, then the longer he waited the less room there was for us to manoeuvre.

"I am happy to receive an offer," Bettman said. He always appears happy, no matter what is going on. "But," he continued, "you understand that I would like to continue to sniff around."

"Sniff around?"

"Sure. Just to see what else might be out there, besides you."

"I understand," I said.

I hung up the phone with visions of Gary Bettman and Ivan Fecan enthusiastically sniffing each other.

We were preoccupied at this point with whether CTV would bid or not. It seemed on its face implausible. CTV usually reserved Saturday nights for the Canadian shows they were obligated to provide as a condition of their licence, and they reserved the more lucrative weekday nights for their bread-and-butter American programs. As well, the playoffs and the Stanley Cup games would require them to displace their U.S. shows at the height of the season, from April through June.

Nevertheless, we were still worried. It was not just that Ivan Fecan had happily overpaid for the Olympics, but he had recently begun buying more U.S. programs than he could ever schedule, to keep them out of the hands of his rivals at Global. It was an enormously expensive strategy but it demonstrated the lengths he would go to achieve national domination. Perhaps he had worked out some diabolical plot with TSN to scoop all the NHL rights. The prospect of Bettman and Fecan not just sniffing each other but actually consummating something was too awful to contemplate.

On July 19, in Montreal, we presented Bettman and Daly with a formal offer. Less than two weeks later, we met again in New York. This time Bettman tabled his revenue model, which had been prepared by an outside group of consultants. The numbers looked absurd to us. They were another world from what we were actually achieving. Bettman, however, seemed quite happy with them. "So," he asked, "now that you see how well you should be doing, how much more can you put on the table?"

"These numbers are crazy," I said. "Your projections are way too aggressive."

"Maybe you just have a lousy sales force," he countered.

"We have a good sales force. They have been selling *Hockey Night in Canada* since the dawn of history. They know the market better than anyone."

"Our consultants say you are priced too low," Gary went on. He smiled cheerfully.

"Perhaps we should meet your consultants," I proposed. "That way we could come to a common understanding."

Bettman thought this a poor idea. Clearly he did not want us beating up his third-party consultants and negotiating with them the ultimate value of his rights.

The conversation drifted along, with us pointing out further absurdities in his study, while he slagged our sales efforts. Clearly no progress was going to be made until we found a way to resolve the differences over revenues. At last we agreed that his man, Steven Hatze-Petros, would meet with our head of sales, David Scapillati, to see whether there was a common ground. Perhaps the two of them could bridge the gulf.

And in fact they did agree. By the end of the month Steven Hatze-Petros and David Scapillati had produced a common revenue number, which was much closer to our own—indeed, it effectively *was* our own.

The next day, I called Bettman. He was his usual sunny self.

"Now," I said, "since we have agreed on the revenues, we should be able to close the deal."

"Nope," he replied.

"Nope?"

"There is no agreement on the revenue number," he said.

"That can't be! Scapillati told me that he and Hatze-Petros had agreed."

"Well, I didn't."

In hopes of breaking the log jam, we went back to New York in early September. There was, however, little movement. Gary Bettman offered some minor concessions but they were of no material value. We argued for about two-and-a-half hours, until we ran out of things to say. Then we shook hands and parted. We were tens of millions of dollars apart. It seemed impossible to imagine that the gap could be bridged. For the first time, I began to think we might not be able to conclude a deal.

That night I reflected on what to do. If we met Gary Bettman's demands, *Hockey Night in Canada* would lose money. If it lost money, it would have to be subsidized from the public funds available to the CBC, at the expense of radio or news or drama. That was unthinkable. It would also have proven that the private broadcasters were right and that we were competing against them using public money. That too was unthinkable. There seemed no way forward.

It appeared that I would end up presiding over a disaster. Having already lost the Olympic bid, the CFL and curling, I would now lose *Hockey Night in Canada*, seventy-five iconic years of the greatest sportscasters and the greatest games. The ghosts of Howie Meeker,

Foster Hewitt and Danny Gallivan frowned upon me. The living presence of Don Cherry scowled.

And of course the loss of *Hockey Night in Canada* meant we could fall into an even bigger catastrophe. We did not have the money to make up those hundreds of hours of Canadian programming, unless we showed endless repeats of *The Fifth Estate* and *Rick Mercer Report*. Our viewers would scream with boredom and abandon us in droves. Our share would plunge from its already enfeebled levels. It would be the greatest calamity in CBC's history, and I would be blamed.

During the negotiations with the NHL, I had lunch with Don Cherry. We talked about how things were going with the league, how the season was unfolding, the problems with the Leafs, the usual stuff. At a certain point, Don said that whatever one thought of foreigners—by which he meant Europeans and Americans—no NHL team could advance significantly in the playoffs, let alone win the Stanley Cup, without a majority of Canadian players and a Canadian captain. To illustrate his thesis, he proceeded to run through the last few seasons of the playoffs, citing which teams had advanced and which had failed. When he was done, he looked at me with satisfaction. Then he spread his arms and asked, "Do you know where we are?" I thought he meant the restaurant. He looked around the room and out the windows. "If you draw a circle from here with a hundred-mile radius, we are sitting at the epicentre of the greatest breeding ground of hockey players in the world. Right here." He smiled, and we finished our meal.

ABOUT TEN DAYS after the fiasco in New York, Hatze-Petros called Scapillati to say we were "inches away." Tens of millions of dollars did not feel like inches to us. But who knew? Perhaps this was some ambiguous olive branch. Perhaps Gary Bettman had concluded that we were genuinely at the end of our capacity to pay. Perhaps he now feared that we might actually go away. Whatever his reasoning, it seemed wise to follow up this peculiar little feeler.

We determined to make one last push. I would meet Bettman in Truro, Nova Scotia, on September 25 for the *Hockeyville* festivities.

Hockeyville is a program sponsored by Kraft, where little towns all over Canada apply to be named "Hockeyville," the Canadian town that most loves and celebrates hockey. Each competing town explains why it should be chosen, and a national vote is held. The winner has its rink rebuilt, and two NHL teams play an exhibition game there. The winner was Salmon River, a town so small that the celebrations had to be held in Truro.

Everyone showed up. Don Cherry arrived on an antique fire engine. The Ottawa Senators and Montreal Canadiens came for the game. The premier of Nova Scotia, much of his cabinet and the local mayors appeared. It was clearly the largest event in the history of Truro.

Tents had been erected outside the rink. The tables in the tents were covered in food; it felt like a church fundraiser. There were sliced meats and coleslaw, three-bean salads and chips, lashings of soda pop, strangely dried-out hamburgers and weird, multicoloured aspics. I found Gary Bettman cautiously examining an implausible food object. He was his usual cheerful self, although he looked a little odd in his immaculate suit and tie, with everyone else wearing jeans and plaids.

We repaired to his car and sat down together. I sketched out a proposal that was a little richer than our previous one, but which was raked, so that CBC's payments would increase in later years. We felt this was manageable because inflation would assist us, and although we would never admit it to Gary, our advertising rates were underpriced. Thus, by pushing the increases to the later years of the contract, we would have enough time to raise our prices without starting a war with the agencies and advertisers. I explained what we proposed to pay year-by-year and the size of the annual increments.

Bettman took a little notepad out of his jacket pocket. He leaned against the dash of the car as I spoke. He wrote down the numbers I proposed for each of the years of the new contract. He used a very expensive pen.

"It sounds good," he said. "I think we are in the right ballpark. I will take it to my board."

A wave of relief flooded over me. Finally it appeared that we would conclude the deal successfully at a reasonable price. A chunk of concrete moved out of my stomach. We got out of the car and shook hands. Gary smiled his endlessly happy smile. We walked back to the tent. The three-bean salad looked delicious. The sliced meats and coleslaw tasted remarkably good.

Two months later, David Masse, the new head of CBC sports, and I went to meet Gary Bettman and Bill Daly at Rao's, a restaurant in East Harlem. Masse had replaced Nancy Lee a month earlier. He is intense and calm. We assumed we were going to close the deal.

Unfortunately, we were running late because the plane was delayed in Toronto. To avoid being rude, we called the restaurant to apologize and tell them we were on our way. The phone rang and rang, but nobody answered. It seemed impossible. We phoned the listed number, checked again with directory assistance, but there was no response at the other end. That seemed absurd. How, at the very least, does one make a reservation if nobody will answer the phone? Bettman had told us in advance that Rao's had a reputation as a favourite restaurant of some mobsters. He noted with what seemed a strangely misplaced enthusiasm that someone had been killed there only three years ago. But, Mob restaurant or not, presumably it still had to take reservations.

When we finally arrived, we were shown down the stairs into the restaurant proper. Bettman and Daly were at a table in the corner. The maître d' came by to tell us the evening's offers. I asked about the phone and the reservations. "Ah, no," he explained. "There are no reservations. The tables are permanently reserved." We looked puzzled.

He explained that each table is committed every night of the week to the same family. Did this mean Bettman and Daly ate every night of the week at a restaurant frequented by mobsters?

"We borrowed a table for the evening," Bettman explained.

Rao's not only took no reservations, it had no menu. The maître d' just listed off what the kitchen was making that evening.

David and I assumed that we were there for a celebratory dinner to conclude our discussions and agree on the final terms of the new contract. The conversation began auspiciously enough, with Bettman saying the league was fine with the financial terms. But— and there was always a "but" with Gary Bettman—they still needed more concessions, giving TSN more playoff games and two more Leafs games. It was like an endless trip to the dentist.

At the same time, it seemed clear that if the league was prepared to close with TSN, then the threat of CTV bidding must not be there. "I guess that CTV's not in the picture," I mused.

Bettman smiled inscrutably. "Well, you never know," he said, apparently implying that Ivan Fecan was somewhere in his back pocket and could be produced if necessary, like a bad rabbit from a malevolent hat.

"I never imagined they would consider it," I went on, ignoring him. "They could never fit *Hockey Night in Canada* into their schedule."

"As I say," he continued, "you never know. But the best course is, of course, just to conclude."

There it was. We should cough up the playoff concessions and two Leafs games, let him close with TSN and be happy. With Gary Bettman one is afraid to have a drink. It's wiser to stick to water. He is always negotiating. Often when he is just speculating or gossiping or asking after the weather report, he is really negotiating. It never stops.

As the evening wore on, the restaurant filled with a big crowd of large, mostly male customers. They looked like businessmen with a penchant for weightlifting, diamond rings and hearty arm punching. The crowd grew thicker and thicker, more and more voluble. I wondered why Bettman had brought us to this particular restaurant. Was there a subtext?

After dinner we walked into the cold Harlem night. Immediately surrounding the restaurant were the limousines of the patrons and their large drivers who stood around smoking and talking. It looked like a convention of garrulous refrigerators. Beyond that, everything was emptiness and desolation. There were no taxis anywhere. Bettman noticed us looking around.

"No car?" he asked.

"No. How do we get a cab?"

"Oh, cabs never come up here. They're afraid," he replied.

"Can you give us a lift?"

"Sure. How about we make it three extra Maple Leaf games?"

So there we were, outside Rao's without a deal. It had been nine months since our first meeting at Nobu with Robert Rabinovitch, when we tried to convince the NHL to conclude quickly for fear of losing us as a bidder. For almost six months we had been discussing revenues and trying to come to an agreement. Neither of those strategies had worked. We were now into the hardest part of the negotiation, since there was no agreement about time frames or the overall business case. We were down to saying no to each other until one side folded. It would be more poker than business. I liked Bettman's hand better than ours.

The ride downtown from Harlem was gloomy and depressing. Even the usually optimistic and cheerful David Masse was strangely silent. The cold New York night enveloped the car, and we drove through the darkness with snow falling lightly.

The conversation with the NHL picked up again in early January 2007. Gary Bettman reiterated the demands he'd made at Rao's, and added new ones: more playoff games for TSN or more dollars from us. We said no. He said no. We were entering new territory, simply eyeballing each other, waiting for cracks to appear in the other side. It was turning into a contest of wills. Did we need them more than they needed us? Bettman ratcheted up the insouciance of his tone; his conversation became more confident and calmer. He affected a note of serenity, of Buddha-like calm. It was getting on my nerves.

January came and went. February dawned, with no movement. The NHL still wanted us to give up more playoff games and Leafs games. As well, they were stubborn on the digital rights for the Internet and wireless. We spoke on a number of occasions, with no result, just more circling and waiting. The pressure within the CBC increased. The president advised that we needed to conclude. The board was becoming restive and unhappy.

February passed. Finally, on March 6, we had another long conversation with Daly and Bettman. We said no again on the playoffs, no again on the Leafs, no again on price increases, and we wanted all the digital rights. After almost three hours, they finally said yes. They dropped the remaining demands and we were done. A hand-shake deal was in place.

It was not as good a deal as the old one; in fact it was a very rich deal, certainly the largest sports contract in Canadian history. But it was a deal nevertheless, and one that should—if everything worked out properly—make the CBC a small but important profit. We realized that there were dangers. We realized that unforeseen events might blow the economic underpinning out of the business case. If the economy collapsed, or the advertising markets went south, or the Leafs never made the playoffs, or the digital rights had no value, then we would face a loss. It might not be a large loss, but even a small one would be embarrassing and difficult to deal with. But the risks seemed remote—the economy was in the midst of a great boom, the Leafs could not lose forever, and the digital markets were grow-ing faster than the economy as a whole. It seemed safe to sign and seek board approval.

On March 21, just an hour before we were presenting it to the board, Gary Bettman and Bill Daly signed the final version, of the agreement. The board received the deal with relief. We walked them through the numbers, reminded them of the consequences of losing the Shrine and recommended it for approval. They asked about the dangers, looked at the projected margins, worried about the pros-pects of the Maple Leafs and agreed unanimously to the contract.

Five days later Bettman came up to Toronto with the Stanley Cup to announce the deal. We held a little press conference, with the Grail between us. Afterward we made arrangements for people to have their pictures taken with the Cup. The line stretched through the Toronto headquarters and almost into the streets. For hours CBC employees and regular folks waited patiently for their moment with the Grail. Many touched or kissed it. They had their pictures taken, arms around it, lips pressed to its silver surface, fingers touching the hallowed names of the winning players of the past. The Rocket. The Flower. The Great One.

➤ Tell me something I don't know.
Rob Russo, Ottawa Bureau Chief,
Canadian Press, 2010

six
NEWS

FOR SIXTY YEARS, *The National* had been the definitive late-night newscast—serious, worthy, preoccupied with the great institutional matters of state. For sixty years, thoughtful middle-aged male anchors had appeared behind a large desk, dispensing the "newscast of record." If a story really mattered, it appeared on *The National*. If it did not appear on *The National*, it did not exist. *The National* defined and reflected the public agenda.

Peter Mansbridge has been reliably there for the last twenty years. Before him, there were the others: Knowlton Nash, Lloyd Robertson, Stanley Burke, names synonymous with maturity and temperance. They would sit in the Big Chair behind the Big Desk and narrate the great national and international events of the day. Administrations came and went: Diefenbaker gave way to Pearson, Pearson to Trudeau, Trudeau to Mulroney, Mulroney to Chrétien. Wars were fought and lost. The economy boomed and tanked. Society shifted and rocked. All was reported and chronicled in the measured, careful voice of *The National*.

At the time of *The National's* greatest power, the country paused at 10:00 each evening. The anchor would appear behind the Big Desk and clarify the complexities of the world. First there would be the News of the Day, often saved until *The National* was ready to

164

reveal it. And then, there would be the Meaning of the News of the Day, sometimes formally separated in *The Journal* of old, sometimes sitting in the back half of the hour.

What happened on *The National* often dominated the priorities of the other news outlets. The papers would see what stories they would be covering the next day. Politicians would discover how Question Period would unfold the following afternoon. Lobbyists and civil servants noted how issues would be defined and structured. *The National* often established the public agenda and the tone of its treatment.

The brand of the CBC was dominated by *The National*. To tamper with *The National* was to tamper with the reputation of the CBC as a whole.

For years, little changed. Generations came and went, but the show stayed as it always had been. The same Big Chair, the same impersonal voice, the same catalogue of institutional stories, the same deliberate pacing and the same thoughtful, slightly ponderous approach.

All around it, the news business morphed and grew at an accelerating pace. Whole new networks arose, offering news twenty-four hours a day. Crazed opinion and debate slugfests appeared from nowhere. The Internet made every story available from anywhere, all the time. The news broadened and expanded. It reached out from the grey groves of government into lifestyle and celebrity. The speed and pacing ramped into bites and clips. Where once five minutes had been too short, a minute and a half was now too long. Outside the CBC, the news business had become a hectic, skittering, ever-evolving panoply of new subjects, platforms, points of view and styles.

The National did not change, nor did the rest of CBC news, which took its cue from its flagship program. The local shows and the all-news network retained the same stately pacing, the same reserved and disembodied tone, the same focus on the major organizations of the government and the same quiet certainty of their superior purpose. As the world accelerated, the audiences for CBC news began to evaporate. Where once the Corporation had been dominant, by 2004 it found itself a sad also-ran to Global and CTV.

The local shows, which had once had been number one or two in their various markets, had been all but destroyed. Collectively, they were down to just over 190,000 viewers nationwide at 6:00 PM, whereas CTV took close to 1.5 million. They were down to a distant third everywhere, except Charlottetown (where they had no competitors).

The American network CNN was regularly beating CBC's all-news network, Newsworld, often drawing twice as many Canadian viewers. And *The National* was regularly being trounced by CTV's late-night shows. Even more ominous, public opinion polls showed that Canadians felt there was little difference between *The National* and CTV in terms of trust or credibility, previously the bedrock of *The National*'s reputation. The situation was grim. The core of the CBC's brand was collapsing.

For me, the news department mattered enormously. My father, Peter Stursberg, had been one of its stalwarts, a correspondent during the Second World War. He had landed in Sicily with the Canadian troops in 1944, a CBC microphone in his hand. As the army fought its way up Italy, he went with them, broadcasting all the battles and terror. Later he entered Berlin with the Canadian soldiers, filing reports and stories from Hitler's bunker. His journalism made him a household name in Canada.

In the 1950s, he opened the first CBC television bureau in New York to cover the United Nations. Every week, he reported on the great events of the Security Council and the General Assembly: the Korean War, the Suez crisis, the Soviet invasion of Hungary. He became even more famous in Canada—now people could see him as well as hear him.

When our family arrived in Ottawa, he furthered his journalism career. He became the Ottawa editor of the *Toronto Star*, co-founded private television in Ottawa and created a syndicated news service. He wrote books on the United Nations and biographies of Diefenbaker and Pearson. Our house was constantly full of journalists and politicians. Don Newman, the long-time host of CBC's *Politics*, claimed that my father got him his job after an evening of raucous drinking at the National Press Club. As I grew up, dinner table conversation revolved around the great events of the day. I was probably the only teenager in the city who felt obliged to read the newspapers so that I could keep up with my father's conversation. Girls and football were infinitely more interesting, but it was essential to be up to date on events in Congo and Czechoslovakia.

Later, I worked in the federal government, rising to become assistant deputy minister of the Department of Communications, where I was responsible for the media relations group. All the press conferences, news releases, speeches, interviews with the minister were my responsibility. Inevitably I spent a great deal of time with journalists, talking to them, briefing them, having drinks with them.

As my career advanced, I became more of a public figure myself, giving interviews, hosting press conferences, writing op-ed pieces. Journalism and journalists continued as a central part of my life. I consumed the news voraciously. At one point, I was subscribing to five newspapers, reading the press clippings wherever I was working, watching *The National* religiously every night and waking every morning to CBC radio news.

Arriving at the CBC, I knew the news department would be hostile to me, as it was to all management, particularly outsiders. And I knew that they were even more likely to resent someone who was actively interested in their operations and who was not himself a journalist. I would be seen as an ignorant meddler. They would doubtless close ranks to keep me out, as they had traditionally done to other members of management who had the temerity to express an interest in their department.

In an attempt to show that I was not unsympathetic, I asked the CBC Archives to find a picture of my father with a CBC microphone in his hand. They produced a photograph of him with a microphone the size of a pineapple, the CBC logo emblazoned across it in huge capital letters. He looked impossibly young and earnest. He was caught mid-sentence, speaking into the microphone, his eyes fixed with alarm on whatever horror he was covering. I put the picture on the wall behind my desk. I wanted to show the news department that far from being hostile, I was sympathetic and admiring of their craft.

THE NEWS PROBLEM paralleled entertainment in that fewer and fewer Canadians were watching the CBC's news shows. But there the parallel ended. Whereas Canadians preferred U.S. entertainment shows, they decisively preferred their own news. Canadians were compulsive and enthusiastic consumers of domestic news. They did not buy foreign newspapers or—with the exception of CNN—watch foreign newscasts.

The other difference was that there was no shortage of Canadian news. There were two national papers in the *Globe and Mail* and the *National Post*, as well as high-quality dailies in all the major markets. Both CTV and Global offered national and local television news across English-speaking Canada. There were all-news radio stations and excellent news websites. Unlike Canadian entertainment, Canadian news was available from many different sources. In no sense was there a market failure requiring remedial government action.

This, however, raised an important question. Since nobody else was providing Canadian entertainment in prime time, the CBC's role was clear and unarguable. But why did the CBC have to offer a news service when there was no shortage of Canadian news? What was the point of spending public money financing a service that the private sector was already providing? The CBC had historically answered this question by saying that its news was different from the private sector's. It was deeper, more thoughtful, aimed at a more sophisticated and better-educated clientele. It was the "newscast of record."

That argument was not achieving much traction with Canadians. They were turning away from the CBC's "deeper and more thoughtful" news in ever larger numbers. They clearly did not feel disadvantaged if they missed it. To the contrary, they were making it clear that the news that mattered most to them was found on Global, CTV and CNN.

And even if the news really were "deeper and more thoughtful," what is the point if nobody watches? It's a bit like constructing a powerful automobile engine for a car that nobody wants to buy. Maybe it's a better engine, but nobody will know, since the car is doomed to sit unloved and unsold on the dealer's lot. Whatever the quality of the news, it needed to have viewers. There is no public broadcaster without a public.

The challenge, then, for CBC news was two-fold. First, we had to reverse the collapse in our audiences. The absolute precondition for anything else was viewers. Second, CBC news had to be genuinely different from the news offered by Global and CTV. If it was the same, there could be no fair and sensible rationale for spending public money on it. Whether this was "deeper and more thoughtful," or something else, *it would have to result in CBC's making a contribution to the public debate that was not only valuable but that would not otherwise occur.*

In 2004, the news department saw itself as the very essence of the CBC. It looked down on the other parts of the Corporation. Sports, entertainment and sales were lesser, unworthy of the news department's attention. When a network launched its new entertainment shows for the fall and winter seasons, its news organizations would cover them—except at the CBC. The news department did not do "entertainment" news. And even if it did, it could not cover other parts of the Corporation for fear of losing its "integrity." When it absolutely could not avoid covering entertainment, the stock response was to sneer.

Fort News was walled off from the rest of the CBC, moated and garrisoned against the entry of outsiders. It believed that it should answer to nobody. It stood at arm's length not just from government interference, but from all interference, from the board, the president and the head of English television. Any incursion or even comment on the news operation was regarded as impertinent and compromising.

Fort News believed in its own superiority. It believed that its news was indeed deeper and more thoughtful than the other networks'. It believed that it served a better-educated and more sophisticated audience. It believed that it was the newscast of record. It believed that the other networks' news involved chasing ambulances. It believed that Global and CTV pandered to less clever audiences by focusing on crime and fires and celebrities. It believed that it set the national standard for journalism and that this was widely recognized.

Fort News did not believe in management. In fact, it was intensely anti-management. This is normal in all news organizations, to a certain extent. Journalists like to see themselves as hard-boiled truth-tellers who see through the duplicity of the Establishment. Their reflex position is that the powerful—not only big corporations and government agencies, but also the people who run the CBC—are wrong or corrupt or compromised. So intense was the anti-management bias that even the top managers in the news department felt slightly embarrassed and uneasy about their own roles.

This combination of defensiveness and self-regard was personified in the great baron who ran Fort News. Tony Burman had been at the CBC for almost his entire career. He had been a working journalist, a foreign correspondent, a documentary filmmaker and a producer. Eventually he rose into management, becoming executive producer of *The National* and for a while the head of Newsworld. In the process, he had won many awards and enjoyed a reputation as one of Canada's outstanding news executives.

Burman was the apotheosis of the news department's strengths and weaknesses. Pugnacious, brittle and clever, he would brook no entry by outsiders to his fortified city. It was his duty to ensure that nobody outside Fort News could influence, let alone change, its editorial priorities, its internal processes or its journalistic standards.

There was no greater blood sport for Fort News' denizens than to try and take down CBC management. This was done simply by passing on information or rumour or gossip to journalists in other news organizations, who would then publish stories revealing the managers' incompetence or venality. The practice had been going on for years, with the result that management grew increasingly secretive, since it could not trust the employees of the Corporation.

When I first arrived at the CBC, Matthew Fraser was the editor of the *National Post*. I had known Matthew for many years, and he would play a little game with me. Whenever I sent out a memo to the staff, he would send me an email telling me how much time had elapsed between its release internally and its arrival in his computer.

He kept a log, chronicling the different times. On each occasion, when a new record was set, he would crow in his email "New Record. Only thirty seconds this time."

At one point, in my attempts to better understand the news department, I suggested to Tony Burman that it might be a good idea for me to have a desk on the newsroom floor, where I would work occasionally so I could meet the journalists, talk with them informally and understand their work process. He dismissed the idea in a peremptory fashion.

"That's a terrible idea," he said.

"Why?"

"It'll intimidate the newsroom staff."

Intimidate the staff? The ferocious journalists?

"How about I simply listen in to some of the editorial conferences on *The National* to see how they approach putting the show together?"

"Another terrible idea."

"Why this time? I'll only be on the line. I won't even say anything."

"It'll intimidate the staff. I never go to those meetings myself."

It was very frustrating. Perhaps my proposals were naive, but I felt strongly that I needed to understand the workings of the news department.

A couple of days after these conversations, they appeared in the *Toronto Star* under Antonia Zerbisias's byline: "Stursberg… has recently and repeatedly sought a desk in *The National*'s newsroom… he is a political appointee's appointee. He has no business in the newsroom of an organization constantly battling to maintain its independence… from the party in power." There it was, fresh from my conversations with the news department, not just my proposals but an attack on my integrity.

It was clear that any attempt to change the news department was fraught with peril. I was afraid that if I made any efforts to halt, let alone reverse, its slide into irrelevance, I would be attacked. It would be like attempting to enter a decrepit house whose sullen residents would prefer to have the house collapse upon them than have it repaired. I was afraid, very afraid.

In 2003, the news department had undertaken a massive survey of Canadians, the largest effort of its kind ever done. It asked about their views of CBC news from multiple points of view. It looked into how they felt about the story selection, the presentation style, the quality of the journalism, pretty much everything. It was an impressive piece of work.

The results confirmed what was obvious on screen. CBC news was seen as boring, static, institutional, narrow, irrelevant and tired. It might be the "newscast of record," but what was being recorded was of little or no interest to Canadians. As Tony Burman said in a note to the news department, "The CBC is seen by many as being for older people, not appealing, not entertaining... too narrow, too focused on 'bad' news that is of little relevance... [as a place] that frequently chooses stories that interest [it] more than audiences." The study was a wake-up call, demanding significant renewal of all the news properties.

Fort News plunged into a huge discussion of what to do to reform itself and respond to Canadians' criticisms. Task forces and committees were established to pore over the study results and make recommendations. Over five hundred employees of the news department participated in workshops and study sessions. They met almost a hundred times, churning out ideas and proposals. The place was a fever of excitement and enthusiasm. The resulting reports called for "bold action." Top management of the news department promised that there would be a "sweeping, even radical (new) beginning."

And then, nothing.

After all the daring talk, there was tinkering at the margins. One set of changes designed to modernize *The National* involved adding some branded segments on particular topics. The news department became anxious that the proposed improvements were too glitzy. They worried that they might alienate the CBC's core Constituency or compromise the show's brand. They wrung their hands, made a pilot and tested it with audiences. Nobody in the test group could tell the difference between the old and the new *National*.

The news department appeared frozen. Despite the precipitous decline in ratings and the devastating results of the research, Fort

News seemed incapable of change. They worked hard, pouring enormous effort and knowledge into renewal, and then ... nothing. The shows simply plodded along, largely unchanged. The news department continued to produce the same old unsatisfactory shows that had brought it to its sad pass.

Why was this?

There seemed to be four interconnected problems.

First, there was no real sense of urgency. Like the frog that is placed in a pot of water raised slowly to a boil, the department could not sense its impending demise. Decline had become the norm—it had been going on for so long that it seemed inevitable. Past efforts to change had failed; the recommendations from the News Study had gone nowhere. Nothing could be done. Resistance was futile.

Second, even if the will to change could be summoned, there was a widespread belief that Fort News did not have the resources to compete effectively with Global and CTV. Everyone in the organization believed that CBC was "outgunned" by the other networks. They believed that the others had more trucks, cameras, journalists and producers. Although this belief would prove to be untrue, it contributed to the sense that very little could be done.

Third, it had become a prisoner of its own internal politics. Virtually everyone in management had been there all their lives. It was well and good to talk about radical change, but effecting it was another matter. It would upset many, many apple carts, belonging to friends and colleagues of very long standing. It is difficult—if not impossible—to tell people that the efforts of many years will not do.

Finally, it was not clear who was in charge of what. Every time I asked somebody how something in the department worked, I would get a different answer. At first, I attributed this to my general ignorance of news operations. Eventually, however, it occurred to me that perhaps there was no agreed set of rules. Perhaps nobody really knew how it worked or who was responsible for what. When I asked external consultants to review the accountability regime, they described it as a "bowl of spaghetti." The news department in effect ran on personal relationships and arrangements rather than clear lines of command. Even if the will and the resources were there and the internal politics would allow it, change would still be impossible since nobody knew how the place worked.

The failure of renewal through the News Study served to reinforce the worst tendencies of Fort News. If change was impossible and there could be no reversal of the ratings decline, it became even more important to believe that the news product was superior to the competitors'. If self-worth could not be validated by the number of Canadians watching the news, another standard had to be found. And that standard was still at hand. The news, although unwatched, was "deeper and better informed."

The net result was a department awash in strange currents and counter-currents. It was vain and defensive. It talked boldly and acted timidly. It claimed pride of place, even as its claims grew increasingly hollow. The employees were not stupid, of course. They sensed the contradictions. They felt the drift and the slow sinking. They came to feel trapped and cynical. The news department was a very unhappy place.

FOR YEARS, the local news shows had been dying. In the 1980s and early 1990s they had posted respectable audiences, being number one or two (sometimes a distant number two) in most major markets. Then, in the 1990s, a series of cuts seriously damaged the local news. Some local newscasts were abolished altogether and others were dramatically reduced. The numbers began to collapse.

In the late 1990s, as part of the new "distinctiveness" strategy, the local news shows were reconceived as local current affairs shows. The argument was that there was no point in duplicating what the private networks did, so the CBC should define its local offerings in opposition to them. Why offer weather when it is available everywhere else? Why offer local crime reporting when it is available everywhere else? Or sports scores? Instead of a punchy local hard-news show, there were long stories on "deeper and more thoughtful" matters. The numbers continued to crater.

In 2000, *Canada Now* was launched with much fanfare. It reduced the local news to one half of an hour-long 6:00 PM program. The other half would be national. It was an odd program. In some parts of the country, the local news was the first half hour of the show; in other parts, it was the back half. In all parts of the country, the local news component was starved and resources were focused on the national half hour. When local stories were deemed of national interest, they were hijacked by the national half hour and did not appear locally. The whole thing was a mess. *Canada Now* further accelerated the downward audience spiral.

As part of my early review of the situation, I toured the local newsrooms and watched the shows. The local half hours were a weird amalgam of local information and "distinctive current affairs." In many cases, hard news had been jettisoned altogether and replaced with long thumb-suckers on topics of marginal interest. My favourite was a Halifax-produced feature—six minutes, an eternity on television—on goat cheese. It was so long that it had a commercial break in the middle. All over Nova Scotia, viewers declined the CBC offering and watched CTV's maritime news.

The same problem existed everywhere. The CBC would not cover the subjects that every market study showed preoccupied Canadians and that every private TV station excelled at. They had abandoned weather, crime, police reporting, local safety—the viewers' top news priorities. In most local stations, scanners—the radios that allow people to listen in on police calls—were removed from the newsrooms or simply turned off. The CBC willfully blinded itself. It was as though it had said to Canadians, "We do not care what local news matters to you; goat cheese reporting is what matters to us."

The turning away from audience preferences, and the redefinition of the "news" as whatever the private sector did not cover, created surreal newsrooms. In all the major local markets, the television monitors were turned to CNN, Newsworld and BBC World, almost never to CTV or Global. The local reporters could follow what was happening in Damascus and Washington but did not see what the private sector was reporting in their own towns.

The local journalists became demoralized. It's no fun producing newscasts that nobody watches. The news department in Toronto—which never had much time for local news—compounded the problem by "big footing" the local journalists. Whenever a story arose locally that was deemed of country-wide importance, a national journalist was dispatched to cover it rather than the local reporters.

The local news departments had always been seen as the farm team for the national news. Now more than ever this was the case. Many reporters and hosts yearned to leave local news. They hoped to be called up to the "network" and have their careers validated by being named "national" reporters and appearing with Peter Mansbridge. Local news was their stint in purgatory.

The local newscasts began to ape the formal style of *The National*. Local anchors and reporters adopted the same serious and chilly tone as Peter Mansbridge at the Big Desk, hoping their performance would catch Toronto's eye and show they were serious enough to be considered for ascension. The effect was stiff and distant. In certain markets it became so cold that it felt almost Stalinesque. The hosts intoned the recent triumphs in meeting the tractor production quotas or the completion of the five-year plan for steel manufacturing. A frosty authority gripped the local shows. They felt unwelcoming.

Often I would ask the local producers and reporters why they were humourless and removed. I would suggest that they think about what they were asking of the audiences. In effect, they were saying, "Please invite us into your house every evening." And who do you invite? The people you know and like, your neighbours, friends and relations. You do not invite people you do not know and feel no kinship with, let alone those who seem distant and cold. The response was always the same. The journalists feared that if they opened up emotionally, they would never be invited to move up to *The National*.

That strangely formal approach served to undercut TV's great advantage over every other medium. Television is the only place where you can see how people respond to events by watching their body and facial expressions. Is the mayor telling the truth? Does the priest really care? Can the principal be trusted? Eyes shift, feet shuffle, heads turn. We can make up our own minds, we can feel how others feel and we can make sense of the stories by understanding their emotional resonance.

The overall diminishment of local news was unfortunate and surprising, since local news is much more important to Canadians than national news. Two-thirds of all news viewing is local, and two-thirds of all advertising revenue sits locally. For Canadians— and this has been true throughout the history of the country—local trumps national.

The privates have always known this. At CTV, local anchors do not pine to do occasional pieces on Lloyd Robertson's show. They aspire to become huge figures in their own communities. In Ottawa, for example, the local host, Max Keeping, stayed in the job for decades. He started at the local station hosting a Saturday afternoon dance party in the early 1960s and became one of the most loved and iconic figures in the city. His newscasts clobbered the competition for years.

To limit the sting of the lost audiences, the CBC continued to insist that its local news, though not popular, offered better journalism. But even this fiction was unsustainable. I used to do a little exercise with the staff in the newsrooms across the country. I would ask them to record their news and their competitors', and the next morning we would watch both shows and see what we could learn. Inevitably the CBC news teams assumed that theirs would be the better newscast, with sharper journalism and more searching analysis. They were often wrong.

In Edmonton, for example, we sat down one morning to watch the previous night's news. Everyone was there: the anchors, journalists, producers, cameramen, director, the lot. It was an exciting time in Edmonton. The Oilers were deep into a run for the Stanley Cup. Every night after the game, people would pour into the streets partying and whooping it up.

The members of the Edmonton newsroom pulled their chairs up to the television set.

"Watch this," one of the reporters said. "It's great. It's my story from last night."

The host of the show smiled with anticipation. They looked forward to showing me how good they were. The lights dimmed.

The CBC newscast came on. There was coverage of the game and then fans raging around in the street, drunk and delirious. "Go Oilers go! Go Oilers go!" they shouted. Police were rounding up the most egregious enthusiasts, handcuffing them and taking them away in wagons. There was a sonorous voice-over from the journalist, deploring the nightly excesses but lavishing warm praise on the Oilers themselves. Go Oilers go. We paused the tape. I looked around the room. Everyone was clearly pleased with the work they had done.

Then we put on the CTV coverage of the same story. It began in a similar fashion, opening with game highlights and quickly moving to the disorder in the streets. Go Oilers go. The police wagons arrived, picking up the unsteady and carting them away. So far, there was no difference between the two newscasts. Then, where the CBC had ended, CTV produced two legal experts, a defence lawyer and a professor from the University of Alberta.

The professor began. "See," he said, "they are being arrested but not charged. How can that be right?"

The defence lawyer replied, "It allows the police to clear the streets without creating pointless paperwork and clogging the courts. It looks to me like a sensible compromise for what are, after all, minor offences."

"But where does it end? So the police have the right to arrest whoever they want without specifying charges? That is arbitrary detention."

The two lawyers went back and forth on the point, countering each other's arguments and exploring the underlying legal issues. Then the CTV piece came to an end.

The newsroom was quiet. I looked at the journalist and the host.

"What do you think?" I asked.

Nobody replied. Nobody was smiling. They looked at their feet.

It was not just the journalism. It was also the stories themselves. Often we would watch the newscasts side by side, only to see that we had missed an important story or that we had got to it late. In one famous moment in Toronto, an OPP sergeant was briefing the media at a major accident scene. The private newscasters were packing up their equipment as the CBC crew arrived. The sergeant looked up as they got to the scene and announced the arrival of "the History Channel." The newsrooms typically reacted the same way they did to the Oilers clip. There was a gloomy sheepishness, with people staring at their feet and looking embarrassed. And that too was the problem. There was no rage.

Journalists by nature are wildly competitive. They will go to extraordinary lengths to get a story. They will work like stink, track down endless leads, sell their mothers, anything to be first to break the news. It is in their DNA. When they are beaten, they despair. Great editors are notorious for raging around the newsroom when their competitors get there first. But not at the CBC. There was no sense of profound failure, just regret.

And this, more than anything else, was the most worrying part. Years of goat cheese stories, of misdirection about the superiority of their efforts and about the irrelevance of the competition, had dulled the newsrooms. The fire to be first and to be great felt almost extinguished.

So there it was. The local news had largely abandoned covering local news, the troops were demoralized, the uninteresting items were delivered in a monotone and the whole enterprise had foundered in ratings. It was not surprising that the president thought local news should be eliminated. During the lockout, he even suggested we could use the work stoppage as an excellent opportunity to throw it overboard.

One day I asked Tony Burman why we were losing.

"We are outgunned," he said.

"Outgunned?" I asked.

"Yes. Just look. They have more journalists, more cameras, more everything. They have helicopters, for God's sake."

Tony Burman glared at me as if he were addressing the willfully blind.

"How do you expect us to win," he continued, "when we do not have anything like the same number of people?"

I pushed on. "How do you know you're outgunned?"

He lost what little patience he had left. "Look, Richard, you're new here. Trust me. We're outgunned. Everybody who knows anything knows that." Given the resources available, they were doing okay.

To test their theory, I hired outside consultants, the Kaiser Group—industrial spies, really—to count the news resources of CBC, Global and CTV. They counted everything: journalists, producers, editors, floor directors and cameramen, both locally and nationally. The results came as something of a shock to the management in the news department. The CBC had more resources than CTV and substantially more than Global.

The difference was that the resources of Global and CTV were distributed in a fashion quite unlike the CBC's. Where CBC was Toronto- and national-centric, the others were much more heavily deployed in the regions. Where CBC had a lot more people sitting inside the building—producers, studio crew—the others had more outside, pounding the pavement. The distribution of the private networks' resources reflected Canadians' viewing preferences: more local and more hard news. However, the privates' national newscasts also beat the CBC's.

This was, of course, both good news and bad news. On the one hand, since we did not have a resource problem, it was possible to imagine doing better, much better. On the other hand, given that we had more resources and we were doing worse than anyone else, it was clear we had a strategy problem.

When I reviewed the findings of the Kaiser study with CBC news management, they looked incredulous.

"Perhaps they're comparing apples to oranges," Tony suggested.

"What do you mean?" I asked.

"They've probably counted in radio news."

"No," I said, "in fact if you count in radio news, the results are more unfavourable. You can see that we have marginally more television news resources than CTV and a lot more than Global. Apples to apples."

Tony looked sour. He spoke darkly about helicopters. I could understand that this was not a comforting conclusion for the management of the news department. At the same time, it seemed to me that there might be an opportunity to rebuild the news offering, starting with its weakest part, the local news. If we were able to rearrange our resources, we could get back in the game.

It would, of course, be a daunting task. We would have to change significantly the tone, pacing, story selection and reporting. We were, as well, confronted with a dramatic shift in the nature of the news business. Everywhere in North America, the production, distribution and financing of news was morphing and changing at a breakneck speed. The emergence of the Internet, blogging and social media was transforming the business. By 2006, the news everywhere was in a state of profound upheaval, nowhere more than in the area of local news.

Across the United States and Canada, the metropolitan daily newspapers had come under tremendous pressure. Their traditional revenue source of classified advertising had begun to vanish. Where people had previously looked to newspapers to lease apartments, buy cars or find jobs, they increasingly went to Craigslist, Monster.com or any number of real estate and automobile sites. Subscription revenue was also eroding. Why pay for a newspaper when one can visit an aggregator website and get all the news one wants for free? Programming one's preferences in Google News provides a cheaper, faster and often more compelling experience.

The local newspapers were facing a double whammy. Their journalism was increasingly picked up by aggregator sites such as Google News, which bore none of the costs associated with reporting the news but made money from other people's efforts. The net effect was to create a financial vise that was choking the life out of the papers.

Something similar was happening to local television news but for slightly different reasons. In Canada, local TV news is offered by Global, CTV and in a few markets, Citytv. These networks rely completely on advertising revenue to finance their operations. The specialty television business that has emerged over the last twenty years, funded by both cable fees and advertising, has drawn more and more viewers away from the big, traditional networks. The result has been an erosion of their financial positions.

As those networks struggled with their financial plight, one of the first places they looked to cut costs was their local news operations. It was widely believed that, with the exception of a few major markets—Toronto, Vancouver, Calgary and Ottawa—all of the local newscasts were losing money. If they could jettison those operations, it would make it easier to improve their financial prospects.

At dinner one evening with Leonard Asper, who was then CEO of Global, and Peter Viner, his head of operations, Robert Rabinovitch and I asked about the performance of their local shows. We sat in a restaurant in downtown Toronto. The mood was amiable.

"How are they doing?" Robert asked.

"Not well," Asper replied.

"We did a little study," I said, "to try and estimate which of your stations are making money and which losing."

"What did you conclude?" Asper asked.

"Well, we think that mostly you're losing money. Certainly Lethbridge, Kelowna, Regina, Saskatoon, Winnipeg, Montreal and Halifax seem to be underwater."

Asper looked gloomy. He sipped his wine. "Go on," he said.

"Our sense is that maybe four of your local shows are profitable."

"That sounds a little high," Viner replied.

All of these problems were dramatically confirmed in front of the CRTC in the 2008 and 2009 hearings on the financial situation of the private conventional networks. It was clear that they were in great difficulty. They argued aggressively that, like the specialty channels, they should receive cable fees; otherwise they would have to eliminate most of their local operations. In fact, they mounted a large advertising campaign called "Local News Matters" to advance their views with the public.

From our point of view in 2006, the financial weakness of the local newspapers and the local news shows looked like an opportunity. If we rebuilt our shows effectively and started to steal share from the privates, perhaps we could force them to start abandoning some of the local markets altogether. This, in turn, would make it easier for us to grow. At the same time, given CTV and Global's desire to get out of the unprofitable markets, the revitalization of CBC news would give them the cover they needed to do so. They could point out that the local audiences were not being significantly disadvantaged because the CBC had increased its coverage. It could be a win-win for both sides.

If local television news was increasingly unsustainable and likely to start disappearing over time from the private networks, it would make sense for the public broadcaster to do what the privates could not. This was then part of the answer to the question, why CBC news? It would *make a contribution to the public debate that was not only valuable but would not otherwise occur.*

Shortly after the dinner with Leonard Asper, I went to see Robert Rabinovitch to discuss what we should do about local news.

He was keen to see them axed and felt I was dithering. "When are you going to wind up the local newscasts?" he asked. "You've been here almost two years and you've made no progress."

"You know, I'm sure this will disappoint you, but I think we should expand the local newscasts."

"Huh?" Robert looked as though I had proposed something reckless. "Expand them?"

"Yes, first to an hour, and then, when we have figured everything out, expand them even more."

He stared at me. It was hard to say whether his look was one of pity or bewilderment.

"An hour?" he said. It was as though I had suggested we swim across the Atlantic, a journey so wearying and implausible that it could only result in hypothermia and death.

"Yes, and eventually an hour and a half. We should also ultimately add local news in the morning and on weekends."

Rabinovitch looked utterly puzzled. "Why," he asked, not unreasonably, "would you bother?"

We went through all the reasons: the imminent collapse of private local news on TV and the newspapers, Canadians' overwhelming preference for local news, the obligation to serve the public, etc. Robert was glum.

"But even if it's right, why would you believe that after twenty years of continuous failure, the local shows can be saved?"

This was an excellent question. We talked at length about what would be required. We talked about the changes in tone, style, story selection, journalism. We talked about the transformation in the newsrooms' culture that was necessary. We talked about respecting the interests and concerns of Canadians, about covering what mattered to them, about weather, fires, crime, pollution, schools and traffic. We talked about how these were the price of entry, the table stakes, if one ever hoped to get to the "deeper and more thoughtful." We talked about how there was almost nothing to lose; the shows could not get much worse.

As we talked about the size of the challenge, the president said, "Exactly. It's overwhelming. What makes you think it can be done?"

By that time, I had hired Magid, North America's most experienced news consulting organization. I had asked for an opinion on whether the local news shows could really be rebuilt and succeed. Their specialty is research. They research everything: public perceptions of news, new platforms, speed and pacing of stories, hair and makeup, sets, lighting, editorial policy. We reviewed their research in detail. We looked at the places where the local news had been effectively rebuilt and where it had not. We looked at what contributed to success and what did not. We concluded that there were indeed good examples of local news renewal, and that it could be done, but it would be hard.

"It will be difficult," I admitted, "very, very difficult. There is no guarantee we will succeed."

Robert looked troubled. He had campaigned for six years to cancel the local news. He had argued before the board that the shows had to go. Now he was being asked to reverse himself completely. He was being asked to agree that he had been wrong on a fundamental issue. We argued off and on for a number of weeks. He probed, questioned, objected, tested and finally said okay.

We went to the board in September 2006. They were also bewildered. One of them, a sensible and thoughtful lawyer with the wonderful name of Howard McNutt, looked balefully at me and said, "You know, Richard, when the horse is dead, it's generally a good idea to dismount."

The conversation went round and round and up and down. Finally the board said okay.

Okay? What had we agreed to? We had agreed to walk into the collapsing and decrepit house. We had agreed to enter Fort News. We had agreed to push past its moats and crenellated battlements, to try and upend its ancient culture and practices, overturn its myths and most cherished beliefs, make ourselves into targets for its barbs and attacks, and to sink my modest career at the CBC before it had really begun.

To move ahead, we extended the contract with Magid. Their expertise lay in combining their research with tremendous practical experience in newsrooms to help their clients become better. At the CBC, they were received with suspicion and hostility. News consultants? They are here to tell us how to do news? And Americans? What fresh hell was this?

The Magid contract was leaked to the press with predictable results. Writing in the *Globe and Mail*, John Doyle savaged the whole effort to improve the local news and strengthen its viewership:

> Right now, the Fort Dork bosses give the impression that they are intensely interested in better viewing numbers and in lighter fare... About the News division, the buzz word one hears from the skeptics inside Fort Dork is "infotainment"...
>
> Apparently CBC has hired the notorious American media consultancy firm Frank N. Magid Associates to shake up its local news coverage... The Magid format [emphasizes] "Ken and Barbie" news anchors [and] a great deal of cheery babble.

The attacks had begun. Fort News was firing back.

To compound the problem, I recruited Derwyn Smith, the ex-news director of CTV's local news in Toronto. For years, Smith had been clobbering the CBC's local Toronto news. He had also rebuilt the local CTV news in London and run CTV's Newsnet (their all-day news network). Smith was one of the most knowledgeable and competitive executives in the local news business in Canada. CTV had let him go recently in one of its obscure internal bloodlettings. I asked him to have lunch.

"Would you like to help me kick CTV's ass?" I inquired.

Smith smiled at me. "That would be very pleasant," he allowed. "What do you want me to do?"

"I would like you to consult to us on rebuilding our local news offerings. You know local news better than anyone."

Derwyn smiled more broadly. He accepted with enthusiasm. He would turn out to be even more competitive than I imagined, a man possessed by the desire to win. He was exactly the transfusion the place needed.

His arrival was greeted with dismay. The private sector teaching the CBC to do news? Was there no end to the nonsense and humiliation?

And so we set off in September 2006 to rebuild CBC's local television news. In every newsroom in the country, we turned the scanners back on, we switched the monitors to the local competitors, we developed ideal newscasts with fixed story counts, we dictated length and pacing of items, we retrained the journalists, we stole hosts from the private broadcasters, we made pilots and tested them with audiences, we coached people on hair and makeup, we rebuilt the sets. We worked on every aspect of the news.

Then in February 2007, just six months after getting the green light from the board, we announced the cancellation of *Canada Now* and the relaunch of the local supper hours. All across the country, from Halifax to Vancouver, *Canada Now* went dark and a full hour of local news came on. We watched in breathless anticipation for the public reaction, for the overnights the next day, the inevitable jump in the ratings. The Canadian public yawned. Nothing happened. It was clear that the relaunch of local news was going to be tough.

THE RELAUNCH OF the local newscasts in 2007 was only the beginning. They were the first flanking movements, designed to test Fort News' defences before making an assault on its most heavily fortified positions. We had moved gingerly to date, careful to avoid inciting too much of the denizens' wrath. The next steps had to move into the heart of the operation: Newsworld, *The National*, the national radio newscasts and the website.

We knew that the changes would have to be massive. We knew that new management was required. The old lords did not see the need for change, nor did they appear to have the skills to accomplish it. It would be unfair to ask them to do what they did not believe in, let alone repudiate their work of the last thirty years. It would have been unreasonable to suppose that they were willing or able to rebuild dramatically all the shows, to gore the oxen of their oldest friends and colleagues.

The first to go probably had to be Tony Burman, the clever, irascible editor-in-chief. He was exceptionally knowledgeable not just about the CBC news but about news in general. He seemed to read a dozen newspapers a day, along with a host of magazines and journals. He also seemed to watch everything, famously bombarding the unwary with scuds of corrections, denouncing inadequacies in the facts or the style of the news. There would be a cry of "incoming" and the missile would arrive, fearsome and exploding, with Burman's signature attached.

I had made a huge effort to cultivate Burman. I wanted him as an ally, and if possible as a friend. We met on a number of occasions for dinner, trying to understand what the other wanted and whether there was any way to create a mutual accommodation. I left all of our conversations impressed with his knowledge, intelligence and commitment, hoping that the following days and weeks would herald a new collegiality and a new spirit of collaboration. Sadly, it was never to be. We differed on too many points.

Burman had tolerated the tinkering with the local news but he had been unhelpful on most other issues. When the lockout came, he made it clear that he did not support it. When there were financial pressures or difficulties, his only response was to resist making any contributions from the news department. When it came time for the Fort to assist the other departments, he angrily denounced the idea. Inevitably there were clashes, with each of us becoming increasingly annoyed with the other. He was a notorious hot head. So was I.

The matter came to a bitter climax in early 2007. We had been working on the relaunch of the local supper hours and had extensive conversations about what to do. Burman had gone to a conference in Turkey. One day, I told him on the phone that we would be moving forward with the next steps of the relaunch. He said I had no right to do anything in his absence.

"Tony," I explained, "we have already agreed to these things."

"You can't move behind my back," he replied.

"We are not. We agreed and now we simply have to move ahead."

"Oh yeah? Well, fuck you."

And he hung up the phone. Perhaps he was tired, since the time was much later in Turkey. I had no idea, but he had crossed a line of simple civility.

The trick was how to get him out. I was afraid that if we simply fired him, he would become a martyr to Fort News' independence. That would help nobody—not me, not the news department. It would freeze things even more, making change an even greater nightmare. Besides, I had no desire to humiliate him. He had served the CBC with distinction and conviction during his whole career. When he left, he needed to depart with honour and dignity. This, of course, could only happen if he retired.

And then, remarkably, he did retire. Burman announced that he was going to leave in June 2007. The CBC issued a laudatory press release, congratulating him on his long and successful career. Farewell parties were organized throughout the news department. Somehow I never made it onto the guest lists.

Over the next few months, we ran an intensive search for the new head of news. We had many spectacular and impressive candidates, the most spectacular and impressive of whom was John Cruickshank, then chief operating officer of the *Chicago Sun-Times* group. A Canadian with a distinguished career as a journalist and editor, he was also a successful manager and businessman. He had become a little homesick, and also tired of the endless grind of working for Conrad Black's collapsing media empire. He wanted a change and to come home to Toronto.

Cruickshank is white-haired, clever and informal. He knew as much about the news as Tony Burman, but had seemingly wider interests. He read novels and philosophy, making a particular study of the recondite work of the mid-twentieth century German philosopher Martin Heidegger. He had, much to my astonishment, actually read *Being and Time*, a book of almost impenetrable difficulty that I had pretended to read when I was in graduate school. Indeed, he informed me that he was ploughing through it for a second time, since it would only yield its secrets over many readings. This alone seemed to recommend him.

We discussed at length the challenges in reforming the news department. We discussed the culture, the belief systems, the work habits, the myths, the editorial stance, the attitude toward competitors, in considerable detail. I painted a dark picture. It was important that he come to the task under no illusions. It was important that he understand the magnitude of the challenge involved. Like me, he would also face the problem of being an outsider. Fort News would inevitably ask the question, why not one of us? Are we not worthy? The danger was that tissue rejection would compound an already formidable task.

After a number of these depressing conversations, I was convinced he was the right person for the job. Although he had no experience in radio or television, he was a skilled manager with excellent editorial judgment, a sunny personality and lots of energy. He seemed the right choice. And if worst came to worst, we could fall back on the consolations of Heidegger.

Cruickshank took over as the head of news in October 2007. His appointment was met with near universal enthusiasm. The board was happy, the president was happy, I was happy, and even— remarkably—Fort News seemed to be happy. He began by touring the news department and the regions, meeting all of the journalists and producers, watching the shows, checking the lineups, looking at the budgets. He went at it with zeal and enthusiasm.

A few weeks after his arrival, we sat down to take stock of his impressions.

"Well," he began, laughing, "it's just as bad as you said." And he laughed again. "They have absolutely no competitive impulses."

He went on in this vein for a while, amazed and puzzled about how journalists could have become so passive at the CBC. In a wonderful turn of phrase, he described them as "news takers, not news breakers." He wondered whether the DNA of Fort News was fatally compromised.

Reporting on his review of the tone and character of the newscasts, he laughed sadly and said that, if anything, I had understated the problem. "They feel," he opined, "like they were designed for sixty-year-old male depressives, while the country is optimistic and outward-looking."

He walked through all the usual complaints: the focus on institutional news, the formality, the gloomy quality of the reporting, the Voice of God, the ponderousness of the items, the "newscast of record" pretensions, the lot. He envisaged a root-and-branch reform along the lines I believed essential.

Shortly after taking office, Cruickshank launched another massive review of the news. He surveyed Canadians in detail about their perception of CBC news and how it compared to that of Global and CTV. He asked them what they wanted from a newscast, how it compared with what they were getting, how they wanted it presented, paced and focused. He asked what mattered to Canadians, which topics were most relevant and important, what they wanted to know more about and what they wanted to know less about. He poked and prodded the Canadian public relentlessly to try and understand what would work and what would not.

The results did not differ much from the News Study of six years earlier. They showed—much to the horror and bafflement of Fort News—that Canadians found little to choose among Global, CTV and CBC. In fact, to the extent that Canadians found CBC news "distinct," it was distinct in being duller and slower than the others. But the biggest conclusion was that Canadians did not care for any of the newscasts very much. They found all of them narrow, phony and old fashioned.

This was both bad news and good news. Since Canadians were dissatisfied with all the newscasts, CBC was not in a particularly dark place. In fact, if CBC could reform itself in a way that Canadians wanted, there might be a significant opportunity to gain a competitive advantage over the others. It was, as well, an opportunity more available to CBC than anyone else. It is always difficult to make sweeping changes when you are number one in a market, as CTV was, or even number two. If, however, you are number three, then you have nothing to lose. It is hard to fall far from last place.

It was also good news because the studies showed what a real public broadcaster should be like, and how the CBC could make a valuable and unique contribution to the public debate. The studies showed that the public was clamouring for much better news coverage. Creating a CBC News for the twenty-first century would break new—and potentially "distinctive"—ground.

The studies discovered two broad demands. Canadians wanted breaking news, when it broke. They wanted 24/7 on all platforms. They wanted to know as soon as the CBC did, and they wanted a CBC that knew things before anyone else. They wanted the news lightning fast. They wanted to know that when they turned on their cell phones, radios, TVs or computers and went to CBC, they would get the real goods right away, ahead of everyone else.

The other demand was for context and meaning. They wanted to know what they needed to know to make sense of the news. They wanted CBC to provide the necessary background, history and explanations for them to figure out how to think about the news. They wanted the tools to allow them to reflect intelligently and make up their minds.

These twin demands also dictated what they did not want. They did not want a CBC that held back breaking news or big stories for *The National* at 10:00 PM, as had been the practice. They did not want *The National*, in other words, to be a newscast of record. They wanted a *National* that assumed that they already knew "the news" by 10:00 PM. They wanted a *National* that would provide background and context. They wanted to know not what had happened but what was going to happen. They wanted depth and investigative materials. They wanted interpretive pieces.

These twin requirements were summarized in the tag line we created for the renewal of CBC news. It should allow Canadians to be Well Informed Now.

The response to the studies and the new directions we decided on was mixed. On one notable occasion, John Cruickshank and I briefed the newsroom on where we intended to go. Perhaps a hundred people crowded around. At one point, Mark Bulgutch, who had produced all the major live events for many years, including the elections, took issue with the idea that the news was ponderous and paced too slowly.

"Brevity," he remarked, "is a recipe for superficiality. Picking up the pace means dumbing down the content."

The place froze. Bulgutch was the voice of Old News. Across the sea of faces, the crowd visibly split in two: those who hated the idea of change and those who craved it.

"It's irresponsible," he continued, "to wreck the country's greatest news organization. It is better to be slow and right than quick and wrong."

"How about fast and right?" I suggested.

The conversation degenerated from there. The vandal who wanted a seat in the newsroom, the upstart who wanted to express a view on editorial policy, was now moving to change all the traditions and practices of Fort News. Battle lines were clear.

Bulgutch and the Old Guard stared angrily at me. The younger members of the newsroom looked alarmed. They wanted change, but these were dangerous waters. The last time change had been promised, when Tony Burman was there, nothing had happened. In fact, those who had embraced the call for new ideas and radical departures had lost. The Old Guard had won, and in winning took its revenge on the others. It could happen again.

The place was tense. When Cruickshank and I left the newsroom, we could hear muted grumbling and muttering. Whispered "right-on"s passed Bulgutch's way. I felt, once again, the terrible strain and anxiety of trying to effect change at the CBC.

IT WAS ALSO essential that the CBC's overall news resources be integrated into one coherent News content offer that ran across all media: radio, TV and online. We wanted, in effect, no longer to have CBC radio news and CBC television news, but simply CBC News.

News was to be the first major area that would transit into a content company model.

To do this, there had to be a common editorial policy, common story priorities, common assignment of journalists and cameramen, so that the CBC could have one efficient, intellectually coherent news service. The big stories should be the big stories across all platforms, with each platform doing the part it did best. If war broke out, it broke on radio, TV and online, ideally with the same journalists reporting to all three. The war would be made sense of across all the context shows: *The National*, *The Current* and *As It Happens*. The reader/listener/viewer deserved an integrated, sustained news experience that ensured they were Well Informed Now, through whatever platform was most convenient for them.

This was a revolutionary idea. It would require the destruction of all the historic silos within the CBC. Years of tradition would be unwound. Inevitably this would cause consternation and misery.

The centrepiece of the revolution was the creation of the Hub. The Hub would integrate the management and assignment of all newsgathering resources—journalists, cameras, trucks, everything. It would determine who went to cover what stories. The journalists would then file back to the Hub, which would make the stories, video, sound and accompanying notes and research available to everyone within the news department. Properly developed and managed, the Hub would become in effect an internal wire service, keeping everyone up to date on everything the CBC knew and reported.

In the past, when major stories broke, each newsroom and news program within the CBC would begin calling for information and interviews. This meant that newsmakers who were already besieged by media would be additionally burdened by calls from CBC radio, TV, local, national, Newsworld and then various individual programs. Each department would also send its own reporter and cameraman to the event. Competitors, politicians and viewers could not believe that a broadcaster with financial problems could send half a dozen people or more to an event ably handled by one or two people from each private station. The Hub addressed this waste of resources.

The Hub needed, in principle, to manage all of the newsgathering resources. Individual shows would no longer have dedicated reporters. They would, of course, have dedicated producers, hosts, floor directors and writers, but they would rely entirely on the Hub for the stories themselves. This freaked everyone out. There was considerable hand-wringing. *The National* in particular was alarmed. It would no longer have complete control over all its news resources. If the Hub failed, *The National* would fail. In effect, the fate of *The National* would be out of the hands of its producers and Peter Mansbridge.

On the other hand, if the Hub succeeded, it would dramatically improve the efficiency and breadth of CBC's newsgathering. If it succeeded, the CBC could leverage the totality of its resources, producing more news on more subjects. It would also permit the shows to pursue a common editorial policy because assignments would be integrated. This, in turn, would allow the shows to hand stories off to each other, advance them consistently and extend them to other platforms, all in an orderly and thoughtful way.

So that was the plan. The entire news department would be reorganized to create the Hub. The shows and platforms would be separated from the newsgathering resources. They in turn would then be redeveloped in terms of the two great pillars of the strategy: Well Informed and Now. Every show would fall into one or another of the camps. *The National*, *The Current*, the new prime-time shows on the all-news network (*Politics*, *The Lang and O'Leary Exchange*, *Connect*) would all be Well Informed. The shows that ran all day on Newsworld, CBC *News Now*, along with the website and the half-hourly newscasts on radio would be the Now. All of the programs would have to be remade to fit the new formats and strategy.

Change of this scale had never been attempted at Fort News before. Everything would be changed, and it would be changed all at once. New shows, new processes, new work assignments, new computer systems, new sets, new graphics, new job descriptions, new roles and responsibilities, new everything. It would involve reassigning a thousand people, almost two-thirds of the total workforce. It was a massive undertaking.

Then, just as we were getting ready to start making the changes, John Cruickshank announced he was leaving to become publisher of the *Toronto Star*. He spoke enthusiastically about returning to his roots in print and taking up the challenges of running Canada's biggest newspaper. He spoke with his usual warmth and optimism. Who could blame him? I thought. CBC news must have felt glowering and immovable. Why should he force the elephant to learn to dance when he could go to the *Toronto Star* and manage a team of professional dancers?

Four months later, his deputy, Jennifer McGuire, was appointed the new head of Fort News. McGuire is an intensely driven, clever and charming person. She is a workaholic who had risen through the ranks of CBC, starting as a radio producer, then moving into television news production. She had produced *Foreign Assignment* with the sainted Joe Schlesinger, *Newsworld Today* and *Sunday Morning Live*. Then she had returned to radio, eventually becoming head of the senior service before returning to the thankless task of rebuilding the news department.

With her customary brio and deep knowledge of the news department, she accelerated the pace of change, pushing everyone even harder. She built a locked war room, where she sat with her senior lieutenants for days on end, planning in detail every move and new position. To get in, one had to knock the secret knock, utter the password and flash the decoder ring. Inside, the walls were covered with diagrams of the new organizational pieces, with a snowfall of coloured Post-it notes showing the proposed names for the new jobs. There was the Hub, with its various structures and all the associated positions. There was *The National*, *The Current*, *The World at Six*, *Connect*, CBC *News Now*, *Politics*, the Ottawa bureau, the Washington bureau, the Beijing bureau, with fluttering Post-it notes crowding around each one. Jennifer McGuire sat there day in, day out, pulling one little Post-it note off one place, pushing it to another and causing a cascade of other changes.

The National, for example, had been reconceived as the centrepiece of the Well Informed part of the strategy. Peter Mansbridge would still host it, but we wanted to surround him with a cast of recurring characters, each of whom would have a specialized area of expertise: the economic whiz, the hardboiled foreign expert, the charming arts reporter, the slightly cynical political specialist, the perky consumer champion. Each of the roles had to be filled by a person of substance and style. Should we put Wendy Mesley into one of these jobs or have her host her own show on the news network? Should Diana Swain become a character here and leave as host of the Toronto local news? What about Ian Hanomansing? Heather Hiscox? Rex Murphy? Evan Solomon? On and on. If we named Diana Swain, who would replace her in Toronto? If we shuffled Ian Hanomansing, who took over Vancouver? Every move implied another.

The War Room had the feel of a nightmare game of three-dimensional chess. Remaking all the shows was complicated. Remaking the newsgathering process and creating the Hub was complicated. But reassigning a thousand twitchy, ambitious, jealous, talented, clever egos was another order of complexity altogether. Each and every one would have to be consulted. Their personal wishes and ambitions would have to be considered; they might then have to be convinced, cajoled or coerced into accepting their new assignments. And all this would have to be done with the union looking over management's shoulder, making sure that everyone was fairly dealt with and that we respected the contract. An unenviable task, not for the faint of heart.

As all of this was going on, the catastrophic economic collapse of 2008-09 hit, causing huge problems for English services. The pressures of austerity exacerbated the traditional tensions within the organization. Fort News was already awash in rumours and uncertainty about the forthcoming reorganization. Cuts on top of everything else would raise the simmer of anxiety to a rolling boil of fear and despair. As word of the financial problems facing us spread throughout English services and it became clear that we would have to make significant cuts, I organized an all-staff meeting to explain what we were planning to do.

The Glenn Gould Studio—a medium-sized theatre, really—was packed with employees from all over the Corporation. The rest were listening and watching on closed circuit monitors throughout the rest of the Toronto Broadcast Centre and in the regional offices across the country. I explained the implications of the economic crisis for the CBC's revenues, the size of the problem confronting us and the difficulty of the decisions we would have to make. I did not sugarcoat the problem. It seemed only fair to be open and candid. At the end of the presentation, I opened the floor to questions.

Among the first to rise were two members of *The Fifth Estate*, co-host Gillian Findlay and the brilliant producer Neil Docherty. "You should not cut *The Fifth Estate* or *The National*," they said. "They are the very heart of the CBC's mandate." There it was, the shameless and brazen entitlement of the news department. Throw everyone else under the bus, but do not touch the peerless and essential news department. I became angry and accused them of looking down on their colleagues.

"That is very unfair," I said. "Are you suggesting that you're more important than the sports department or the kids department or the music department?"

"We didn't say that."

"Oh no? What then? We have to make cuts, and you say don't cut us. Doesn't that mean you are more important than your colleagues?"

"No. No. We never said that."

The situation grew heated. It was getting out of hand. To try and defuse the tension a little, I jokingly said, "Maybe we should take this outside and settle it like men. Could someone hold my jacket?" The meeting deteriorated further.

Outside the Glenn Gould Studio, the argument continued. "We didn't say the others were second rate," Findlay and Docherty said.

"Yes, you did, actually," I replied. "It's shameless to say you're better and more deserving than the rest." It looked as if fisticuffs might ensue. Cooler heads took me by the arm and led me away. Everything was getting harder as the financial pressure mounted.

Over the next few days, employees from across the Corporation sent me emails or buttonholed me on the elevator to say thanks. Thanks for standing up for them. Thanks for not toadying to the vanity of Fort News. Thanks for recognizing their worth. All of which was nice, but no help with reorganizing the news, the cuts or the gigantic reassignment of personnel.

Jennifer McGuire redoubled her efforts. She had to now relaunch CBC news while incorporating significant cuts to her budget. She cut back some of her plans, reduced staff on various shows and postponed expenditures. She did this while performing all of her other daily tasks. The thousand employees were reassigned, with only two union grievances. All the sets were rebuilt, the graphics changed, the musical signatures rewritten, the shows reformatted, the Hub shaken down, the egos massaged, the tears wiped, the disappointed consoled. Jennifer did all this, and all on time.

On October 26, 2009, everything changed. When Canadians tuned in that morning to Newsworld, it had been rechristened the News Network. The shows were all new, the set a sparkling white with enormous smart screens, a reconstructed graphic wrap, new anchors, a breaking news desk in the middle of the newsroom itself, and a much wider array of subjects. There were still political developments and international news, but there were also more movie reviews and human interest stories. The languor of the past was replaced with zippier pacing and shorter story lengths. It felt quicker, more of the moment.

The News Network roared through the day, with *CBC News Now* breaking stories continuously from the moment it came on air at 6:00 in the morning through to 5:00 in the afternoon. Then up popped *The Lang and O'Leary Exchange*, freshly stolen from the Business News Network; the new version of *Politics* in Ottawa, with Evan Solomon taking over a longer show from the venerable Don Newman; and on to 8:00 PM, where Mark Kelley was to *Connect* with folks making news, involved in news, touched by news. Zip. Zip. The smart screens swirled with background information. The wraps popped important facts.

At 9:00 PM, the revamped *National* appeared, with its new set and—God help us—Peter Mansbridge standing up. The Big Desk was gone. Mansbridge was standing and reading the news. The cast of characters started to appear in their new roles. The smart screens on

The National's new set were illuminated. They swirled graphics and information, charts and illustrative video.

And so it went. Boom. Overnight everything changed. The radio newscasts as well. Boom.

The reactions of the chattering classes, the Constituency and the professional reviewers were predictable. Oh dear, oh dear. They have Americanized Newsworld. It is being turned into CNN. Oh dear. Oh dear. And Peter Mansbridge is standing. Standing! Oh dear. Somebody get the man a chair. And those smart screens! There is so much going on. It is all so quick and busy and different. Oh dear. Oh dear!

The *Globe and Mail* whined that it all looked derivative of CNN. "CBC News Network, or CBC NN. That name... Doesn't it strongly resemble that of a certain American cable news network? And then there's the network's new look: busier, brighter sets festooned with huge TV monitors; a greater emphasis on star reporters; multiple, ever-changing camera angles; and news anchors talking directly to those monitors as they chat up reporters delivering their missives from the field." Worse yet, "reporters are filing shorter, punchier news hits throughout the day... [with] a greater focus on younger prime-time anchors."

But the most troubling aspect was Peter Mansbridge standing up. The *Toronto Star* mocked the transition: "Gone is the pomp and circumstance of old, the age-soaked wisdom the national broadcaster oozed at 10:00 PM... Its now unseated anchor plays a cross between a wandering, gracious maître d' and... an avuncular publican." It was all a little too modern and too busy and too quick: "What *The National* has gained in speed and visual wallop seems to be at the expense of the appearance of reality. It was all a little, sad to say, self-satisfied and contrived."

In fact, the idea to have Peter Mansbridge stand up was his own. He had pioneered it during the previous election's coverage and liked the freedom and mobility it gave him. The Canadian public, too, liked it. We tested the new shows immediately. Viewers responded extremely well. They liked everything: the new look, the new hosts, the accelerated pacing. In fact, unlike the Constituency and the chatterati, they saw faster as better. Where the elderly members of the Constituency seemed overwhelmed by the changes, the public at large asked for more, faster still.

And best of all, CTV and Global looked unnerved by the changes. It seemed unimaginable, but the Corporation had actually reformed its news. My colleagues at the private networks told me that they never believed it capable of change. Now, however, they were beginning to worry. What if CBC became a real threat to their dominance? Jennifer McGuire had done a remarkable job.

Over the next couple of years, the changes proved their value. The old Newsworld had been regularly beaten by CNN, often seeing CNN take twice as many viewers in Canada as Newsworld, but the revamped News Network regularly clobbered them. As the months went on, the numbers continued to climb. Eventually the News Network's audiences grew by 40 percent, a remarkable feat in an intensely crowded environment.

The National, as well, began to pick up numbers. From an average of just over 600,000 viewers at 10:00 PM during the 2009-10 season, it moved to over 640,000 in 2010-11. While the improvements were not enormous, the trajectory was correct. *The National* was growing. The key question was how far it could go being stuck at 10:00 PM, the most competitive time slot in television.

The local shows also climbed off their death beds and started to become serious challengers. When the old *Canada Now* was axed, the local shows were at a low of 192,000 viewers nationally at 6:00 PM; by the end of the 2010-11 season, they had grown to almost 500,000. While still in third place, their trajectory was completely different. They were now gaining viewers rather than losing them. Their total share moved from 3 percent to 7.2 percent of the available audience. It was the first time they had grown their share in more than thirty years.

THROUGHOUT THE OVERHAUL of the news, there was an urgent requirement to address the issue of bias. It was not a new issue. Over thirty years earlier, the Trudeau government had accused the CBC of a separatist bias in the French network. The prime minister had said in the House of Commons that Radio-Canada was "propagandizing" separation. "The overwhelming majority of employees in Radio-Canada are of separatist leaning."

Jean Chrétien, then justice minister, and a host of other members of the Liberal cabinet expressed similar concerns. André Ouellet, then urban affairs minister, claimed, "Every night there is bias and every night it's in favour of the separatists." He demanded that Al Johnson, then president of the CBC, "fire the bloody guys who are working separatists."

Eventually the CRTC was asked to look into the matter. They issued a report that satisfied nobody. It said, in effect, that there was no evidence of separatist bias, and if anything there was a problem in the English network, which failed to cover the country in its entirety, particularly Quebec.

I was a junior analyst at the Department of Communications when the CRTC report was issued. My job was to read it quickly and prepare a summary for the minister, Jeanne Sauvé. In drafting my note, I followed the CRTC line, explaining that while there may have been individual examples of apparent sympathy for the Parti Québécois, there was no evidence of active bias as a policy of the Radio-Canada news department. There was, I recall writing, no *mens rea*. As the note worked its way up the line, the deputy minister, Max Yalden, signed it, but wrote in the margin to Mme. Sauvé that he found my assessment "tendentious." When we appeared to brief the minister, it was clear that she agreed with the deputy's view and found my reasoning, along with the CRTC's, tendentious.

The concern about separatists at Radio-Canada never went away. The controversy of the late 1970s calmed down, but senior Liberals continued to believe that Radio-Canada was subversive. The French all-news network, RDI (Réseau de l'information), was widely mocked as the "Réseau de l'indépendance." When I worked in the federal government in the 1980s, both Liberal and Conservative cabinet ministers would express their frustration to me at what they believed was continuing bias in favour of the Parti Québécois and the Bloc Québécois. They would express astonishment that nobody seemed to be able to do anything about it.

Even Stephen Harper's government is troubled by this question of bias. In conversations with members of the Prime Minister's Office, I would be told how Radio-Canada remained a hotbed of separatists and fellow travellers. Like their predecessors over the last thirty years, they were concerned that the CBC's French arm was undermining the federalist cause.

At the same time, they expressed even stronger reservations about the English news service. They were convinced that Fort News had a left-liberal bias and was actively hostile to the Conservatives and what they stood for. The more zealous believed that the place reflected the values of downtown Toronto rather than the country as a whole. They felt it was anti-family, anti-religion, anti-American, anti-military, anti-capitalist, anti-Israel and anti-anything worthwhile in the fabric of Canadian society. They saw it as an elitist, vaguely socialist, pro-Palestinian, tree-hugging, bicycle-obsessed collection of liberals. When pushed, they admitted that this was clearly not true of the whole place. Television, they allowed, was better than radio, but they still felt it was not balanced in its coverage or its attitude.

They were not alone in their views. The *National Post* had historically regarded the CBC as a hotbed of unreliable lefties. They had even started a weekly column called CBC Watch. In it, they would list and mock what they took to be egregious examples of CBC news' bias.

Earlier this month, the *National Post* editorial board invited readers to email us their complaints about bias at the CBC. In coming months, we'll highlight some on these pages. Taxpayers subsidize our national broadcaster to the tune of $850 million every year. Too often, that money goes to subsidize anti-U.S., anti-Israeli propaganda.

Often the slant creeps in subtly—a refusal to call Palestinian terrorists "terrorists," for instance. (In CBC speak, they are all "militants.") But sometimes, the bias hits you squarely in the face. On CBC radio's *The Current*, there have been a few appalling instances of late . . .

Similarly the *Sun* chain regarded the CBC as hopelessly compromised. They spent a great deal of time not only denouncing the Corporation's deviations from orthodoxy but also trying to show it was wasteful and ill-run. They took to calling it a "state" broadcaster rather than a public broadcaster, as though it were *Pravda*. The drumbeat of criticism went on and on.

In 2006, Stephen Harper and his Conservatives won their first minority government, defeating Paul Martin and the Liberals. The CBC's practice at the time was to monitor its election coverage in two ways. First, it had ERIN Research count the number of stories about the different parties on CBC news and on the competitors. They then compared the results to see whether the Corporation had given more air time to one party over the others. They looked at the total amount of time allocated on the CBC and the time given by CTV and Global. The results were almost identical.

The second practice was to establish a panel to review the coverage and comment on its overall fairness. The panel was made up of people of widely varying political views; it was designed to try and include the full range of opinion in the country. The panel members were asked to watch television, listen to the radio and read the website. They were then asked their opinion. Although not as rigorous as the ERIN studies, the panel's opinion was more interesting.

The panel agreed that the election coverage had been pretty fair, with the exception of some of the views expressed on social values. "Social values" meant opinions on issues like abortion, gay marriage and the place of the church in society. In these areas, the panel said, the coverage was worse than biased. Canadians—particularly Albertans—who were opposed to abortion or gay marriage were treated by the CBC as uninformed hicks. They were lampooned as bible-thumping, born-again Rapture-o-philes who, like their equally unsophisticated cousins in the Republican party of the United States, believed extraordinary things. Who knew what all? Creationism? Flying saucers? Serious, intelligent people could not possibly hold such views. The tone was patronizing and dismissive.

After the new government settled in, Rick Mercer phoned me one day. He called in confidence. Mercer has no discernible political views; he mocks everyone equally.

"I have been talking to the PMO," he said. "They are very upset."

"About what?"

"Well, it sounds small, but it shows how seriously they take things."

"Yes?"

"If you go on the website, you will find a part of it with potted bios of all the prime ministers. Check out the one of Mulroney and his picture."

"Where is it?"

"In a section designed to help teachers explain Canadian history."

"Whoa. That's obscure."

"I know, but I think they're right."

After much digging around, I finally found the part of the site he was talking about. Everyone was there, from Sir John A. Macdonald to Paul Martin. They all looked suitably prime ministerial, with photographs capturing their thoughtful dignity. All, that is, except the photograph of Brian Mulroney. He looked wild and demented.

I asked Tony Burman to come and look at it with me. He professed to see nothing wrong with it. I asked him to look again. Prime Minister Mulroney leered out of the website, dishevelled and peculiar. "Really?" I asked.

"No. He looks fine to me."

"Come on, Tony. All the others look noble and serene. He looks like he just emerged from the madhouse."

"Sorry. I can't see it. He looks fine to me."

When I continued to insist, Burman objected to my meddling in the news department and questioning his editorial judgment. Pushing the matter any further was going to create an enormous row.

There were similar arguments over the word *terrorism*.

"Why," I asked, "do we characterize terrorists as 'militants'?"

The news boffins would sigh with exhaustion at having to go through the arguments again. "We don't want to take sides, Richard. One person's terrorist is another person's freedom fighter. We are a news organization. We don't take sides."

"But what if the UN and the Canadian government and everyone else characterize certain groups as terrorist organizations?"

"Well, we report that they are so characterized but do not do so ourselves."

"Okay. If the courts convict someone of murder, we report the fact of the judgment but do not characterize him as a criminal or a murderer?"

"You're being silly. The charge of terrorism is a political charge and we don't take sides."

"Why don't we call terrorist acts 'terrorist acts,' at least?"

"How can we know they're terrorist acts?"

"Because they conform with the international definitions of terrorism and involve the targeting of civilian populations."

"How can we know they were targeting civilians?"

"Because the job of journalists is to find out the truth. Either they were or they were not targeting civilians. In most cases it's pretty clear."

"As I said, we don't take sides."

All this was pretty frustrating. It went to the heart of the conversation about our coverage of the Middle East. It seemed wrong-headed to espouse a journalistic policy that created moral equivalencies where there were none. That was a disservice to our viewers and listeners. It fed, as well, the general perception that the CBC was systematically anti-Israeli and anti-American.

Beyond questions of active or passive bias, the range of subjects the news department covered seemed too narrow. There were lots of stories about politics, for example, but almost nothing about business. Despite the fact that the overwhelming majority of Canadians make their livings in private business, there was almost no coverage of the economy or the fortunes of major companies or the workings of modern capitalism. To the extent there was coverage, it was most often to expose corporate malfeasance (which is okay) or consumer rip-offs (which is also okay). The net effect, however, was to make it appear that governments were generally the source of solutions and businesses the source of problems. As a friend of mine noted, "The standard CBC reporter's question is always what is the government (usually the federal government) going to do about *x*, *y* or *z*?"

Sensible people can have differing views on what is fair or reasonable about the CBC's news coverage. My views on the treatment of Brian Mulroney's picture, the use of the word *terrorist* or the Corporation's anti-business bias could be disputed. Others might feel, with justification, that there was nothing wrong with the way in which the CBC handled the issues. Journalism, after all, is not an exact science. It is, in fact, not a science at all, but an exploration of the most complex and contentious aspects of human life.

This does not mean that there cannot be coherent discussion of the questions of fairness and bias. To the contrary, given the intellectual difficulty of these questions, and the nature of the passions they awake, it is absolutely essential that we find ways to talk about them. We must create a framework for dialogue, or we simply end up with people shouting at each other, with no standards by which to resolve the issues. The creation of such a framework is particularly important at the CBC, because unlike the other great news organizations, it is partly financed by the general public. It can and should be held to a higher standard of transparency and openness on how it deals with these questions.

The importance to the CBC of being—and being seen as—fair and balanced is a political necessity and potentially a major competitive advantage. It is a political necessity since the CBC's funding depends on the whims of the government in power. If the government feels that the Corporation is actively hostile to its agenda, it is unlikely to increase its financing. Indeed, it is much more likely to reduce its resources. Unfortunately, all the governments of the postwar period, whether Liberal or Conservative, seem to have felt that the CBC was unfair.

Some would argue that since the CBC has been disliked by both parties almost equally, it must be doing something right. Others would say it's just in the nature of the relationship. No government will ever like the Corporation's news coverage, nor should it. The job of the CBC is to be disliked by the government of the day. It demonstrates that the CBC is doing what it ought to do and is speaking truth to power. Perhaps. But these arguments rather miss the point.

No sensible person, whether in government or not, suggests that the CBC should bend its knee and compromise the integrity of its news coverage to get more money. I have never heard a single cabinet minister of any stripe argue that the CBC news should cover the government favourably. Nobody wants to turn the Corporation into *Pravda*. Nobody wants a state broadcaster.

So where to begin? The CBC already had some mechanisms in place. There is a handbook of journalistic standards, which is fine as far as it goes, and it goes pretty far. It defines how individual stories need to be sourced and balanced, how to deal with anonymous tips, what to do about point-of-view pieces, what is appropriate and inappropriate behaviour in chasing stories, how journalists should conduct themselves. It is an excellent handbook.

There are also ombudsmen, one French and one English. If a person or an organization feels they have been unfairly treated by CBC news, they can appeal to the ombudsman, who will look into the matter and make a finding. The ombudsmen are completely independent from the news departments. They are hired by and report to the president.

While both of these arrangements are useful and important, they are also notable for what they do not do. They do not systematically review CBC's news coverage to see whether it is meeting its own standards and ensuring an appropriate breadth of coverage of the most important topics. Apart from the machinery put in place to monitor election reporting, there is no regular, statistically reliable review of the news. There is nothing to show the staff or the outside world whether the CBC is producing a news offer that is genuinely fair and balanced in all its dimensions.

So central is the issue of bias to the CBC that it seemed like a good idea to initiate a new study that would go well beyond the elections work done with ERIN, a study that would look at the totality of our news coverage. Properly done, we could find out whether the complaints of our critics had merit. If they did, we could then put in place measures to deal with them. If not, we would have the tools to defend ourselves. We could show everyone that we had mounted the largest independent study ever undertaken and it had concluded that CBC news was fair. Either way, it would help the organization.

When the idea of the study was first broached, there was much moaning from Fort News that the idea was insulting. It called into question the journalists' professionalism and the wisdom of the editorial policies. Eventually, after the general unhappiness died down, it was agreed the study would go forward. It would be characterized, however, as a review of the "diversity" of CBC news, rather than a look at "bias." We would see whether the news covered the full diversity of topics and points of view. The undertaking would be communicated to the denizens of the Fort not as an accusatory initiative but as a tool to help them do a better job.

To mount a major study of the news would, of course, require a parallel effort on the French side. It would be strange to have only the English news examined. Inevitably this led to delays. The French news department was even less enthusiastic than its English counterpart. It snarled and grumbled, trotting out all the same reasons why this was a bad idea, insulting to the journalists, intrusive and generally unacceptable. Eventually, the French news department agreed to participate. It would, however, do its own study, a distinct study for the Distinct Society, thereby ensuring that the results could not be compared. On the English side, we hired five top international experts to help design the study. They included eminent scholars from the University of British Columbia, York University, the University of Washington, the University of Amsterdam and the Pew Research Center's Project for Excellence in Journalism.

In the early months of 2008, there was much concern at the CBC that the Conservative government was planning to cut the CBC's budget. Its fundraising arm jumped on every perceived gaffe by the Corporation to animate its base. It would write letters to its supporters soliciting funds to ensure the party could stay in power and keep the CBC in line.

Doug Finley, the Conservative Party's campaign director, would write to his party's members on a regular basis, deploring the CBC's bias and claiming it was in bed with the Liberals. In a typical sally, he wrote:

> And now it has been revealed that representatives of the CBC—the CBC that you and I pay for with our taxes—worked with Liberals to attack our government's record on a House of Commons committee...
>
> The CBC even admitted to Canadian Press that its behaviour in this instance was "inappropriate" and "inconsistent" with the Corporation's policies and practices.
>
> Sadly, this is not the first time our taxpayer-funded broadcaster has found itself caught up in an embarrassing anti-Conservative controversy.
>
> During the 2004 election campaign, it was revealed that CBC tried to stack a town hall style meeting with Stephen Harper with people who were "scared, freaked out or worried about the Conservatives, the Conservative agenda or its leader."

Every time one of those letters was released, it felt like a dark omen, hovering over the CBC's future financing.

At the same time, the government was subjecting the CBC to a review of its operations. It had asked the Corporation what it would do if its subsidy was reduced by 5 percent. The Treasury Board wanted to know what our lowest priorities were and where the cuts would fall. The fact that they were asking these questions increased the sense of impending doom.

It seemed a good idea, therefore, to visit one of the Most Powerful Ministers in the Conservative government. I wanted to explain to him that I too shared his government's concerns about the fairness of Fort News and was taking steps to review it. I wanted to explain the study we were putting together, how extensive it would be and how we would use the results. It was important that the government understood that its concerns were not falling on deaf ears and that work was underway to address the issues involved. I hoped to deflect further attacks, at least for a while.

The visit had to be carried out in complete secrecy. If Fort News discovered I was meeting One of the Most Powerful Ministers it would have the perfect ammunition to destroy me. They would charge that I was a toady of the government and that I was conspiring to compromise their independence. The story would be circulated to all the other news organizations in the country and I would be finished. The minister also wanted discretion. He did not need to be seen consorting with unsavoury characters.

We met at an anonymous office building. The arrangements had been set up through a third party, so that there would be no record of it whatsoever at the CBC. Nobody except the president of the CBC knew I was there. The minister was accompanied by his chief of staff.

He smiled. One of the Most Powerful Ministers in the government is clever and gracious. He poured coffee.

"This meeting is not happening," he said.

"I agree," I replied. "It never took place."

His chief of staff looked slightly menacing. I assumed he was a hard case, one of the *pur et dur*. Doubtless he was an avid reader of the party's fundraising newsletters and a keen student of the CBC's erroneous ways.

"I know there are concerns about the fairness of the news," I began. "I understand that people in the government feel the CBC is actively hostile to your agenda," I went on, hoping to draw out the minister a little.

He said nothing. He sipped his coffee. He looked at me inscrutably.

"I myself," I continued, "do not think the news department is self-consciously hostile. Certainly there is no organized attempt by anyone to try and attack the government's agenda or promote another one. Rather the issue is whether—quite unselfconsciously—it casts its stories in a particular way, whether it has a particular slant that results in it favouring more left-liberal points of view."

I feared I was wandering into the same territory as the CRTC's review of the French news service of thirty years ago. Perhaps he was finding my remarks "tendentious." He said nothing. I waded further into it.

"The problem," I explained, "is that it is hard to make a judgment. Singling out particular stories or commentators does not give the whole picture. Just because Judy Rebick [a famous left-wing feminist] is on TV does not mean the network shares her views. The real question is whether Ezra Levant [a famous right-wing non-feminist] is also on. The test is: do we have balance?"

The chief of staff frowned at the mention of Judy Rebick but seemed comforted at the thought of Ezra Levant.

"To figure this out, we have to look at everything. We need to examine the total output of the organization." I went on to explain the nature of the study, the experts involved, the fact that everything would be public, the timing—the works.

One of the Most Powerful Ministers smiled and finished his coffee. I promised to send him the final terms of reference for the work, thanked him for his time and left. He had said almost nothing. The chief of staff walked me to the door. He glowered.

We met again a few months later. This time I briefed the minister on the results of the research, which had come to be known as the "Fairness and Balance" study. The research revealed no particular bias by the CBC against the Conservative government. To the contrary, it showed that—if anything—the CBC treated the government more positively than either CTV or Global did.

Among many other things, what the researchers had done was count the amount of time the three big networks allocated to the various political parties. It also sorted all the stories into three big buckets, on the basis of whether they had cast the parties and their positions in a positive, neutral or negative light. Remarkably, the results showed that the CBC not only allocated more time to the Conservatives than either Global or CTV, but we tended to treat them more positively as well. This, for me, was unexpected.

As I explained all this to One of the Most Powerful Ministers and his ferocious chief of staff, I had the feeling that I was not making headway. They looked at me sadly. I feared once again that the work was being deemed "tendentious." They did not comment on the result. I promised to send them the full study as soon as it was completed. They thanked me and let me out of our secret meeting room. I have no idea what they thought, although there were no cuts to the CBC in the next round of budget reviews.

Later, when we released the study publicly, we released everything, including the raw data on which the study was built. This would allow anyone to reanalyze the results themselves and make sure we were not rigging them. We also included contact information for the experts who had supervised the work. They were happy to take calls and be interviewed.

I looked forward to the resulting coverage and debate. After all the jabbering on the part of the other media outlets (most notably the *Toronto Sun* and the *National Post*) and the unrelenting attacks by the Conservative party, various right-wing bloggers, aggrieved fundamentalist ministers and Ezra Levant, it would be fascinating to see how they responded to real information. At the very least, I expected the study to ignite a firestorm of debate about the CBC's place in the Canadian political landscape. The bigger the debate, the better, I thought, since it would provide an excellent platform to discuss the research and its conclusions.

We released the results, complete with descriptions on the front page of the CBC website and press releases to the other media. We smacked our lips at the prospect of the upcoming debate. We even prepared for attacks from the Liberals and the left, who we thought might interpret the results as indicating that the CBC was kowtowing to the Conservatives. How else could we explain the fact that we were treating them more positively than the other networks were? But no matter the nature and direction of the conversation, it would inevitably throw the spotlight on the research itself. When that happened and people saw how meticulous, thoughtful and extensive it was, they would realize that the CBC was taking its responsibility to be fair very seriously. That conclusion alone would be a small victory.

The results were released and we waited to field the calls from the rest of the media. Our plan was to direct them to the experts, rather than comment on them ourselves. We felt that the experts were best positioned to comment credibly and objectively on the work. The important thing was for everyone to understand that we had made the best effort anyone could to assess as scientifically and independently as possible the quality of our journalism. Even if we were not perfect, we were working hard to get it right.

Then, nothing happened. Nothing at all. The phones did not ring. The experts were not interviewed. Nobody was asked any questions. The *Sun* and the *National Post* shrugged with indifference. The right-wing bloggers, the fundamentalist ministers, the aggrieved Liberals, Ezra Levant—nobody took any interest in it. After thirty years of debate about the bias in CBC news, after thirty years of outrage and hand-wringing, nothing. The report fell stillborn from the press.

THERE IT WAS. We had managed a complete overhaul of news. The results had been encouraging. Canadians responded well by watching in larger numbers. The employees of the news department were excited and pleased by the new directions. The only concern we had was to ensure that the relaunch of the news was seen as the first step, not the last, in rebuilding CBC News. Jennifer McGuire and I feared that the news department would be tempted to down tools after all of the work that had gone into the rebuilding of the shows and the restructuring of the processes. The danger was that they would declare a great victory.

The truth was that the hard work lay ahead, not behind. The purpose of the relaunch was to build a platform that would permit the news department to increase its audiences and *make a contribution to the public debate that was not only valuable but would not otherwise occur.* Until the audiences were significantly larger, and the promise of Well Informed Now fully kept, the hard work and heavy lifting had not only to continue but to accelerate. The news department needed to push harder if it was to take advantage of the changes that it had made and keep its promise to Canadians.

> Perhaps the time hasn't yet arrived.
> Let's not force it: haste is dangerous.
> Premature measures often bring remorse.
>
> C.P. Cavafy, "In a Large Greek Colony, 200 BC"

seven
RADIO

AH, RADIO. The senior service. It is known inside the CBC as "Tiny Perfect Radio," the service that works. Unlike its vulgar, expensive younger brother, radio is everyone's dream of what the CBC should be: thoughtful, funny, intelligent, distinct, charming and popular. Everyone thinks it's great. The Constituency loves it. The public at large, the taxi drivers, the firefighters, the models, the bakers and the physicians all listen with avidity.

Just listing the iconic national shows captures the breadth and resonance of Tiny Perfect Radio: *As It Happens*, the *Sunday Edition, Cross Cou ntry Checkup, Quirks & Quarks, The Current, Q, Ideas, Writers & Company, Afghanada, The Debaters, The House, Definitely Not the Opera, The Next Chapter*. It's an extraordinary collection of programs. Every week they show the country in all its variety: our books, our preoccupations, our sense of humour, our worries and our hopes. The hosts of the programs are important figures in their own right. Barbara Frum, Peter Gzowski, Lester Sinclair, Vicki Gabereau, Michael Enright, Shelagh Rogers and Jian Ghomeshi are brilliant, highly regarded cultural figures.

The same is true of the local shows. *Metro Morning* in Toronto, *The Early Edition* in Vancouver, *Eyeopener* in Calgary and *Ottawa*

214

Morning in Ottawa are the number one shows in their markets. Their hosts have become personifications of their cities. Andy Barrie, before his retirement from *Metro Morning*, was Toronto. He seemed to feel all of its anxieties and enthusiasms. He loved to explore every part of it. Each morning he introduced the city to itself. The whole place was there: the troubled gangs of Jane and Finch, the matrons of Rosedale, the Korean pastry chefs, the cheese vendors of Kensington Market, the art galleries on Queen Street, the South Asian Urdu poets association, the Lords of the Universe on Bay Street. Every morning Andy Barrie oozed empathy for them in his warm, intimate baritone. The city loved him.

In early 2008, I was appointed head of English services, overseeing radio as well as TV. I was thrilled. The most sophisticated, charming and entertaining cultural service in the country, and I would have the honour of leading it. Remarkable! The only problem was that there appeared to be almost nothing to do. The senior service was by any standard extremely good. Messing with it would be a mistake. Unlike TV, it presented no great challenge of salvation. It was already saved; it was already what it needed to be. I loved it and had loved it for a long time. Being named head of all English services felt like coming home.

The raison d'être for merging CBC English services under one person was the challenge of creating a content company. The idea was to move away from being a radio and a TV company to becoming a company focused on particular genres. The CBC would be in future a news company, a music company, a sports company and a talk company. To get there, all of the assets had to be integrated in a single structure. When they were unified, we could move our focus from the platforms to what really mattered, the content.

There were, of course, questions. Why is radio so well received, and why does TV struggle? Why can't TV be more like radio? Why can't it be as smart and as funny and as thoughtful? It's strange that they should inhabit the same company: the admired senior service and the despised junior one. Is there no way for TV to learn from radio? The successful service is just down the hall, just around the corner. Why can nobody seem to draw the appropriate conclusions and make TV as good as radio? This surely was the great mystery of the CBC. Perhaps, being in charge of both, I could learn the answer.

RADIO HAS TWO markets: talk radio and music radio. Approximately 20 percent of all radio listening in Canada is to talk radio. The other 80 percent is music radio.

Within the talk segment, CBC Radio One is unique. The private stations in talk radio principally follow all-news formats. They feature a "wheel" of weather, traffic and information that repeats every half hour and is updated as the day progresses. Sometimes the news will be supplemented by call-in shows, where opinionated listeners telephone opinionated hosts and engage in shouting matches. The whole effort is local in character and relatively inexpensive.

There is no national private talk-radio network. There are no national talk-radio newscasts or sportscasts, let alone national talk shows on science, current affairs, drama, books, culture, politics or humour. There are simply none. There are local private talk-radio wheels of news and call-ins with peculiar arguments. That is it.

In this sense, CBC Radio One has no competitors. The private sector does not compete with the CBC in talk except at the local level, and even there the shows are totally different. They both offer news, weather and traffic, but there the similarities end. CBC's local shows during the "drive" hours from 6:00 to 8:30 in the morning and 3:00 to 6:00 in the afternoon do not run on "wheels." Rather they follow a magazine format, offering local current affairs, documentaries, interviews and investigative pieces. They cover everything from municipal politics to the local arts scene and developments in social services. Their range of materials and topics is far wider than that of their competitors in the private sector.

In this sense, CBC Radio One is in a class by itself. For many of its listeners, the private radio stations do not constitute an alternative at all. If they turn on Radio One and they do not like what they hear, they turn off the radio. They do not go elsewhere. They do not turn the dial to see if there is something else they might like.

As a result, Radio One is astonishingly dominant. By 2010, it was taking a 13 share, which means that 13 percent of all Canadians listening to radio were listening to Radio One. This is the highest in its history, the highest in its seventy-five years of existence. To put this in perspective, Radio One's 13 share is for 100 percent of the market. In the talk radio market, it takes a 65 share—in other words, of all the listening to talk radio in Canada, almost two-thirds is to CBC radio. There is no other medium in the country that so completely dominates its segment.

The success of Radio One is a relatively new phenomenon. Just over thirty-five years ago, it was nothing like what it is today. By the early 1970s, it was a disaster. Its share had sunk so low that practically nobody in the country was listening. Serious consideration was given to winding it up altogether.

The share had become so low, in fact, that the management of the period decided to drop the advertising they were then carrying. They did this not because they hoped it would help revive radio's fortunes but because it was less expensive to be ad-free. The audiences were so low that the revenues generated could not cover the costs of maintaining a sales force. The abandonment of advertising was a sad testament to how far CBC radio had fallen and how irrelevant it had become.

This is a poorly understood point. In the mythological versions of CBC's history, revisionists claim that the period's far-sighted management realized that CBC radio could only flourish if it was freed from the dead hand of the market. They saw—as nobody has been able to see clearly at CBC TV—that advertising was anathema to quality, that commercials were ruinous to good programming. Once they were gone, and the dead hand removed, CBC radio would become the revered and admired service that it is today. In fact, of course, CBC did not abandon the market; the market abandoned the CBC.

CBC radio's hitting bottom had a liberating effect. Realizing that things could not get worse freed up the service to take risks and try new things. Suddenly it could pursue any mad notion it wanted because anything would be better than where it was. This set the stage for what became known as the Radio Revolution. The Revolution had two broad waves to it. The third, which was planned, never occurred, but the first two completely remade the service.

Although it is ancient history now, it is worth spending a moment on the origin of the Revolution. It was led by a remarkable woman by the name of Margaret Lyons. Lyons is a Canadian of Japanese descent, and like many of her contemporaries, including David Suzuki, she was interned during the Second World War as a potential enemy alien. She emerged from the camps, married and went on to become a radio producer for the BBC between 1949 and 1960.

While at the BBC, by some small accident of fate, she ended up with George Orwell's old desk. His initials were carved into the surface: E.B. (Eric Blair, his real name). She too made her mark on it, writing in Japanese. She cut into the wooden surface: "All producers are created equal, but some producers are more equal than others." She would go on to be the most equal of all, and arguably the greatest media executive in CBC history.

When she returned to Canada, she went to work at CBC radio. After the senior service reached its nadir in the early 1970s, she was asked to reinvent it. Her point of departure was to jettison the old voice of the CBC. As CBC journalist Barbara Frum described it, the old voice "was ponderous, a sort of university of the air... it talked down to people and was patronizingly intellectual." The new voice was designed to be the opposite. It was "identified with the lives of real people and... made a commitment to being fun." This was the crux of the change. Radio was moved from being a snobby, self-important, elitist service to one that was much more informal, populist and engaging.

To effect the changes, Margaret Lyons surrounded herself with a number of young producers, some only in their twenties. The most famous of these was Mark Starowicz, who along with Barbara Frum established the current format for *As It Happens*. The show moved into its new style in 1973 and has changed little since. It begins with a terrible pun and then works the phones to talk to people all over the world about stories that range from the political to the silly. The tone is informal, funny and intensely personal. It set the standard for all the other Radio Revolution shows that were to follow.

And there were a host of them. Under Margaret Lyons, Tiny Perfect Radio created *Sunday Morning*, now the flagship show of Michael Enright, a former host of *As It Happens*. *Quirks & Quarks*, Canada's most influential science show, emerged at the same time. And perhaps most famously, *Morningside*, which began its run as *This Country in the Morning*, with its incomparable host, Peter Gzowski, was launched. That show, more perhaps than any other, captured the new spirit of CBC radio: intimate, funny and warm. It covered all parts of the country, focusing not on the Worthy and Important, but on the Small and Charming. It had a rural, small-town feel, as though you were listening to a family conversation with your favourite uncle.

The Radio Revolution was not just a change in programs, although it was certainly that. It was even more a dramatic change in tone and manners. It recognized, as television had great difficulty doing, that society had changed. The old distinctions between the high arts and popular culture had eroded to the point of meaninglessness. There was no cultural elite whose job it was to educate or lift up the sad unwashed. There were only Canadians, all equally interesting, funny and important. The Radio Revolution was fundamentally a democratic revolution. It embraced everyone.

When we were working on redoing the CBC brand for English services as a whole, the promise that we wanted to capture was that the Corporation was there to reflect "how fascinating Canadians really are." It was not there to educate Canadians; it was there to celebrate our history, accomplishments, sense of humour and sophistication. The CBC should stand in a relationship of service and equality. This was the real meaning of the Radio Revolution. If television could learn the same lesson, it might pull itself out of its nosedive. We captured the new brand message in the slogan "Canada Lives Here." It became the signature sign-off for all the shows on both the junior and senior services.

We accompanied our new tagline with a musical mnemonic. In what we thought was a cheeky appropriation, we took the first four notes of "O Canada." Before doing so, however, we asked Canadians if that would be okay. They said yes, without hesitation. They were happy for the CBC to clothe itself in the national anthem and promise that Canada would live there. This reflected, no doubt, their hope for the Corporation's future as much as their celebration of its past.

THE REVOLUTION THAT Margaret Lyons began with the national shows continued into the second revolution and the reform of the local shows, which had begun in the mid-1990s. Here, the overall strategy was the same. Make the tone and character democratic. Broaden the shows to reveal the full character of the cities they serve. In Calgary, "Calgary Lives Here"; in Ottawa, "Ottawa Lives Here"; in Toronto, "Toronto Lives Here." The shows needed to become reflections of the fullness of the places they served.

These changes were controversial and difficult. In Toronto, for example, plans were made to ensure that *Metro Morning* reflected the extraordinary diversity of the city. The idea was to show the multicultural character of the various neighbourhoods. No longer would it reflect the preoccupations of the Annex intellectuals and the plutocrats of Rosedale; rather it would reach out into all the communities. It would cover the issue of honour killings in the South Asian community and the emergence of Toronto Bollywood stars. It would look into the youth problems in the Somali community and celebrate K'naan. It would explore the shops and cultural activities, the civic preoccupations and triumphs of the resident Chinese, Turkish, Greek, Nigerian and Palestinian communities.

There were worries that such a change would alienate *Metro Morning*'s core listeners, the matrons of Rosedale and the pipe smokers of the Annex. Maybe they would be put off by the bhangra music and the goat curries and the Urdu poetry festival. Maybe they would switch off. Maybe the other communities would not come. Maybe the Somalis and the Jamaicans and the Portuguese would say no thanks to CBC radio. And then what? Nobody would be listening.

They pushed ahead anyway. They changed the production staff, bringing in people from the communities they were trying to explore. They changed the story selection. They changed the music. Now there were specialists on mango salads and Pakistani family formation appearing on air. There was music in languages other than English. There were ragas, salsas, high life music and Afrobeat, in Hindi, Spanish, Fon.

And the Rosedale matrons liked it. They did not go away. They were thrilled, in fact, to see the city opened up. They were thrilled to discover the neighbourhoods and people they might otherwise never have met. And for their part, the Sikh taxi drivers and the Chinese ginseng merchants were equally pleased. They were thrilled to have their cultures and their place in Toronto society recognized and validated.

The changes took *Metro Morning* to the number one position in the Toronto market. Toronto lives here.

Similar changes were made to the other local shows. Vancouver focused more on its Chinese and South Asian communities. Ottawa reached further into its French population and the denizens of politics-land. All across the country, the shows were broadened and their voices made more natural, more informal, more relaxed. Throughout the country the response was the same. Even in places like Calgary, where CBC local television was dead in the water, *Eyeopener* was number one. Vancouver Lives Here. Halifax Lives Here.

The strengthening of the local shows had an interesting impact on the national ones. When the local shows drew larger audiences, they also drew larger audiences for the national shows locally. In Toronto, when *Metro Morning* gained greater audience share so too did *The Current*, *As It Happens* and the *Sunday Edition*. We discovered that there was an important relationship between doing well locally and doing well nationally. The two sorts of shows supported each other.

This effect can be seen particularly clearly in towns that are adjacent to each other. So, for example, *Metro Morning* in Toronto takes a 14 share between 6:00 and 8:30 AM. In nearby Barrie, where there is no local morning show, Radio One takes only a 6 share. The effect holds all through the day, even when there are no local shows being aired. Radio One takes a 10 share for the day as a whole in Toronto and only a 5 share in Barrie. The same relationship holds true in Alberta. *Eyeopener* in Calgary, the local morning show, takes a 13 share. In Red Deer, where there is no local show, Radio One takes a 5 share. Again, the relationship holds all day.

The effect was startling. It meant that if the senior service was to expand to its full potential, it had to strengthen its local footprint.

This relationship between local and national success in radio also suggested another reason for rebuilding our local television news offerings. If the same effect could be seen, then the rebuilding of the local newscasts should also strengthen the performance of *The National*. When we looked to see if that was true of CBC's rivals Global and CTV, we found it was. Where their local newscasts were strong, their national ones performed better.

The CBC local shows are strangely distributed in Canada. Tiny places like Corner Brook, Goose Bay and Gander, Newfoundland, have their own local shows. So too do Thompson, Manitoba; Sydney, Nova Scotia; and Saint John, New Brunswick. At the same time, large cities like London and Hamilton have no local radio shows. The situation is particularly odd if we compare New Brunswick to Hamilton. New Brunswick has three local radio shows (Moncton, Fredericton and Saint John) and a local TV show (Fredericton). Hamilton has no local radio or TV shows, despite having a population larger than all of New Brunswick.

There are no doubt historical reasons that account in part for these anomalies. When radio started in the 1930s, western and central Canada were more heavily populated than the east. It was perhaps not surprising that as the senior service was established, it was over-represented in the Atlantic provinces. Strangely, however, as the years went on, little or nothing was done to rectify the problem. No new English local radio stations have been created for years.

There are fundamental issues of equity involved in the distribution of local radio. All Canadians pay for CBC radio, but some receive no service. A number of very small towns receive service, but others do not. Some large towns and cities receive service, and others don't. It is not clear why.

Part of the problem seems to be that the CBC has never been clear on its policy for providing local service. Sometimes the Corporation has argued that its job is to serve towns that would otherwise not receive local service from the private sector. If that were correct, the local services in Toronto, Vancouver and Calgary should be wound up and their resources deployed to Wawa and Olds and Saint-Louis-du-Ha! Ha! But of course this does not happen.

The alternative view is that the Corporation should try to maximize the number of Canadians receiving local CBC service. If this is correct, then Corner Brook, Sydney and Saint John should be wound up and a local service started in Hamilton. But that does not happen either.

These two different views of the matter are contradictory. Within the CBC, there have been innumerable efforts to pretend that the contradiction is not there. The result is another of the muddles for which CBC is famous. The problem with muddles, of course, is that they lead inevitably to incoherence and unfairness. This confusion became particularly vitriolic and unsettling when it came time to decide what to do during the financial crisis.

WHEN I BECAME head of English services, the idea was to lay the basis for CBC's emergence as a "content" company. In pulling everything together in a single organizational structure, we could—as we had with news—lay the basis for more coherent, subject-specific offerings. We would, for example, be able to create CBC Music and make sense of all the music assets scattered across the Corporation. The music of Radio 2; the interviews with musicians on Q and The Hour; the music news on television; the vast music archives of the Corporation; the online music service, Radio 3; and the occasional television specials could be seen as a whole and organized in a thematically integrated way. Instead of music on CBC TV, CBC radio and CBC.ca, there would be CBC Music.

At the same time, drawing radio and television together under one roof would make it easier for them to learn from each other. The more informal, democratic, confident and populist culture of the senior service might reassure the junior service that it was okay to show a little leg and have a little fun. It would lay the basis for the two sides helping each other. Television could promote the radio shows and the radio shows could promote TV. The sum would be greater than the parts.

I was under no illusions that this would be an easy sell to radio. The announcement that the head of television was taking over radio was indeed met with cries of fear and revulsion. The fear was that Tiny Perfect Radio would be taken over by its slobbering idiot younger brother. The admired, clever and popular senior service was being sacrificed for some strange management idea to the failed junior service. Doom.

To explain the change, we organized a Town Hall. This is a CBC event in which management offers the employees an opportunity to ask all the tough questions on their minds. It is slightly phony, since most employees take the sensible view that aggressively grilling management may not be a path to career success. To avoid this, we asked the tough old birds of radio to ask the hard questions. We knew that Andy Barrie and Michael Enright were afraid of nothing. In fact they rather enjoyed the CBC blood sport of showing up management for the fools they clearly were. Barrie and Enright were to pose all the tough questions that the radio folks wanted to ask but might be too timid to pose.

Interim head of radio Jennifer McGuire and I met the assembled. The radio folks were all there or watching by closed circuit. They are a little woolly. Where the television types tend to be somewhat flashy, the radio crowd is more Birkenstocks and scented candles. I started with a little speech about how I loved radio, my father was an old CBC radio hand, television could learn so much from radio, blather, blather. Then Jennifer reassured them she was still there, it would make radio's priorities more central to the organization's, blather, blather.

We opened the floor to questions. Barrie and Enright came out swinging.

"What do you know about radio?"

"Nothing. I hope you will teach me."

"How do we avoid getting swallowed?"

"This should get you more resources, not less. Now I have to think about how to ensure radio is a success, not just TV. It should make it easier, for example, for me to convince myself that you should be properly promoted."

"Are you going to dumb us down like TV?"

"I didn't think we were dumbing down TV. What I hope is that TV can learn from radio, which is more successful."

"Are you putting ads on radio?"

"No."

And so it went. On and on. They asked the hard questions that the others might be uncomfortable posing. By the end, I thought it had gone okay. But the real tests would come later, depending on what I did. Inevitably the radio folks would judge the acts, not the talk.

The first order of business would be to find a new head of radio. Jennifer McGuire was moving to news, and whoever replaced her would have big and much-loved shoes to fill. We started a national search. Brilliant resumes poured in from across the country. I begged a number of people to apply. Most notably I asked Denise Donlon. She had been the "pop princess" of MuchMusic, then rose to become the architect and boss of the CHUM group's very successful music channels and went on to become president of Sony Music Canada. When I tracked her down, she was working for the Bill Clinton Foundation. Our first conversation was unsatisfactory.

"Would you consider applying?" I asked.

"No," she said.

"Why not?"

"I'm happy where I am. I only came to see you because I thought it would be rude to say no on the phone."

"It's a great job."

"I know. I used to work for Gzowski."

"So why not think about it?"

"No, thanks."

"No, thanks?"

"Nope."

It was often this way when trying to convince people to come to the CBC. The Corporation had a terrible reputation, and most sensible people shied away from it. The only way forward was to beg Denise Donlon so insistently that she would eventually grow tired of me and give in. That is exactly what I did. After a while, she buckled and accepted the job.

We discussed at some length the Next Wave of the Radio Revolution and settled on the key things we needed to do. First, we had to continue the work of the two original revolutions. This would require further strengthening the national shows and expanding the footprint of the local shows. For the third revolution we wanted to position radio as the leader in transforming the CBC into a content company.

To continue the original revolution, we began with the national shows. Shelagh Rogers's morning show, the inheritor of Gzowski's iconic *This Country in the Morning,* continued to do well, but the audience had not increased in years and continued to age. The show itself had a slightly antique air. It continued to feature a small-town sensibility, with charming stories from the remote parts of the country. It felt lovely, but a little twee.

For her part, Shelagh Rogers was tired of the show. For reasons that made little sense given the time zones involved, it was being produced out of Vancouver. Since it appeared in the morning in the east, Shelagh Rogers had to do the show in the middle of the night Vancouver time. This was grinding her down, and the rest of the production staff with her. It seemed a propitious time to make a change.

We thought about moving Jian Ghomeshi and *Q* into the Rogers/ Gzowski time slot. *Q* could not have been more different from its predecessors. Jian Ghomeshi is anything but small-town twee. He is an urban hipster with a contemporary sensibility. In a previous life he had been the drummer in the band Moxy Früvous. Most recently, he had hosted the afternoon cultural magazine show on Radio One. It was a strong show, very much in the moment, exploring the ins and outs of the zeitgeist.

We liked the idea of moving *Q* into the Rogers/Gzowski slot, not only because it was an excellent show but also because the move would signal a shift in direction for the network. It would indicate that we were pursuing a more urban and more contemporary feel, along with a younger demographic. Denise Donlon and I met Ghomeshi. We talked about moving his show to the Rogers/Gzowski slot.

"Put me in," he said.

I looked at Ghomeshi. He was a little rumpled.

"It's radio," he said, "nobody can see me."

I laughed. It was a private joke. Occasionally we would comment on how each other was dressed.

"Put me in. We'll move the numbers."

"A big claim. Nobody has moved them in thirty years. You think you can beat Gzowski and Rogers?"

"Yes. Guaranteed."

"Guaranteed?"

"Oh, yes."

Ghomeshi is so clever, so charming and so driven, I did not doubt he was right. We put him in. After some mild moaning from the Constituency, *Q* caught fire. For the first time in well over a generation, the audiences increased for the time slot. He may be the best interviewer on radio. Arguably he has already eclipsed Gzowski.

We looked, as well, at continuing the second revolution by expanding the local footprint and strengthening the existing local shows. We knew that if we could provide local service in the large underserved cities, we would lift the ratings for the network as a whole. This became the subject of huge debate over the course of the next year, as the financial crisis fell upon us.

At the same time, we wanted to push the local morning and afternoon drive shows to grow further. We were convinced that the strategy of fully reflecting the communities they served was the right one, but it had stalled. To take *Metro Morning* as an example again, there was no doubt that it reflected the ethnic diversity and multicultural character of the city much more effectively than in the past. There was also no doubt that Toronto had responded favourably to the changes. But it seemed to have run out of gas in its ambitions. It seemed to have fallen into a CBC comfort zone that could ultimately prove self-limiting.

The show had become a little self-righteous. It championed end-less social causes, from environmentalism to public transit and bicycles. It was preoccupied with social ills: bullying at school, unhappy teenagers, abused dogs, the lack of bicycle paths. These were all worthy, but the tone was relentlessly earnest and hectoring. So many ills, so little time.

There was no sense in the show that Toronto was one of the five great growth centres in North America. There was no coverage of its most important industries, where the vast majority of people made their living. The greatest financial hub outside of New York never appeared. Canada's media centre did not exist. The software and technology businesses were not there. The extraordinary drive, cre-ativity, wealth and optimism of the city was never covered. It was not true to its own strategy of opening up all aspects of Toronto to itself.

To move forward we needed to continue to push both the national and local shows. They needed to be more daring and more open to the full character of contemporary Canada. There is a natural—perhaps inevitable—tendency for Tiny Perfect Radio to become smug and self-congratulatory. After all, if *Metro Morning* is number one in the Toronto market, it must be doing something right. The danger of success is self-satisfaction.

AS PART OF the transition to a content company, and the start of the third revolution, we chose to focus on books and music. The senior service has more important book shows than anybody else in the country—*Writers & Company* with Eleanor Wachtel, *The Next Chapter* with Shelagh Rogers, *Canada Reads* (the national literary competition where Canadians pick a favourite book), not to mention the books that are covered or reviewed on *Ideas*, *Quirks & Quarks*, *Q*, *Definitely Not the Opera*—and sponsors the CBC Literary Awards. CBC television also had lots of literary content. Authors were inter-viewed on George Stroumboulopoulos's show and the News Network. Television adaptations of famous novels appeared on a relatively reg-ular basis: *St. Urbain's Horseman*, *The Englishman's Boy*, *jPod*.

Despite the CBC's extensive book holdings, much of it is invisi-ble. The CBC Literary Awards, for example, are the oldest in Canada, apart from the Governor General's Literary Awards, but utterly unknown. I asked Michael Levine, Canada's preeminent literary agent, what he thought about the prizes. He stared at me blankly. He had been representing authors for forty years and he had never heard of them.

"Really?" he asked.

"Really," I replied. "In French and English."

"Remarkable," he opined. "Who knew?" Who knew, indeed!

To check out the prizes, I went to the awards ceremony. It was held in a restaurant of unparalleled obscurity in an undistinguished neighbourhood in Montreal. It was very dark. I was told that I was the first head of English services ever to show up. Shelagh Rogers was hosting the English prizes. She giggled in her madly enthusiastic way and introduced me to the nominees. They were all young and charming. The crowd seemed mostly made up of their girlfriends and boyfriends, their parents and their hangers-on. There were also enthusiastic marketing people from *enRoute*, Air Canada's in-flight magazine, who were going to publish the winners. There seemed to be no journalists, literary critics or publishers. Over the next couple of days, I scanned the French and English papers in vain for any mention of the event.

This was typical of CBC radio. Many of its most wonderful properties languished unknown and unloved, blooming in a night of promotional darkness and aridity. Despite this, the CBC remained for English-Canadian publishers the most important vehicle for promoting and showcasing their authors and new books. Perhaps this is not surprising, since there is so little else. Book reviews in the *Globe and Mail*, the *National Post* and obscure literary magazines aside, nobody else really covers books. CTV, Global, CHUM, Astral— none of the big radio and television broadcasters bother with literary matters. The CBC is pretty much all there is for Canadian publishers and readers.

We thought, therefore, that it might be a good idea to pull together in one place all of the CBC's book assets and build a portal for Canadian book lovers. We wanted to gather up all the scattered bits and pieces of book interest and make something that was much bigger than the sum of its parts, a place where Canadians could find the best and most comprehensive coverage of books. We wanted to be CBC Books, the Canadian Home of Books.

CBC Books would be a place where readers could go to find everything bookish they wanted: bestseller lists, reviews, all of our interviews and book talk, prize information, book clubs, contests, promotions, authors' tours, literary festivals. It would be one-stop shopping for bookworms. Properly done, it would also provide an opportunity for Canadian publishers and retailers to sell more books. We wanted a place where Canadians could come, read a review, hear a talk, check the prize-winners and order the book right away online. It would be nice for everyone, and—who knew?—perhaps the senior service could make a little money.

To build the Home of Books, we wanted to encourage everyone to join in the project. The more of the literary community we could bring to the party, the more comprehensive and attractive the offering would be. The more comprehensive the offering, the bigger the platform for the promotion of Canadian books and authors. The bigger the promotion, the more Canadians would come to CBC Books. The more they came, the better the associated book clubs, prize debates, votes and contests would be. We thought a heretical and unworthy thought. We thought an un-Canadian and un-literary thought. We thought it might be nice to do something attractive and exciting about Canadian books.

To begin assembling the pieces, I went to have lunch with Eddie Greenspon, then the editor of the *Globe and Mail*. We ate at Le Sélect, a traditional French bistro a block away from the *Globe*'s headquarters. I was interested to see whether he would agree to put the *Globe*'s book review section on the site. It would drive more traffic (and ultimately more advertising dollars) to their reviews and add to the prestige and comprehensiveness of the Home of Books.

Eddie Greenspon is a lovely guy, but I knew the conversation would be tricky for him. At that time, the *Globe and Mail* had a relationship with CTV. A series of transactions led by Bell a number of years earlier had fused the telephone company to CTV, its stable of specialty channels and the venerable *Globe and Mail*. The result was that the *Globe and Mail* was in fact owned by CTV, although majority control continued to remain with the Thomson family. I was worried that the relationship to CTV would limit his enthusiasm to do anything with the CBC.

Le Sélect had been a landmark of the Toronto restaurant scene for many years. It started on Queen Street in the 1970s, opening next door to the headquarters of the Communist Party of Canada. To this day, its business cards show an old black-and-white photo of the original establishment. It takes a certain amount of effort—and, for those with poor eyesight, a magnifying glass—to read the Communist Party sign on the building next door. But there it is.

I ordered the steak tartare.

"Can we work together?"

People at adjoining tables looked in our direction. I lowered my voice.

"Well, I would like to," Eddie began. "The CBC is a much more natural home for the *Globe* than CTV, but realities make it difficult." He looked sad.

"It's just the book section," I went on. "CTV does not have a book show. In fact, I think they discourage reading."

"Still," he allowed, "... still."

"Besides," I said, "I thought your boss [*Globe* publisher Phillip Crawley] reported to the Thomsons. Why does he care what CTV thinks?"

Greenspon looked at me in dismay. Clearly he was surprised that I had missed an important fact about the realities of Toronto business. "No. You're wrong. Phillip Crawley reports to Ivan Fecan."

"Really?"

"Ah, yes," he sighed.

"Well, what sort of man is Phillip Crawley?" I asked.

Eddie Greenspon looked at me, licked his index finger and stuck it in the air.

Ivan Fecan! Everywhere I turned, no matter how obscure the undertaking, he was there, grinning from dark corners, pursuing his relentless quest for media domination.

"I take it that means no?" I asked plaintively.

"Pretty much."

Continuing our search for partners, we decided to try and team up with Chapters, the country's largest bookseller. We thought it would be nice for both parties. We could do some of our book shows out of the Chapters stores and they could promote our shows on their ads and flyers. We would pull more people into their stores and they would attract more people to our shows. As well, we could feature their online bookstore at the Home of Books. Every time someone came to the Home and bought a book, Chapters would make some money. Even our brands were aligned. Chapters' great slogan—"The World Needs More Canada"—celebrates Canada's stars and authors, while ours—"Canada Lives Here"—holds a mirror to the country to show how fascinating it is. A natural marriage, if ever there was one.

Denise Donlon and I prepared a pitch describing the Home of Books and sent it off to Chapters. I called Heather Reisman, the CEO, to describe the idea. I described how great it would be for them. They would sell more, we would cross-promote, it would strengthen the publishing industry (God knows the industry needed it), it would add prestige and credibility to Chapters' cultural bona fides, and it was the right thing to do. I worked myself up into such a fever of excitement that I was more than a little disappointed when Reisman said no.

It is hard to know exactly why she declined. She said they were busy, working on other things. Certainly she was facing significant financial challenges, like all booksellers. But I suspected it was something else. Serious people in private business do not like to venture into collaboration with the CBC. It has a reputation for being difficult and capricious. Its motives are unclear (often commercially unsound), its directions obscure and variable, its senior executives unbusinesslike. One never knows from one year to the next who the president or board will be, or whether they will be reliable. Perhaps Reisman declined because the CBC seems a peculiar partner, too arbitrary to invest much time and energy in.

As it became clear that big partners were not available to us, we searched out smaller but nevertheless valuable ones. Eventually the literary magazine *Quill & Quire* joined, giving the Home access to its huge archive of book reviews. Simple, standardized click-through deals were made to sell online. The CBC's shows were inventoried and organized in a searchable fashion. We made plans to add games and book clubs to CBC Books.

CBC's other main content area was music. The Corporation is—and has always been—extremely involved with music. Most of the best-known Canadian musicians had their careers made through the CBC. In many cases, they were largely unknown before the CBC found them and put them on air. From Ian and Sylvia Tyson through Gordon Lightfoot to Leonard Cohen, Arcade Fire and Chantal Kreviazuk, the list of distinguished alumni reflects the who's who of Canadian music. Much of Glenn Gould's astonishing career was spent at the CBC, after he retired from touring. His best-known recordings and his experiments in sound poetry were made late at night at the CBC studios. The senior service was famous for housing and breaking new artists and musical innovators.

The most important cbc musical asset is Radio 2, the transcontinental, all-music fm network. Over the years, it had been widely admired for the breadth of its coverage and the daring of its shows. By the time I arrived in 2004, however, it seemed to have lost its mojo. Some years earlier, it had been transformed into an all-classical network and had turned its back on contemporary Canadian music.

Its audiences were modest. Typically it would take about one-third the audiences of Radio One. At the same time, Radio 2's audience was aging. The market for classical music is at best limited and very grey. The CBC's internal studies showed that the average age of Radio 2's listeners was increasing by a year for every year that passed. If the average age was sixty in 2004, it was sixty-one in 2005, sixty-two in 2006, and so on. If the senior service was not careful, it would lose the listenership of Radio 2 not to competitors, but to the grave.

There was, however, a bigger problem at Radio 2. It was not at all clear why the CBC would give itself over completely to classical music. The music played was almost exclusively eighteenth-, nine-teenth- and early twentieth-century European music. There was lots of Mozart and Brahms, Beethoven, Tchaikovsky and Shosta-kovich, masses of Verdi and Bach, Debussy and Ravel. There were no contemporary Canadian composers. Occasionally R. Murray Schafer might appear, but not much more. Radio 2 had become a museum for the celebration of famous old European masterpieces.

This was surprising, since the contemporary Canadian music scene is by any international standard extraordinarily vibrant. Every month it seems a great new band breaks both in Canada and around the world—K'naan, Broken Social Scene, Feist. It is not as though Canada is short of musical talent. To the contrary, it is—as it has always been—one of the great incubators of contemporary music in the Western world.

And yet it was not on Radio 2. In fact, there was little of it any-where except campus radio stations. Private radio long ago splin-tered into highly specialized musical niches that featured heavy rotations of popular standards, along with extensive airplay of one or two really successful artists, more often than not American. It did not matter what splinter was considered: oldies rock stations, heavy metal, country, country rock, easy listening—the formula was always the same. The radio doctors had established rigid formats: a couple of old favourites, followed by three or four current hits, fol-lowed by a couple of old favourites and maybe something new. The exact balance varied from splinter to splinter, but the result was always the same. Programming safety lay with the tried and true and the massively popular. There was little or no room to introduce new artists, let alone Canadian ones.

The situation had become so bad by 2004 that of the 30,000 pro-fessional music recordings released in Canada in any given year, only 250 received regular airplay on private radio. This meant that the aural soundscape of the country did not exist on radio, the musi-cal medium par excellence. Neither the private stations nor the CBC were prepared to take any chances on new music. They remained grimly wedded to the enthusiasms of the past, whether Bartók on Radio 2 or Buddy Holly on Hot Rocks FM.

For all of these reasons, the head of radio in 2006, Jane Chalmers, and her irrepressible deputy, Jennifer McGuire, decided it was time for a change. They had carried out extensive studies and on the basis of them resolved to transform Radio 2 from a dying network devoted to long-dead European composers into a present-day platform for the release and exploration of new Canadian music. They wanted to make Radio 2 once again culturally relevant and important to the vast majority of Canadians, who never listened to classical music.

They knew this would be a dangerous undertaking. Much of the Constituency was made up of classical music enthusiasts who were convinced that contemporary music was rubbish and that classical music was what really mattered. They believed that abandoning Beethoven would mean abandoning quality. They believed that electric guitars meant nothing but bad manners and loud noise. They knew that if the gates were opened, a rush of cacophonous filth would pour in. It would be all Johnny Rotten, Sid Vicious and the Sex Pistols. It would be raucous, drugged-up, meaningless horror. Once again, the CBC would be dumbed down; once again, it would fall into the disreputable trap of celebrating popular culture and appealing to a younger audience.

This potentially horrid outcome was captured eloquently in a *cri de cœur* from Jeffrey Simpson in the *Globe and Mail*:

> The last islands of the sustained appeal to intelligence lay in CBC radio, which remained free from commercial pressures and, until recently, from the fixation to "solve" the CBC's problems by maximizing its audiences through programs aimed at younger people. The most redoubtable of these islands—a refuge, really—was Radio 2.
>
> Radio 2's distinguishing characteristic was its intelligence. It emphasized classical music because that kind of music was not easily available in private radio and because, through the ages, that form of music appealed to the intelligence and deepest emotions of listeners.
>
> Other musical forms can be intelligent and emotional, but the classical genre has endured and evolved through the centuries as the deepest exploration of the human dilemma through music.

Whew. There it was.

Chalmers and McGuire realized that convincing the president and the board to change direction on Radio 2 was fraught with peril. Despite the fact that the audience was dying off, despite the fact that it had nothing to do with Canadian culture, despite the fact that there was a huge need for a great platform for Canadian music, the board would balk. They would—in the wearying way of CBC boards—anticipate the criticism that would result and refuse to go along. They would prefer a quiet life.

Some of the board members were also deeply committed to classical music. Peter Herrndorf was the head of the Nationals Arts Centre, whose prize possession was the National Arts Centre Orchestra, with its internationally famous conductor, the violin virtuoso Pinchas Zukerman. George Cooper, another distinguished board member, had been the chairman of Symphony Nova Scotia. All the others generally moved in circles that valued and admired classical music. If they did not go to the opera themselves, their friends did. They would have to explain why they had joined the vandals and agreed to sack the city.

The best hope for convincing the board lay in the fact that the CBC French radio had already made the same change. They had taken their all-classical FM network and transformed it into "Espace musique," which was relentlessly contemporary in orientation. They had also done it quickly. One night the citizens of Quebec went to bed listening to Bach, the next morning they were greeted by Garou. Just like that. There was some rumbling from the French Constituency, along with the predictable anxiety about the loss of quality and standards. And then it settled down. Musicians who had not previously been heard on Radio-Canada, along with their enthusiastic fans and listeners, leapt to the defence of the new strategy. Within a few months, the audiences increased and grew younger. It was a huge success.

Nevertheless, Jane Chalmers and Jennifer McGuire approached the shift gingerly. The English board members probably had no idea what had happened on the French side; that history would be of little value in helping them make their case. The statistics on decline and irrelevance would be brushed aside in favour of personal preference and fear of controversy. It would be tough.

They met the board in Moncton. It was worse than tough. I found McGuire and Chalmers outside the boardroom, having been ejected so that the board could debate the proposal in private. They looked pretty bad. They were bruised and cut. One of them had a black eye and the other was walking with a cane. I tried to buck them up as best I could, but they had been mauled.

When the board finally decided the matter, it proposed a compromise. Instead of taking off all the classical music at once and immediately introducing the new offering, they wanted to move slowly, one step at a time. A little classical music would come off, and then a little more, then a little more, until it was eventually all removed some years later. The band-aid would be pulled off as slowly as possible. Unlike the case of Espace musique, where the advocates for the new strategy would immediately be available to defend the CBC against the enraged classical music enthusiasts, the board contemplated no counterweight to their anger. Instead, it created a situation where Jane Chalmers and Jennifer McGuire would have to stand naked in the field, without allies or friends, while the enraged members of the Constituency threw rocks and insults at them.

It was never clear to me whether the board insisted on this death by a thousand cuts because it believed this was the best way to transform Radio 2 or because it was consumed by its fears of criticism. But whatever the reason, the result was a disaster. The new service was a mess. It had no coherent brand or rationale. Its programming swung wildly from shows for the retired to shows for the indie-rock hipsters. Not surprisingly, the ratings sank and the level of criticism rose. No matter how hard everyone tried, it was impossible to make sense of the new direction.

By the time I became head of English services, the transformation of Radio 2 had been going on for about a year. At the moment of my arrival, the plan called for pulling off the second band-aid. Classical music would be relegated to daytime and the CBC Radio Orchestra would be cancelled. New shows would be built around the "drive" periods, weekends and evenings. Once again, it would satisfy nobody. It would simply further enrage the Constituency, without allowing a clear break to bring on supporters. Nevertheless we plunged ahead.

We hired new hosts for the revamped shows, some of whom had no radio experience but were extremely knowledgeable professional musicians. We wanted people who could maintain the informed voice that had characterized Radio 2 in the past. We wanted people who could introduce the music, explain why it mattered and what to listen for. On weekend mornings, for example, the brilliant jazz singer Molly Johnson would act as host. The rapper and musical encyclopedia Rich Terfry, also known as Buck 65, would host the afternoon drive show. We made similar changes everywhere, except for daytime, where we kept the classical music format but attempted to modernize it by having the great mezzo-soprano Julie Nesrallah host it. She is young, charming and brilliant. If we were stuck with classical music, we hoped she might give it a more contemporary feel.

To insulate ourselves from criticism, we decided to put up four streams of music that would be available twenty-four hours a day online: one was all classical, one was all contemporary Canadian composers, one was all jazz, and one was all singer-songwriter. We figured that if the Constituency complained about the loss of classical music, we could point to the twenty-four-hour streaming.

"You want classical music?" we would ask. "Just go to the CBC website and stream it to your sound system. There it will be. No commercials. No annoying commentary. Just classical music, twenty-four hours a day."

Of course, this was no help at all. The classical music enthusiasts were not mollified. They moaned and wailed. I met one elderly gentleman at a cocktail reception who was much aggrieved by the changes. He berated me furiously. When I explained that there was a classical music stream available to him all the time, he looked at me blankly.

"It's a stream," I said.

"A stream?" he asked.

"Yes. Just plug your computer into your sound system and all will be well."

"A stream?" he asked again.

"Yes."

"A stream. I don't want to get wet."

Whenever I bumped into the head of the CRTC, the formidable Konrad von Finckenstein, he would berate me. Konrad von Finckenstein is very tall, very imposing and speaks with a thick Prussian accent. He is known in the industry as the Baron.

"Ach," he would say to me, "ven I get up in ze morning, zer is only vulgarity and noise on ze radio. Das ist nicht gut."

It is never a good idea to enrage the Chairman of the CRTC. Achtung baby.

Meanwhile the situation in Vancouver was going from bad to worse. The CBC Radio Orchestra, the last of its kind in North America, was made up of players from the Vancouver Symphony Orchestra (VSO). They supplemented their meagre incomes by playing for the CBC Radio Orchestra whenever it was called together. Eliminating the orchestra would be a blow to their incomes. It would also be another point of outrage for our detractors. The members of the VSO and the Constituency joined forces to stop us.

From deepest Vancouver, the war drums could be heard pounding. They beat out rhythmic invocations to the fearsome gods of quality and good taste. They mocked the new directions. They threatened savage reprisals. We sent Jennifer McGuire out to confront them. She explained the new directions, the fact that the CBC Radio Orchestra was the last of its kind in North America, the fact that we could no longer afford it. All to no avail. The torrent of abusive emails, letters and phone calls continued to pour into Audience Relations. Impossibly, it seemed, the classical music fans were even more intemperate than the curling fans.

Once again, I trooped down to the windowless warren of Audience Relations. The shell-shocked veterans looked, if anything, more frightened than they had during any previous scandal.

"How bad is it?" I asked, as gently as I could.

A little moan went up from the assembled. Their leader spoke. "It's not just that we are knuckleheads. It's worse. We are vulgar cretins."

The outpouring of rage had been savage. The classical music enthusiasts had been cruel and toxic in their remarks.

"They called me an idiot with no class, a stupid knuckle-dragging barbarian," one of Audience Relations' denizens complained.

"Worse. Much worse," said another. "We are killing the country. We are dumbing everything down. We are turning it over to savages and teenagers."

Many of the employees stared blankly into space, a little slack-jawed, burned out.

Through this dark period, we consoled ourselves with the thought that the vitriol would eventually end. We would finally eliminate the last of the classical music and create a coherent cultural experience. Then we would have a terrific offering that people could understand. Canadians would flock enthusiastically to the new Radio 2, musicians would be thrilled, the labels would be ecstatic and the critics would congratulate us. The darkest hour is just before the dawn.

To enhance what we were doing, we decided to expand the music strategy beyond radio. We thought we could—as we had tried with books—create a place that would be CBC Music, the Home of Music. Like CBC Books, it would feature everything that Canadians needed. There would be reviews, interviews with artists, searchable concerts, playlists of important musicians, opportunities to discuss and vote on the best music, contests, prizes, music news and an opportunity to purchase whatever was heard on the CBC. We planned to weave in video from the TV shows that dealt with music and make games for children. When Canadians came to CBC Music, it would all be there.

We already had some experience with creating a music portal. Radio 3 had been established a few years earlier. It was a music service that existed only online. The focus was Canadian independent bands of one variety or another. It featured lots of charming social media activity, including shared playlists, voting on favourites, band blogs, potted biographies of the musicians and easy access to the music. It had been a great success both in the independent music community and in the online world, winning many Webbies for its innovation and general hipness.

The work on CBC Music began with even more gusto than the work on CBC Books. The idea was to launch it at the same time as the final iteration of Radio 2 was launched. With the last of the classical music gone and CBC's commitment to contemporary Canadian music absolutely clear, we would be in a position to make a culturally coherent brand promise. We would provide Canadians with the broadest, most accessible, most carefully curated exploration of modern music available anywhere in the country. It would run consistently across radio, the Internet, social media and television. We hoped to make CBC Music one of the key new offers in CBC's transition to a content company.

Ultimately CBC Music would become the place to break new artists, promote them and build their fan bases. It would become what the CBC had been for Joni Mitchell, Leonard Cohen, Gordon Lightfoot and Ian and Sylvia. It would be the place where Canadian music—but not just Canadian music—was celebrated, explored, shared, tweeted, discussed and denounced. The renewed Radio 2 would act as the great promotional vehicle for CBC Music, while Radio 3 would be expanded to host the full variety of the new offering. CBC television would link its music strategy with that of CBC Music and the whole would be much greater than the sum of its parts. If the board was prepared to approve the changes, we thought we could be ready to roll out CBC Music in 2011. Alas, it was not to be. CBC Music was a bridge too far.

> All happy families are alike;
> each unhappy family is unhappy
> in its own way.
> Leo Tolstoy, *Anna Karenina*

eight
MONEY

IN MID-JULY 2008, I set off for France for my summer holiday. When I left, our financial projections showed that we were running about $12 million light on advertising revenue. This was principally due to the wretched performance of the Canadian teams, most notably the Maple Leafs, in the hockey playoffs. As well, the Toronto Blue Jays had failed to attract much interest from the audiences. But $12 million was not a particularly big deal in the context of English services as a whole, a $750-million operation. It represented a small proportion of our anticipated advertising revenues, and we had more than $20 million in free cash reserves. The problem was annoying, but not serious.

As the summer wore on, reports began to arrive that the $12-million problem was growing. By mid-August, it had grown to more than $20 million. Revenues had begun to dry up beyond the sports properties and were beginning to hit our projections for news and entertainment. We had created aggressive targets for 2008–09, so I was not surprised that we were having some difficulty. Still, I did not worry. The $20-million shortfall was covered by the $20-million reserve.

Then, as August turned into September, the situation darkened further. What had appeared as mere slippage in revenue during the summer now began to look like a collapse. The advertising agencies were dramatically slowing their commitments as the economy began to contract. The vibrations coming out of the United States were grim. Previously unknown financial products were causing severe difficulties. Credit and inter-bank lending were starting to dry up. Companies were starting to hoard cash in anticipation of a downturn.

By the middle of September, the $20-million problem had grown to $40 million. Our revenues were falling off a cliff. I phoned around to my friends at Global and CTV to see if they were experiencing the same thing. They said they were. Executives with many, many years in the advertising business said they had never seen anything like it. Nobody was buying. The entire business was grinding to a halt.

Outside our little parish, the economy went from bad to worse. Through September, the drumbeat of bad news from the United States increased in volume and intensity. It became clear that an economy built on debt and inflated house prices was beginning to unravel. The big banks that had encouraged the spending spree realized that many of the loans and mortgages they had issued would never be paid. They began to worry that the other financial institutions to which they regularly extended credit were in the same situation. They stopped lending to one another. Credit began to evaporate. Where three months earlier there had been money in abundance, now it was increasingly difficult to find.

The banking and credit crisis spread as a contagion through the rest of the economy. Solvent, well-performing companies could no longer get loans for simple operating requirements. They began freezing whatever cash reserves they had, knowing that they would have to finance their operations themselves. The first place they looked—as they do in all recessions—was to their advertising and marketing budgets. The cash is there, liquid and uncommitted. It is the easiest saving to make quickly.

As the economy continued to slow, panic began to appear in the markets. Throughout the industrial world, the stock exchanges registered precipitous and catastrophic losses. The Toronto Stock Exchange fell over seven hundred points in a single day. Life savings were wiped out. The value of great companies was cut in half. Major corporations had to be bailed out or they would fall into insolvency. The governments of Canada and the United States had to refinance the big automobile companies, and the U.S. moved to recapitalize the banks. Even the most sanguine economic observers realized that the situation was perilous. There was talk of a depression that might rival the 1930s.

Many of the companies that were in the deepest difficulty—General Motors, Chrysler, the retail banks, the credit card companies—are among the biggest advertisers. They had to pull back radically on their spending. The cuts hit us hard. By late October, the hole in our advertising revenue had reached $70 million. In less than three months, what had seemed like a small but manageable shortfall had morphed into a gigantic and cavernous pit. Seventy million dollars represents almost 10 percent of English services' total budget. It was a colossal amount of money.

At the CBC, the problem of managing revenue shortfalls is aggravated by the fact that it operates with no margins. Whatever money the Corporation has, it spends. Aside from the small reserves that are built into each year's budget, there are no profits or dividends to be forgone. In a normal company, the $70 million loss could be managed—at least in part—by earning less money. Not at the CBC. There are no earnings. This means that costs must be cut to keep the ship afloat.

While revenues can vanish quickly, costs cannot be removed at the same speed, since they consist for the most part of fixed contracts for rights, buildings, equipment and people. When the CBC's hockey revenues are not as large as the Corporation hopes, that is not the NHL's problem; it is the CBC's problem. The contracts for the television rights to the hockey games must still be honoured. The same is true of buildings. Whether the CBC's revenues are strong or weak, the facilities must be heated and maintained. The only cost that can be pulled quickly is people. When the CBC has financial problems, it inevitably has to make layoffs. The only question is how severe the layoffs need to be.

In the fall of 2008, despite the size of the shortfall, I hoped we would be able to minimize the job losses. If the downturn was cyclical, the best strategy might be simply to borrow some money to cover the losses and pay for the inevitable severance costs. We could then pay the loan back when the economy improved and the advertising revenues recovered. That way we could also maintain the momentum we had developed. It was discouraging to have to contemplate losing ground after all the efforts we had made to reverse the CBC's historic multi-year decline. After taking so much abuse and working so hard, we desperately wanted to approach the financial crisis in a way that would least damage the growth we had achieved. This would require imagination and daring, qualities that are often in short supply at the Corporation.

THE CBC IS quite unlike the companies it competes against. It is much more constrained, both in terms of how it can raise money and in its attitude toward doing so. Some of the limitations are imposed by legislation and some are self-imposed. Collectively they make it difficult not only to respond to financial problems, but in fact to manage the Corporation responsibly at all.

The CBC is a peculiar hybrid. It is a public broadcaster in the sense that it relies in part on public subsidies from the federal government. Radio, for example, carries no advertising and is completely dependent on public money. Television, on the other hand, receives more of its money from private sector sources than public ones. Approximately 55 percent of the total budget of television is raised through private sources, principally advertising revenues and fees paid by the cable companies for the Corporation's specialty channels—Bold, Documentary and, most importantly, CBC News Network. This puts CBC television in direct competition with the private networks.

The competition takes many forms. CBC television must compete for advertising revenue. To be successful at this, it must compete for audiences. To compete for audiences, it must compete for the best talent—hosts, journalists, producers, executives, engineers and managers. It must also compete for the best Canadian shows, searching out the best scripts, producers and stars. If it does not compete successfully, it will fail.

Over the years, there has been much lamentation about the requirement to compete. Many of the CBC's top executives have believed that competition is unhealthy, that it forces the Corporation to pander to Canadians to achieve larger audiences, that it forces it to abandon "quality." Inevitably this leads to a terrible schizophrenia within the culture of the organization, where people are asked to compete, but not too hard, where competition is to be pursued reluctantly, as a necessary evil. But asking people to compete while denigrating the desire to win is a recipe for failure. The reluctant competitor will almost always lose.

The alternative has been to moan about the inadequacy of government funding. Almost every president since the founding of the CBC has complained about the niggardliness of government support. They have noted—correctly—that the Corporation is by international standards poorly financed. They draw up charts and graphs showing the unfairness of it all; they make speeches decrying the problem; they create elaborate cultural and economic arguments to justify more funding. And then, nothing.

For the last forty years, the CBC has not only had no permanent increase in its parliamentary appropriation, it has been subject to rounds of savage cuts. In the mid-1990s, the Chrétien government stripped hundreds of millions from the budget. Since then, the slow drip-drip of inflation has eroded the value of what is left. The public subsidy shrinks and shrinks, with its purchasing power growing smaller with every year.

If past is prologue, it would seem best not to base any financial strategy for the Corporation on the assumption that new money will be forthcoming from the federal government. It has not happened in two generations. There is no reason to believe it will happen in future. In fact, to assume that anything other than further reductions are in the offing would be extremely imprudent.

That being the case, it seemed unwise to spend any time lobbying for an increase in the appropriation when I joined the CBC. Rather, it seemed a much better idea to focus on earning more money. It seemed wiser to focus on what all the other broadcasters have to do: convince Canadians to watch their shows, and advertisers and cable companies to pay for them. We settled, therefore, on a growth strategy. Beginning in 2006, after the lockout and the return of hockey, we focused hard—as any other company would—on "growing our business." That had never happened before at the CBC. In fact, the relentless decline had made a growth strategy seem absurd and impossible. Nevertheless, since the value of the public subsidy declined in real terms every year, it was essential to do something.

Fortunately the growth strategy fitted naturally and coherently into the audience strategy for television. If the singular cultural challenge was to make Canadian drama and entertainment shows that would connect with audiences, then pursuing growth in revenue and growth in audiences would be mutually supportive. The same was true of news. If the news audiences had to be rebuilt before the news could become more distinctive, there would be no contradiction between our programming goals and our financial ones. Unlike administrators of the past, I had no sense that there was a mutually exclusive choice between money and cultural success.

In thinking about revenues, we knew we had certain advantages over our competitors at CTV and Global. Whereas they bought most of their shows ready-made in the United States, we commissioned or produced most of our own from scratch, which meant that we could incorporate advertisers and sponsors directly into the shows as they were being produced. We could do product placements, website extensions or games and contests that were integral to the shows themselves and helped sell the sponsors' products. Advertisers were happy to pay a premium for that, and our competitors could not match it.

One of the best examples of how this could be done was *Kraft Hockeyville*. In the show and the online voting, Kraft was woven into everything. *Hockeyville* appeared on Kraft products in supermarkets, and everybody was pleased. To extend the idea further, we commissioned an episode of *Little Mosque on the Prairie* for Kraft. *Little Mosque* takes place in a fictional small town called Mercy,

Saskatchewan. In this particular episode, we had Mercy apply to be named Hockeyville.

Nobody else in Canada can do product placement like the CBC. As we grew better at it, we caught the attention of the advertising agencies, who became increasingly impressed with our imagination and responsiveness. In 2009 and again in 2010, *Marketing* magazine named CBC Media Player of the Year for its innovations. That had never happened before.

We also knew that there was room for revenue growth even if our audience share did not increase. Advertising spots are sold based on what are called CPMs (costs per thousand pairs of eyeballs delivered). When we compared our CPMs with those of Global and CTV, it was clear we were not getting as much money for the same thousand pairs of eyeballs. We were in fact at the bottom of the pack. There was room for us to raise our prices.

So the growth strategy focused on three pillars: growing audiences, innovating in servicing the advertisers and raising prices. We reckoned it would take us some time to execute the strategy, but at least it provided an alternative to endless lamentation about the inadequacy of government funding. Our plan, then, was to save ourselves. We would improve our finances by hard work and imagination, rather than relying on the kindness of strangers.

We knew the growth strategy flew in the face of decades of CBC culture and rhetoric. Over the years, the Corporation had created a whole series of elaborate impediments designed to make it harder to sell advertising. Many of these had a Mrs. Grundy quality to them. CBC policies, for example, forbade the Corporation from advertising dating services. The Corporation apparently took the view that it was improper to encourage lonely people to meet each other. The CBC's policies also placed bizarre restrictions on selling infomercials, political advertising and anything remotely religious.

To begin to unpack some of this, we decided to see if we could convince the board to abandon one of its silliest policies.

The CBC board is a peculiar institution. It is not like other boards. It does not hire and fire the CEO. It has, therefore, little power to initiate new directions or discipline the president. Its powers are essentially negative. It can block things from happening by refusing to vote for them. It can decline to endorse things. It can refuse to vote the budget; it can refuse to delegate spending authorities; it can decline to change policies. It can slow things down, but it cannot—unless the president wants to—accelerate things. And if the president does not want to accelerate things, there is nothing the board can do. The board cannot fire the president.

Unlike the members of most private sector television boards, the CBC's board members are rarely expert in the media businesses. In fact, they may not be expert in any businesses at all. They are typically friends of the government of the day, who are rewarded for their loyalty by enjoying the prestige of being on the CBC's board of directors. They are never briefed on what the government wants the CBC to do and how they should guide it. They are simply asked to sit on the board and do their best.

The board at this time was fairly typical. The wild Guy Fournier had been replaced as chairman by the sober Tim Casgrain. Casgrain is an accountant with an impressive business background in a number of different areas, none of which touched on media, let alone broadcasting. The same is true of the other members, most of whom were accountants or lawyers, all distinguished Canadians with long and successful careers who wanted to do the best they could for the CBC. The only two board members with experience in broadcasting were Peter Herrndorf, who had held my position many years earlier, and Trina McQueen, who had been head of news during the 1980s. They are both charter members of the Constituency.

Most of the board members do not watch television. To the extent they do, they watch news. The CBC, for them, is most centrally Tiny Perfect Radio. They often have little idea what is actually on TV. And like most of the previous presidents, they do not want a CBC preoccupied with ratings and grubbing for advertising revenue.

The policy we wanted changed related to infomercials. Infomercials are long-form commercials that are typically didactic in character. We had been approached over the years to see whether we would consider putting them on after 2:00 AM so that people could sell things to insomniacs. Most recently, we had been asked by a

Korean manufacturer of pots and pans and by Time-Life Records whether we would be prepared to sell them infomercial time. We reckoned we might make as much as $5 million, enough to commission a full drama series or hire another seventy or seventy-five employees (or save seventy or seventy-five jobs).

I explained all this to the board. I explained that Time-Life wanted to sell music box sets from the 1970s and that the Korean pots and pans manufacturer needed to explain his pots and pans in some detail to sell them (apparently they constituted a complex cooking system). There was nothing offensive or compromising about either offer.

The board rumbled. Herrndorf led the charge, arguing that infomercials were a bad idea. They were incompatible with the CBC brand. They lacked gravitas.

Gravitas?

I asked the board members if they were familiar with the ads we were running. "Currently we are touting Lakota medicine. We also have speculative mining ventures and reverse home mortgages designed to turn old people into spendthrifts."

The board members looked blankly at me.

"I think you'll agree with me that pots and pans are better than these products."

"No," Herrndorf insisted. "Infomercials are not right for the CBC."

"How about I promise to review every infomercial personally before it is accepted, to ensure that it is not vulgar."

"No," Herrndorf repeated.

The rest of the board agreed with Peter Herrndorf. The policy on infomercials did not change, and the $5 million went elsewhere.

In a similar vein, the CBC's policies ban political ads outside election periods. If the Liberals, the Conservatives, the NDP or anybody else (the Raving Loony Party) want to buy ads on the CBC to advance their views, they cannot do so unless an election is in progress. The chief electoral officer of Canada and the chief electoral officers of all the provinces have no problem with political advertising. The CRTC has no problem. All of the other broadcasters accept political ads. Arguably they are of value because they contribute to public debate on the issues of the day. Refusing to carry them seems incompatible with basic standards of freedom of expression.

Again I trooped down to the board to explain why the CBC's policy on political advertising was restrictive and unwise. I noted that, like infomercials, political ads were probably worth another $5 million to our beleaguered treasury. This time, they asked me to leave the room so that they could debate the matter in private. When they had finished their deliberations, they advised me that they regarded my views as unsound and declined to change the policy. Taking political ads, they explained, was incompatible with the CBC's independence.

The financial problems created by the sense that the CBC should be above gross money-grubbing are compounded by its organizational status. Unlike any other broadcaster trying to adapt to rapidly changing circumstances, it has no access to capital. It can neither issue shares nor go to the bank and borrow money. It has absolutely no ability to raise money independently of the government. This means it cannot make investments in new businesses or acquire existing ones. In fact, even if the CBC had money of its own, it could not buy or sell a single share without approval of the federal cabinet.

This freezes the Corporation and makes it very difficult for it to succeed. For example, all the big broadcasting groups own significant blocks of specialty services. CTV, Global, Rogers, Corus and Astral own multiple channels. They have assembled all of these channels not only because they are excellent businesses in their own right, but also because the various businesses help each other. When a group owns many channels, it can share the rights costs and back office costs among them. It can, as well, bundle the advertising inventory and make better pitches to the agencies. This allows them to improve their cost structure and diversify their revenues, making them financially more stable.

When the Alliance Atlantis assets came up for sale in 2006, they included the History Channel and Showcase (an alternative drama channel). Both would have been excellent complements to the CBC's documentaries and drama, as Newsworld is for the news department. They would have helped stabilize the CBC's finances (potentially reducing its dependence on government), expanded its ability to serve Canadians and improved its cost structure. The CBC could not even contemplate bidding on them because it could not access the capital markets without government approval.

If it decided to seek government approval for such a transaction, and assuming the government wanted to help, the processes would be too slow. They would involve working with the relevant government departments to prepare the necessary documents and then seeking approval from the federal cabinet, an extremely laborious and time-consuming business. It would be unimaginably fast to conclude such a process in six months. While private broadcasters interested in bidding on such assets can typically line up financing in a few weeks, the CBC would still be wandering around Ottawa months after the seller had sold. Ted Rogers famously bought Citytv over a weekend.

These fantastic encumbrances aggravate the CBC's already fragile finances by rendering it incapable of making effective decisions in a timely fashion. All these problems emerged in even higher relief as the Corporation confronted the financial collapse and economic meltdown of 2008. To make matters even more challenging, we were dealing with a new president right in the middle of the financial crisis.

THE ANNOUNCEMENT THAT Hubert T. Lacroix would become the new president of the CBC in January 2008 had provoked a frenzy of curiosity. I had never heard of him. When I called round to friends in Montreal media circles, nobody knew who he was. The same was true in Toronto. His name meant nothing to people in the broadcasting, program production or new media industries. I drew a similar blank with my investigations in Ottawa. He appeared to be unknown to people in the Conservative Party and the upper mandarinate. He was a great mystery.

As my research continued, I discovered that he was a well-respected lawyer at the distinguished firm of Stikeman Elliott. He had an MBA from McGill, where he had coached the women's basketball team. He was also an occasional basketball commentator on Radio-Canada. His only other connection to the media business seemed to be that he had helped the de Gaspé Beaubien clan sell some radio stations. None of this seemed terribly relevant to being president of the CBC.

Generally speaking, presidents of the CBC need to know three important things. They need to know something about the media, and ideally the broadcasting business; they need to know how to run a large corporation; and they need to be wise in the arcane and Byzantine ways of Ottawa. Most previous CBC presidents had at least two of these three qualifications.

Robert Rabinovitch had been deputy minister of communications and chief operating officer of Claridge (which owned Cineplex Odeon, the Sports Network, Discovery Channel and other media properties, as well as the Montreal Expos). His predecessor, Perrin Beatty, had been minister of communications and much else besides in the Mulroney government. Gérard Veilleux (president from 1989 to 1994) had been deputy minister and secretary of the Treasury Board in the Trudeau and Mulroney governments. Pierre Juneau (1982 to 1989) had been head of the National Film Board and chairman of the CRTC. All of them had some passing knowledge of media issues (except Veilleux), considerable management experience and a deep understanding of Ottawa. Hubert T. Lacroix's background did not resemble that of his predecessors.

In December 2007, just before he took up his new duties, he invited me to have dinner with him at his club in Montreal. It was the beginning of winter and very cold. Snow was beginning to fall as I arrived at the Mount Royal Club on Sherbrooke Street. I was let into a private room, where he was waiting.

Hubert T. Lacroix is tall. He has the build of a marathon runner. His hair is thinning and combed over in a sandy-coloured, greying fringe. He affects a three-day stubble, which makes him look slightly grizzled. He greeted me warmly.

We exchanged the usual pleasantries. How are you? Congratulations on your appointment. Thank you. I have heard good things about you. Me too. I look forward to working with you. Yes. Me too. It is a great organization. There are important challenges. Very exciting. Yawp. Yawp.

Finally, when enough time had passed, I pushed the conversation to where I really wanted to go. It was my assumption that there must be some special reason why he was appointed. His background was too far from the norm for him to be considered a routine choice. There had to be a secret and compelling reason why the new Conservative government had chosen him. There had to be a new vision involved or a new set of directions for the future of the Corporation. I asked him what he wanted to accomplish as president.

"I would like a great team," he said.

"A great team?" I asked.

"Yes," he said, "I am a great believer in teams."

He sipped his glass of white wine. I would never see him have more than a half a glass of wine.

"Well, I agree. Certainly a great team is always a good thing," I replied, wondering where the conversation was going.

"Yes," he said, "a great team is very important. Teamwork is the key to success."

He went on for a while longer extolling the virtues of teamwork. I thought perhaps he had not quite understood my question.

"Teamwork, yes indeed," I said, "But what would you like to accomplish for the Corporation? What would you like to get done?"

"Well, as I said, I would like a great team."

It was clear that we were not making much progress. I wanted to know if he had particular views about sports or news or entertainment or radio, but he seemed to be playing his cards close to his chest. I was not getting any sense of his goals for the CBC. I decided to change tack and see if I could flush him out another way.

"What did you agree with the prime minister about the future of the Corporation?" I asked.

He looked a little startled.

"The prime minister?" he asked.

"Yes. How did you leave it with him?"

I wondered if he was being evasive because his mandate was a secret.

"I did not talk to the prime minister."

"No?"

"No."

"Well, what about the minister of heritage? What did you agree with him?"

"I did not talk to the minister of heritage."

"I see."

It seemed a good time to move the conversation along. It was becoming a little awkward. We moved on to his enthusiasm for basketball, when he might come down to Toronto, how he would like to be briefed and the prospects for Les Glorieux. It was all friendly and salubrious, but I left uncertain where we might be going.

When Lacroix arrived at the Corporation, I organized a number of detailed briefings for him on all aspects of English services. We explained the sorry history of television's long decline, the focus on popular Canadian shows, the growth strategy and its accompanying revenue targets, the revival of news and its integration into a single multi-platform news offer, the recommitment to local shows, the book and music initiatives. Hubert Lacroix listened carefully and pronounced himself a supporter of the directions we were pursuing.

I was reassured. Our first dinner had not filled me with confidence that he had a clear sense of the direction he wanted. If he agreed with me, however, I had no cause for complaint. We should get on very well indeed. At the same time, I tried to be clear that the path we were following was regarded by many people, including many members of his own board, as unsound. He needed to be prepared for the criticism.

We had already had indications that the board might be unhappy. Some of the longer-serving members had been doubtful from the very beginning about the emphasis on popular shows. A number of the newer ones shared their concerns. They feared that English services had moved too far away from the core of its mandate as a public broadcaster. They were worried that there was no arts programming on television, that classical music was being eliminated from the radio, that the new reality shows were indistinguishable from those on the privates. They wanted a more traditional CBC, one that stood for more sophisticated, more cerebral fare.

In his early meetings with the board, the new president was told about their anxieties. He shared their views with me. I, of course, pooh-poohed their arguments. We went through all of the traditional reasons why I felt we were on the right course. I noted as well the remarkable growth in audiences we had achieved, the improvement in employee morale and the generally improving perception of the Corporation among Canadians at large. Even our critics and the other broadcasters were showing us some grudging respect.

Hubert Lacroix was in a tough spot. I sensed that he was struggling with the overall direction of English services. The board pulled one way. I pulled another. Something might have to give. At the board meetings the members would meet with the new president in private, where they would express their concerns. In May 2008, only five months into his presidency, the board held in-camera meetings in Quebec City. I do not know what they discussed, since I was not invited to participate. Afterward, I was told that they had once again expressed their reservations about the direction of English services. They reiterated their desire that we get back to being a "real" public broadcaster.

The new president was getting quite a bit of this on all fronts. Governor General Michaëlle Jean had advised him that we needed to get back to basics. In her case, this meant putting the Governor General's Performing Arts Awards back on TV. We had chopped them some time back because they made for poor television and nobody watched the show. Nevertheless, the governor general's views are not to be taken lightly.

Nor, for that matter, were those of other important members of the Constituency. Patrick Watson, the famous co-host of *This Hour Has Seven Days* and ex-chairman of the CBC's board, had written that "the real public broadcaster will seek out and program the best that Canadians have to offer, in the arts ... science, journalism, documentary, policy discussion, comedy and theatre (when did you last see anything from Canada's prolific regional stages on CBC?)... It will leave big ticket sports to the private broadcasters... while taking its cameras into the myriad wonderful sports venues that really occupy citizens—like children's soccer."

In a similar vein, Carole Taylor, another distinguished past chair, opined, "For me, my preference is to do broadcasting that is different from what the privates do, that is not going for ratings but is providing a service that cannot be found anywhere else... I think there is a danger people... look at ratings numbers as a measure of success... If you do that, that inevitably draws public broadcasting into straight competition with American shows."

Hubert Lacroix heard from many sides that English services was losing its way.

The financial crisis would test his resolve, as it would that of the board and everyone else. Financial crises have a wonderful way of exposing all the fissures and cracks, driving wedges into the papered-over compromises. When it comes time to choose what to keep and what to let go, everyone's real preferences surface. The financial crisis would force everyone to show their hand and decide between the quick and the dead.

IN SEPTEMBER OF 2008, before the full horror of the crisis became apparent, we imagined that we were facing a steep but manageable cyclical downturn. If that was the case, then the key strategic problem was to figure out if we could bridge it without compromising the growth strategy. If we could get a loan or a line of credit, we would be able to minimize the size of the cuts we would have to make and retain more of our shows and people. When the downturn ended, and the advertising revenues recovered, we would pay off the loan.

That seemed simple enough, except, of course, that we had no access to the capital markets. We could not, therefore, go to the banks and borrow the money, so at the beginning of 2009 the board authorized the Corporation to approach the government for a bridge. We reasoned that the government could, if it wanted, simply advance the parliamentary appropriation faster than it normally would. That way we could use the "extra" money for the bridge, without having to make a greater call on the Treasury. It seemed a modest request and one that would help avert significant layoffs.

By the beginning of 2009, it had become clear that we were in a really tough spot. The revenue situation had become unbearably grim. The $70-million hole, which was only the English side of the problem, looked like it might become larger still. If there was ever a time to seek a lifeline, it was now. But regardless of the size of the lifeline, we would still need to make painful cuts.

In January 2009, the Corporation made a formal request to the government for a bridge. The president met with the responsible officials and the minister of heritage on a number of occasions. All the arguments were laid out. We explained that we needed the money to help cover our losses until the economy recovered. We explained that we needed extra money to pay the severance costs of the employees whose jobs were to be cut. This latter point was particularly important. If there was no money to cover the severances, we would have to cut even further to generate it. These cuts in turn would generate more severance costs. And on and on in a vicious downward spiral.

At the end of February, the government said no. Why the government declined was never made completely clear, certainly not to me. They just said no.

Hubert Lacroix became upset. He could not understand why we had been turned down. At the end of the month, he made a speech at the Empire Club in Toronto and said, quite simply, "What I am looking for, as the president of CBC/Radio-Canada appointed by this government, are the same tools that others in the industry have to manage... Canada's largest cultural institution through this unprecedented period. I have asked for a meeting with the prime minister to explain the impact this decision will have on our services."

Alas, it was to no avail. Prime Minister Stephen Harper declined to see him. He declined, in fact, to respond at all.

Meanwhile our advertising revenues had sagged so far that it was clear drastic action needed to be taken. Even our most lucrative property, *Hockey Night in Canada,* was in trouble. The problem was compounded by the fact that the Toronto Maple Leafs decided to continue their long and venerable tradition of failure, missing the playoffs yet again in 2008. When Toronto does not make the play-offs, revenues decline sharply. This is partly because the Toronto audience—Leafs Nation—tunes out, and partly because the buyers, the vast majority of whom are in Toronto, grow depressed and buy less. The same thing happened in the 2009 season.

Thus our worst fears came to pass. The recession deepened though the winter of 2008 and into 2009. The Leafs duked it out for last place in the division, and almost last place in the league as a whole. Every bad thing that could happen did happen. Even the other Canadian teams—except the Montreal Canadiens—expired in the early rounds of the playoffs or failed to show up at all. Canadians throughout English Canada switched their interest away from the Game. The advertisers pulled their belts tighter and tighter. The projected margins vanished, and *Hockey Night in Canada* became a drag on the network as a whole.

With enormous reluctance, in the middle of February 2009, amidst the raging storm, I dismissed Dave Scapillati, the head of sales. The decision was difficult. Was it wise to unload the captain when the ship was taking on water? Scapillati was a charming guy. We had worked closely on the NHL deal and on rebuilding the sales force. I was extremely reluctant to see him go.

We replaced him with Scott Moore, the ebullient head of sports. Moore is jovial, tenacious and competitive. He had come to the CBC a couple of years earlier and had made a big impression with his energy and infectious enthusiasm. When I asked him to consider taking over, I understood that it was like being asked to pull the boat back just as it is about to go over the falls. If you fail—and fail you certainly may—you will still be blamed. Nobody will understand how perilous and difficult the task was.

He told me that he went home that evening and consulted his father, a successful businessman. His father advised against accept-ing. It was a sure loser, he said. Moore had a glass of wine. His wife was doubtful. Moore had another glass of wine. He was doubtful. He had one more glass of wine. Finally, sufficiently fortified, he decided to agree. The next morning, much to my pleasure and astonishment, he said yes. Like me, he is a man who savours a futile gesture.

Moore was joined by the equally remarkable Jack Tomik, who agreed to act as a consultant. Tomik had been the head of sales at Global during its glory days. He had made so much money for Global that he was widely regarded as a magician. Between the two of them, they set about trying to put a floor under our losses. They began by repricing our advertising inventory and restructuring the department. It was a daring and difficult set of manoeuvres to try and execute in the middle of the ongoing economic collapse.

WITH NO LIFELINE from the government and a new team in sales, we turned our attention to the inevitable requirement to make cuts. This would be where the real tension points would arise. This is where we would see the real fights over the role and meaning of the CBC. The debate about what to jettison and what to keep would reveal what people thought mattered most about the Corporation. Inevitably the ancient cleavages and contradictions would re-emerge: popular or elitist; small town or big city; radio or TV; French or English; local news or national; *Battle of the Blades* or *Opening Night*. The resulting debate would flush out where the board and the president stood on the future of the Corporation.

The debate would inevitably be complicated by political considerations in both the large- and small-*p* senses of "political." The government was in a minority and struggling with the overall financial crisis, and would want us to cut in a way that would cause the least political fallout. We assumed that their preference would be to maintain local jobs and the radio service to the maximum extent possible. From the government's point of view, cuts that were not visible immediately were best, which would mean focusing on the entertainment shows on television, since cuts there might result simply in fewer shows and episodes. Job losses here hit the independent production community, but not the CBC itself.

The board's normal instinct would be to agree with this general approach. The majority of them had been appointed by the government and would not want to compound the problems facing it.

Besides, it had become increasingly clear that although they had formally approved the overall strategy for English services, their hearts lay elsewhere. Like most members of the Constituency, they believed that television was secondary and that what mattered most was radio and the small towns. They were of the old school, in their heart of hearts believing that ballet was better than situation comedies and classical music trumped hip-hop.

Within English services, the view was quite different. There was a strong feeling that since the growth strategy was finally yielding results, we should stay the course. It had been years since CBC television had grown its audience. After thirty or forty years of continuous decline, when we had finally turned the corner and even beaten Global in prime time with our Canadian shows, it seemed unimaginably sad to have to go backwards. We also knew that if we hacked aggressively at the TV schedule, we would compromise our ability to generate more revenues in future. We would, in fact, end up digging ourselves a bigger hole.

CFO OF ENGLISH services Neil McEneaney and I spent enormous amounts of time looking to see how we might manage the cuts with the least damage to the future of CBC English services. McEneaney is a terrific financial advisor. He was determined to manage the problem in ways that compromised the growth strategy as litt le as possible.

To assist our deliberations, we built a number of financial models that showed the likely outcomes of different choices. The models specified where we would land if we cut one thing, but not another, if revenues recovered more slowly rather than sooner, if we placed more or fewer shows in inventory, if our severance costs were at one level or another. The models also showed the cash requirements associated with each choice, and the size of the loans or credit facilities required. McEneaney worked endlessly, green eye shades in position, sharp pencil at the ready, to make sure we understood clearly our choices and made the wisest choices possible.

We concluded, not surprisingly, that it would be better to close the small stations in the parts of the country that were already over-served. How did we justify three stations in New Brunswick and none in Hamilton? If we dropped two, the province would still be better served than Hamilton, which has a larger population than the whole province. Similarly, we should jettison the block of pre-school shows for children in the mornings. They carried no advertising and had very small audiences. Besides, there were alternatives. Treehouse, a specialty channel owned by Corus, provided similar fare for the same age group, also without ads. We looked too at unloading the Cross-Cultural Fund. It was worth $10 million and was nice to have, but there had been very, very few successes out of it. It was just too difficult to make shows that worked effectively in both the French and English markets.

We went further. How could we justify the gigantic transmission tower infrastructure? It is the largest in the world. There are more than seven hundred towers supporting television and radio transmitters all over the country. In the 1970s the government decided that every town with a population of more than five hundred people should be able to receive CBC over the air. That was when the CBC was rich, and even then the government had to give the CBC money to build all the towers. Now the CBC is poor. Besides, there are all sorts of ways to receive CBC signals now—satellite radio and satellite TV—that never existed in the 1970s. Maybe it was time to enter the twenty-first century.

We looked again with longing at the possibility of changing our policies on infomercials and political ads.

We felt strongly that the focus should be on saving—as much as possible—the prime-time schedule on TV, the major national radio shows and the regional news and "drive" shows in the biggest markets in the country. We focused on finding cuts that would result in the smallest erosion of our overall audiences. The important thing was to save the dog and sacrifice the tail.

The French services shared that view. I had discussed the matter extensively with my counterpart, the charming Sylvain Lafrance. We felt it was important to have a common position. That way it would be easier to resist what we were sure would be the board's instincts to do the things we felt to be wrong for the Corporation, the things that would further weaken it but be politically easier to swallow. We feared the triumph of the Constituency.

The first board meetings on the cuts began in early March 2009. The conversation went precisely where I feared it might. The exchanges were often difficult.

"Perhaps," a board member would suggest, "we could pull down one or two of the big prime-time shows. They are expensive. A couple of series could save $10 million."

"Yes," I would reply, "but we could just as easily find $10 million by cancelling the Cross-Cultural Fund and not compromise the entertainment strategy."

"But surely that is what we are most centrally about: encouraging better understanding between French and English Canada."

"Yes, we are. But if we cut our successful shows, we also lose more advertising revenue. Not so with the Cross-Cultural Fund."

"Really? Are you really saying that *Battle of the Blades* is more important than bridging the Two Solitudes?"

"Yes," I would reply, "I suppose I am."

Similar exchanges would occur around radio. I would suggest we get rid of the small stations.

"How," I would ask, "can we justify four stations in Newfoundland and none in Hamilton?"

"These people don't have much," the board would reply. "The people in Gander have nothing else."

"True, but neither do Canadians in hundreds of other small towns."

"Two wrongs would not make a right."

The same problems arose everywhere we turned. The board members were not wrong. They simply had a very different view from mine about what mattered most.

In fairness to them, the exercise was very difficult. They had almost no room to manoeuvre. Many of the costs were locked in and impossible to shed in the short term. At the same time, the government—the principal and only shareholder of the Corporation—had not given them any direction when they were appointed. It never said this matters to us but not that, please safeguard one thing but not another. They had absolutely no idea what really mattered to the government. To the extent it had any views, they were general and communicated in gnomic private utterances. "Try not to cut radio and the small stations" was apparently the whispered instruction, transmitted secretly in the dead of night.

To compound the difficulties of the exercise, the board decided to continue to hold most of its discussions in-camera; they would ask Sylvain and me to leave the room while they discussed the Corporation's priorities. They would sit there with the president, reviewing what needed to be done. It was hard for Sylvain and me to imagine how those conversations might be unfolding. With nobody in the room having any deep understanding of broadcasting, the CBC, its economics or its competitors, we were concerned that the outcome of their deliberations would end up being arbitrary. As Sylvain described it, the whole process was "hallucinant."

Throughout that period, Hubert Lacroix and I would meet privately from time to time in his office to discuss the situation. His office is spartan, the furniture modern. There is an enormous painting by James Lahey on the wall that shows a vast horizon of the sky and the sea with no people.

"The board is not happy," he would say. "They want to save the small stations."

"That's unwise," I would reply.

"They don't think so and neither do I. I have made it very clear that local matters to me."

"You said you supported the strategy. Why would we cut the entertainment shows to save the small stations?"

"The board doesn't see it that way."

"Then you should convince them otherwise. It's hardly fair to characterize me as anti-local. I convinced everyone we should expand the local television news when everyone thought it was a dead dog."

As the exchanges went on they became more and more heated. I felt betrayed. The president found me difficult and insubordinate. We clashed repeatedly. I began to doubt that he was serious enough about endorsing the directions we were pursuing. I feared he was joining the Constituency.

"The board wants to keep the Cross-Cultural Fund," he went on, "and so do I."

"It doesn't work very well and it's pure cash. We can cut it and not incur layoffs," I replied.

"I believe in building bridges between the English and French cultures," he went on.

"Me too. I have done more and tried more than anyone else."

"It has to stay."

The conversations became more intemperate. The president grew increasingly frosty. I became more difficult. As they unfolded, they began to reveal the gulf between us. They began as well to erode our relationship.

TO ADD TO the CBC's woes, the government decided to subject it to a strategic review of its budget. It was asked to identify what it would do if the parliamentary appropriation was cut 5 percent: which programs it would shed, which services it would suspend, which stations it would close. The parliamentary appropriation was roughly $1 billion, so the cuts would amount to a further $50-million pressure on the Corporation.

Quite apart from the difficulty of having to contemplate a further $50-million cut while we were navigating the worst economic crisis since the Great Depression, the request significantly compounded the complexity of the problem. We now needed to expand the model Neil McEneaney had built to contemplate further reductions. By now McEneaney and I were inseparable. We seemed to spend all of our time huddled together, poring over spreadsheets in darkened boardrooms. Fortunately, McEneaney is positive, even in the face of terrible problems. Many CFOs are gloomy, even in the face of great success.

The outside world grew increasingly remote. We sat endlessly exchanging ideas.

"What if we eliminated all the transmission towers?" I asked. "What if we simply said we cannot afford them anymore?"

"How do people get their services?" Neil asked.

"By satellite," I replied.

"Right," he said and began querying his computer. More spreadsheets emerged, showing the costs of maintaining the towers and the transmitters. The numbers looked good.

"But if we abandon them, we will have to decommission them," he noted, "and that will cost money."

"Maybe we can sell them?" I suggested.

"Maybe in Toronto and Montreal, but who wants towers in the middle of nowhere?"

On and on we went. We pored through everything we could imagine, searching for ways to accommodate the board's views, while not compromising the growth strategy. We wanted also to minimize the impact on the employees. We lived only for the numbers. It was like a fever dream, pressing, intense, vivid and frightening. No matter where we looked, horrid choices confronted us. No matter how hard we worked, we could find nothing but painful and ruinous options. We grew increasingly miserable and worried.

As we worked away on responding to the economic crisis, it became clear that we would have to reduce total expenditures across the Corporation by more than $170 million and eight hundred jobs. English services would have to absorb $80 million of cuts and get rid of four hundred jobs. These were enormous numbers, more than 10 percent of the Corporation's entire budget. If we also had to absorb the $50 million in reductions to the parliamentary appropriation, we would be really cooked.

And beyond these disastrous possibilities, there was another $60 million up in the air. Early in his presidency, Robert Rabinovitch had convinced the Liberal government of the time to increase the CBC's appropriation by $60 million for programming. This was a significant accomplishment, since the Liberals had earlier subjected the Corporation to the largest cuts in its history. The $60 million amount was supposed to increase every year by another $60 million for a further three years, augmenting the Corporation's budget by a total of $240 million. The last three years never happened, and the original $60 million was never put into the CBC's "base." Rather, the government had to decide every year in the context of the budget whether the Corporation would once again receive the $60 million. Every year, representations had to be made, along with submissions to the Department of Finance and the Treasury Board, for the money.

It was never clear as we approached the Strategic Review whether the $60 million would be forthcoming the following year. When asked, the government was silent. So we did not fully understand the fiscal context within which the Strategic Review and the economic crisis cuts were being considered. If the $60 million was not forthcoming and the government took the $50 million from the Strategic Review, and you factored in $170 million of cuts on top of that, the CBC would have to make expenditure reductions of almost $300 million, or roughly 20 percent of its base. The uncertainty and the size of the potential cuts were extremely intimidating.

To approach all this in an orderly way, we focused first on the most urgent and difficult set of cuts, the $170 million in lost revenue from the economic crisis. The others we decided to address later.

To begin to prepare everyone, I started with management. The most difficult place would be news. They were in the middle of the biggest reorganization in CBC history. Now it would not be enough that Jennifer McGuire had to reorganize the entire news department. It would not be enough that she had to rethink all the shows, redesign all the workflows, reassign all the egos. Now, in the middle of everything else, she would have to manage a significant cut. We met in my office.

"You have to chop $7 million out of the news budget," I said.

"That's at least seventy jobs," she replied.

"Yes," I allowed.

"We don't have enough resources as it is," she said.

"I know."

"You understand that everyone is doing two jobs: keeping the existing newscasts on the air and planning the new ones?"

"I know."

"You understand that we actually need *more* people, at least for the next year, while we make the transition?"

"I know."

Jennifer looked at me as though she were inspecting a particularly malevolent and obdurate enigma.

I adjusted the arms of the Don Cherry action figure that sat on my coffee table. It seemed particularly important that they be placed at the correct angle to the plastic replica of Blue, his dog that sat by his feet.

"This is very difficult," she said.

"I know," I replied.

"I have no idea how to do it," she went on. "I scarcely knew how to get done what we are already doing."

"Think about it," I said unhelpfully. The truth was that I had no good ideas as to how she should approach the problem. I had proposed to the president that we take two cuts separated by a year to give Fort News a chance to get through its reorganization without having to reduce its resources at the same time. Once the relaunch was complete and the new shows had settled down, we could take money out of the news department. He had said no.

McGuire left my office looking shaken.

To prepare the employees, and in the interest of transparency and fairness, I briefed everyone in English services on March 26, 2009. It seemed only fair to level with them, since it was their livelihoods that were at stake. Apparently this was a departure from the way these things were normally approached at the CBC. The tradition was to tell nobody anything until all the decisions were taken and the pink slips were ready.

On that horrid day, I appeared at the Glenn Gould Studio. The place was packed. Everybody knew what was coming. The meeting was carried across the country by closed circuit. The room crackled with anxiety and unhappiness. When I stood up to speak, an anticipatory hush settled across the rows of worried faces. I felt like the Angel of Death.

I said, "The situation is very bad. Our revenues are collapsing. The advertisers and agencies are not buying."

The room was completely silent. There wasn't a cough or a whisper.

"We are not the only ones in this boat. The situation appears to be—if anything—even worse at Global and CTV. Unfortunately, we have no idea how deep the recession will be or how long it will last. You follow the financial news. You can see what's happening in the States. You know about the bail-outs and the collapse of the stock markets."

Still there was not a sound in the room. I looked around. My mouth was dry. Everyone looked grim.

"We will have to make some very deep cuts. We need to eliminate four hundred jobs in English services."

There was a collective intake of breath.

I tried to soften the blow. "This does not mean there will be four hundred layoffs. We are trying to minimize layoffs. We won't fill vacant positions. We have created a voluntary retirement plan..."

I went on. The room seemed to shift around me. The fear had become palpable. It broke my heart.

Over the next month, I set off to see the people who were most likely to be affected. It seemed only fair to explain to them personally why they might lose their jobs. It was through no fault of theirs. They were the victims of circumstance. They were going to lose their jobs not because they had failed to perform well. To the contrary, many of the people who were to lose their jobs had worked very hard and produced excellent results. They were going to lose their jobs because bankers in New York had over-reached. They were going to lose their jobs because American financial regulators and ratings agencies had failed to do theirs.

I stopped in at the CBC office in Saint John, New Brunswick. It occupies just a single floor in a nondescript office building. It has a radio studio and a tiny television studio. They produce a local morning and afternoon show on radio. They also do hits into the New Brunswick television news that originates in Fredericton. They produce a remarkable quantity of material for such a small group.

As the only counterweight to the Irving family, the CBC is very special in New Brunswick. Apart from owning all the gas stations, food stores and major businesses in New Brunswick, the Irvings control the local newspapers and radio stations. It may be the most concentrated media market in the Western world. The CBC is the only independent, alternative voice.

We gathered in the boardroom, which, like the office, is very small. I explained the situation and said that some of them would likely lose their jobs. At this point, we could not say who because it would depend on bumping arrangements, on whether some people took early retirement, and such like. They looked grim.

One young journalist spoke up. "If we could sell ads," he said, "perhaps we could save some jobs and keep up the journalism."

"No," I replied, like an idiot. "That's not our policy. Radio is commercial-free."

"But why not?" he persisted. "Why not make an exception?"

He was very young, in his mid-twenties. He loved what he did. He sparkled with commitment and enthusiasm. He lived to do journalism and tell the truth. Without seniority, he would probably be among the first to go.

"Our policy," I repeated, "is not to take ads. I don't claim it makes any sense in this circumstance, but it is our policy."

One of the older journalists chimed in. "You know we are the only alternative to the Irvings," he said.

"I know," I admitted.

"So?" he went on.

They were right. I should have taken up their argument, but I did not. I was already at daggers drawn with head office and the board on where to cut. My views were regarded as too competitive and too commercial. This fight really seemed too much. But it was a mistake. They were right and I was wrong.

"So, nothing," I said. "You understand that to propose such a thing would be to propose desecrating the holiest of Holies?"

"Yes," the older journalist replied. "But if not, what is your alternative?"

I had no alternatives. We would cut the station. The journalism would be reduced. The level of service would decline. The voice of the Irvings would become more dominant.

I felt not only like the Angel of Death but like a fraud as well. They were right, and I was too timid to take up their cause. Some boss.

The conversation carried on for a while longer. They could see how unhappy and disconsolate I had become. Then it turned. They decided to cheer me up.

"You know," the older journalist said, "you're the only senior executive in my thirty years here who has come to talk directly to us when these things happen. Normally they hide. Thank you."

Thank you?

They thanked me for coming and telling them I was going to cut their jobs. They even gave me a special Saint John coffee mug and bucked me up. It was remarkable.

Back in Ottawa, the debate about where to cut ground on. The board seemed to be in almost continuous session. It met in late March, a couple of times in April, and what seemed permanently in May. Sylvain Lafrance and I would reiterate our belief that the board should safeguard the big things and cast the little ones adrift. We would plow through the same arguments.

"Surely you could chop one show in prime time and save the little stations," a board member would say.

"Yes, we could. But when the economy recovers where will we be? We will have a little station that yields no revenue and no way of making up lost ground."

"But surely we should be for the small towns," the member would counter.

"Why?" I would reply. "Is it more important that they have local service than the big ones?"

"That is an unfair way to put the choice."

"Why? What is our policy? If we want to serve little underserved towns, we should wind up *Metro Morning* in Toronto and set up in Wawa and Sturgeon Falls, places that have nothing else."

The board members found all of this arrogant and unhelpful. They would thank me for my views and boot me out of the room to continue deliberating in private. Occasionally the president would emerge, looking grim, and scowl. The conversation was clearly difficult. Apparently they would go over the same ground again and again.

My relationship with Hubert Lacroix—and, I presumed, with the board—continued to deteriorate.

"You need to focus more on what the board wants," Lacroix said to me one day.

"I know what they want; they want to go backwards."

"Don't be absurd. They are the board. They are, in effect, the Corporation. Not you."

He was right, of course. But the prospect of going backwards appalled me. After working so hard and suffering endless name-calling and public abuse, I could not bear the thought. The CBC was finally winning and nobody seemed to care.

The discussions were demoralizing. I wondered, not for the first time, why I bothered. I thought seriously that it might be time to go.

WHILE THE DETAILS of the cuts continued to preoccupy the board, we still needed to find some money to help "bridge" the revenue decline and pay for the severances. Since the government had declined to help us with a line of credit, we had to look elsewhere. When we looked, we could find only one thing to sell that might generate enough cash to cover the money we needed. It was called the Ontrea payments stream.

When Robert Rabinovitch was president, he made it his business to try and develop alternative sources of money for the Corporation. One of the areas he addressed most successfully was real estate. A number of years earlier he had sold to Ontrea Inc. a piece of land adjacent to the Toronto Broadcast Centre that belonged to the CBC. It was very valuable, prime real estate, right downtown. Instead of taking the money in a lump sum, the CBC took it in a stream of payments extending over many years. That way it would generate supplementary income annually of about $12 million to help offset the inflationary erosion of the parliamentary appropriation. This was the Ontrea revenue stream.

Selling the Ontrea stream was obviously not ideal. In selling it, we would lose the annual supplement to our revenues and make our financial problems worse. Unfortunately, there was nothing else left to sell. All the family silver, jewellery and precious heirlooms had been hocked long ago. The cupboard was bare. We thought about selling some buildings, but then where would we make the shows?

We thought about selling the transmission towers, but nobody wanted to buy them. It was the Ontrea stream or nothing.

The board agreed to the sale in March 2009, and we approached the government for the necessary approvals. Not only can the CBC not access the capital markets or buy and sell shares without government approval, it cannot dispose of major assets. The government officials and ministers were briefed. We explained that we needed the money to pay the severances, so that we could make the cuts. We explained that time was of the essence. The longer it took us to make the cuts, the greater the hole we would have to fill and the greater the cuts we would have to make. We explained that the transaction was straightforward. We were simply selling a stream of payments.

Three months after the matter was originally raised, nothing was resolved. The officials mulled it over. The ministers (I presume, but do not know) mulled it over. Perhaps the Ontrea stream really belonged to the government and not the CBC (which in a sense, of course, it did). If so, why should the CBC be allowed to benefit from the sale? How was that different from the CBC proposing to sell some other government assets—fighter jets for example—to pay its severances? That would not be right. Hmmm. Complicated. Very complicated. Perhaps it required longer and more profound consideration.

And even if the CBC was allowed to sell the Ontrea stream, presumably whoever bought it would require the CBC to guarantee it. But if the CBC guaranteed it, was it not providing a government guarantee and trading on the government's credit? And if the government's credit was involved, then perhaps it was not a sale but a loan. Except that the government had already decided not to give the CBC a loan or a line of credit. In which case the Ontrea could not be sold.

The strangeness of these deliberations slowed the process interminably. What would have taken a normal company a month or two to resolve ground on and on. Opinions were sought, calculations were made, debates were held and the clock continued to tick. The longer we waited, the bigger the financial hole became. The bigger the hole, the bigger the cuts.

Eventually the government decided that it was acceptable for us to sell the Ontrea stream. The length of the deliberations and the complexity of the approval process meant, however, that almost a year would pass before the money became available. The Byzantine manoeuvrings within the federal government also consumed endless time and energy of the Corporation's senior officials. How can a company possibly survive, let alone compete, when it is forced to move so slowly?

WHILE ALL THIS was going on, the board deliberations about where to cut continued. The two schools of thought narrowed slightly when we realized that new production technologies would allow us to reduce the local stations without closing any of them. Whether or not this was a good idea was another matter. Keeping them open meant that the stations would not actually be closed, so we could not realize the savings associated with winding up the real estate commitments. It also meant that while they would continue to operate, the small stations would be on life support, with deeply compromised journalism and production quality. The larger ones, while still viable, would also be forced to produce weaker shows. I thought it wiser to accept some closures rather than weakening everyone. But the desire prevailed to avoid the controversy associated with shutting down operations in places like Corner Brook and Sydney.

The rest of the argument raged on. Sylvain and I continued to insist that we had to jettison the marginal properties while saving the biggest ones. For its part, the board and the president continued to insist that money be chopped out of the television schedules, from prime time if necessary. They recognized that this would potentially cause greater revenue problems in the future but felt strongly that television entertainment shows were secondary. The issues separating us were becoming clearer and clearer and the gulf more and more unbridgeable.

The debates about the possible 5 percent Strategic Review cuts and the cuts to deal with the recession inevitably flowed together. However we dealt with the cuts, they had to be inspired by a consistent and coherent view of the role of the Corporation. If we were to avoid looking like complete idiots, we needed to be able to articulate a clear philosophy that guided our efforts.

Eventually a big compromise was reached. For the purposes of the $80-million cut to English services, no stations would be closed. They would be made smaller instead. Windsor, Thunder Bay, Sudbury, Quebec City, Moncton, Saint John, Sydney, Corner Brook, Gander and Grand Falls would all be reduced. If we had to go further and implement the Strategic Review cuts, then we would start closing them.

We also compromised a little on the programming side. We would not, for example, get out of kids' programming immediately. We would instead defer our kids'-programming expenditures and make no new shows until the economy recovered. But again, if the Strategic Review was implemented, we would chop kids' programming altogether.

In a similar way, we compromised on the television schedule. We would reduce the number of episodes of our flagship shows (*Little Mosque on the Prairie*, *The Border*, *This Hour Has 22 Minutes*), but the beef would remain. We would not take out the Cross-Cultural Fund now, but we would remove it if the Strategic Review was implemented.

We also wound up much of our promotional spending and our travel budgets, froze hiring, extended the life of our equipment, stretched our accounts payable, trimmed our production budgets, cancelled some daytime shows, increased the number of repeats in the schedules, chopped the executive bonuses and planned to eliminate four hundred jobs.

We felt that if everything worked out properly and the creek did not rise, the changes might see us through the recession without damaging the growth strategy. They might—just might—allow us to maintain the momentum we had built in strengthening CBC's audiences.

AFTER ALL OF this agonizing deliberation, the question arose of what the government would do with the 5 percent Strategic Review. The board had agreed that if we had to go further and implement that cut, we could jettison the programs that Sylvain and I had originally argued should be killed. This was a significant concession on the board's part. I knew that that they had come to the decision reluctantly and with many reservations. In their heart of hearts, they felt closer to the small-town stations than to *Battle of the Blades*; they preferred shows made for both the French and English markets to *Being Erica* or *Heartland*; they wanted kids' shows more than independent punk bands. Nevertheless, they agreed in the end with the overall directions we had proposed.

We needed to know about the possible government cuts before we could finalize the decisions on which jobs, shows and activities would have to go. If it was just the cuts for the recession, that was one thing, but if we had to include the 5 percent, then all of the bumping arrangements would have to change, the size of the severance packages would increase and we would find ourselves in a much tougher spot.

Fortunately, the decision came relatively quickly. The president appeared before the Treasury Board ministers. He began by running through the $170 million in cuts we would make to cope with the recession. He observed that we had already given at the office. He then ran through the 5 percent Strategic Review cuts. The Treasury Board president apparently thanked him for the presentation and moved on to the next subject. There were no questions. It was over in ten minutes. After all the endless work and agonizing, the government sensibly decided not to impose a further cut.

This opened another question. If the areas in which we were going to cut 5 percent were genuinely the lowest priorities of the company, why would we not make them anyway? If we did, we could ensure that we had a $50-million cushion in case the recession proved deeper than we anticipated. Alternatively, if the recession ended, we would have an extra $50 million to invest in new priorities. Since we were constantly poor and never had enough money to do anything big, it might be wise to bury the $50 million within the bigger cuts. It would be invisible against the backdrop of everything else and give us some serious flexibility for the future.

I raised the issue with Hubert Lacroix. He looked at me like I was demented.

"The board has already approved it," I said.

"No," he replied. "The board said that if it was imposed, we would do it. Not otherwise."

"The board said that these were our lowest priorities. Just as a matter of good management, we should chop our lowest priorities."

The president looked grim. I pressed on.

The last thing he wanted was to start winding up small stations and the kids' shows. These were the very cuts that he and the board had resisted in the first instance. "We'll make the government angry," he said. "They give us a pass on the 5 percent cuts and we do it anyhow? How does that work? Surely that's a recipe for making them look like fools."

"We never mention the government," I said. "We make the cuts at our own initiative."

I could see he was growing impatient. It was just another crazy, impertinent suggestion. Only an imbecile would think it was a good idea. He was probably right.

We set about working through the big cuts. The first thing was to meet the union and develop a joint plan for moving forward. Four hundred jobs had to go, but we hoped to dismiss as few people as possible. We had developed an early retirement plan for those who wanted to take it, to help reduce the numbers receiving pink slips. We would not fill vacancies and count on a certain amount of normal attrition. The union could not have been more helpful. They recognized immediately that it was in the interest of all concerned to work hand-in-glove with management to drive down the number of actual layoffs.

The situation was complicated. We not only had to eliminate four hundred jobs to meet our targets; we had also to conclude the reorganization of the news department, which involved reassigning close to a thousand people, as well laying off some in the department itself. The job reductions and reassignments would involve the largest reconfiguration of CBC's labour force in its history.

We briefed the union in detail on the overall approach and made sure they understood the financial engineering involved. For their part, they worked diligently to counsel us on how to move forward and to make sure that their members knew we were working in concert. The result was that four hundred jobs were eliminated but significantly less than a hundred people were dismissed. That was not only a victory for the employees; it also reduced the severance we needed to pay.

The overall approach proved very successful. By keeping to the growth strategy and preserving the most important shows in the prime-time schedule, we were well positioned to benefit from the recovery when it came. Fortunately, it came sooner than we had originally planned.

As we came through the cuts in 2009, the schedules held up remarkably well on both radio and television. We were thrilled and astonished to discover that in 2009-10 CBC radio posted its highest share in its almost seventy-five-year history. The momentum of the previous years had not been lost at all. To the contrary, the dominant local morning shows increased their grip on the top spots, while the national shows strengthened as well.

The same was true of television. We had finished the 2008-09 season with an 8.7 share in prime time, and we closed 2009-10 at 9.3. At the same time, we once again trounced Global's U.S. prime-time schedule with our Canadian one. The 2009-10 season marked the fourth year in a row that we had managed to improve television's prime-time share. That had never happened before in the history of the Corporation.

The fact that our share strengthened and that the recession ended earlier than we anticipated dramatically improved our financials. By the end of the first quarter of 2009-10, our revenues were running ahead of forecast. By August of that year, it was clear that we could afford to start bringing back shows that we had suspended or cancelled. The first to return was *Steven and Chris*, the charming afternoon lifestyle show on how to be fabulous. Ultimately we ended up coming in $20 million ahead of plan.

THE CUTS, THE 5 percent Strategic Review and the sale of the Ontrea payments had consumed almost a whole year of management time. In the process of working through the issues, we learned many things, some good and some worrying. The good thing we learned was that there seemed to have been a sea change in the culture of the organization. There had been almost no whining from the employees or the union. Despite the extraordinary difficulties we faced, everyone rolled up their sleeves and worked together. The sense of entitlement that had infected many parts of the organization appeared to be gone. There was almost no finger-pointing or name-calling. We were all simply adults facing a tough problem with maturity and discipline.

The manner in which the cuts were handled and the fact that the network continued to perform also dramatically improved morale. The managers and employees were confident in the future of the CBC in a way they had never been in the past. According to a survey we did, in 2006 only 41 percent of the employees had been "optimistic about the future of English services," but 74 percent now believed we were on the right track and that we would succeed.

Despite that, it had become very clear that the president, the board and I were not in agreement. The directions they wanted to pursue seemed to be more or less the opposite of where I thought we should go. That had led to very difficult and rancorous conversations. If we did not come to a better understanding, it would be impossible to make further progress.

> Where there is no vision,
> the people perish.
> Proverbs 29:18

nine
THE PLAN

WHEN HE FIRST arrived, Hubert Lacroix said that he supported the directions we were pursuing for English services. He claimed to be a champion of the entertainment strategy, including the acquisition of *Jeopardy!* and *Wheel of Fortune,* which he had voted for. He had also expressed his enthusiasm for the overhaul of the news and the rebuilding of CBC's presence in the major local television markets. He had spoken out in favour of the new directions for Radio 2.

After the cuts decisions in 2009, however, it was not clear that he agreed with the strategy. He had asked repeatedly to cut the prime-time television schedules and had insisted that we not cut very small stations even if that imperilled our ability to deliver service in the larger regions. As well, in our private conversations he had reflected a desire to re-introduce the high arts on television and return to the CBC's "mandate." All this had created significant tensions between us.

I was not sure how much his apparent change of heart reflected his personal views and how much it reflected the board's. Many, if not most, of the board meetings during that period had been held behind closed doors, without either Sylvain Lafrance or myself present. The same was true of the board dinners, where presumably more informal discussions of overall direction took place.

I did not have a clear sense of where the board stood on many of the issues, let alone their overall view of where the Corporation should be going. All I knew was that, according to Lacroix, they were unhappy. They wanted "higher-quality" shows; they wanted more "mandate" shows.

I was concerned that despite all the work that had been done and the vilification that the senior management of English services had endured, he was not with us. I was concerned that we would lose many years of hard-won success and that he would not support the next necessary steps for the growth strategy.

For Lacroix's part, he had come to doubt my loyalty and my willingness to follow his instructions. He no doubt thought, with good reason, that I was difficult, arrogant and often insubordinate. One evening we sat down to have a drink at the Place d'Armes, a pretty boutique hotel in Old Montreal. He asked me bluntly: "Do you want to be on my team?"

I knew that having a good team meant a lot to him, but I had to confess that I was not sure.

"I don't know," I replied. "I think it depends on what game you want to play."

"What game?" he looked at his glass of white wine.

"Yes," I said. "I don't know what game you want to play. You told me that you agreed with where we were going with English services, but now I'm not so sure."

"Well, the key thing," he replied, "is whether you want to be on my team."

"How can I answer that if I don't know what you want to achieve for the CBC? How can I know if I want to play for you if I don't know your game plan?"

He gave me a wintry look. "We have a plan. It's the three Ps."

Sometime earlier Hubert Lacroix had propounded a personal vision for CBC/Radio-Canada that had come to be known as the three Ps. The Ps stood for People, Programs and Pushing Forward. They were meant to describe the priorities for the company.

"That's not a plan, Hubert, it's a slogan."

I had an unfortunate history of being dismissive of the Ps, and intemperately I let my scorn for them show again. Lacroix looked annoyed. I'm often rightly accused of being undiplomatic.

"What we need," I went on, "is a real plan, the sort of plan you would do if you were going to market to raise money for a private company. A plan with clear directions, teeth and targets." I attempted to appeal to his background in mergers and acquisitions and find an analogy that would resonate with him.

"We need something like an offering memorandum: a plan that describes what business we are in, where the competitors are, what we need to do to succeed, how we will finance it. You know, a real plan."

Lacroix looked displeased. Like me, he does not like to be told how to do his job. I went further.

"That's your job, Hubert. Only you can develop a plan. Only the president can do that."

He seized the moment.

"If we do a plan, and we know what game we are playing, then you will have to decide whether you want to part of the team," he said.

"I agree. Once we have a plan, I'll be happy to tell you whether I want to play that game."

"And if you do not, then you will have to go," he said.

Lacroix stood up, bid me good night and left the Place d'Armes. He had barely touched his wine.

I had been a partisan of developing a plan for the CBC for some time. It seemed to me essential that we be very clear where we were going. We needed to be able to explain in a compelling way to everyone what the CBC was about. We needed a sharply articulated vision for the employees, the board and the external community. Without it, we were rudderless and had no way of deciding how to move forward. We had seen the problems associated with not having a plan during the cuts exercise and the 5 percent Strategic Review. The absence of a plan had made the board deliberations more rancorous than they needed to be because there was no consensus on where the Corporation should be going.

The absence of a plan also made it difficult to explain to people why the CBC mattered and what the Corporation would do if it had more money. Whether the money came from the government, levies on the cable companies or access to the capital markets, nobody would grant new resources unless we could be clear what they would finance. A coherent and compelling plan was fundamental to the future financing of the Corporation. Without it, there was no chance to make a claim on greater resources.

BY THE END of 2009, the environment confronting the CBC had changed dramatically. A host of new platforms had emerged that challenged the traditional dominance of radio, television and the web. Facebook had come out of nowhere and over a few short years had amassed hundreds of millions of users. On Facebook people can share everything: email, photos, videos, algebraic formulae, music. For many people, it had become the place where they lived their online life, where they went to be entertained and informed, where they went to see funny things or learn the news. It had become the place where people went increasingly for things that had been the prerogative of traditional media.

Twitter too had emerged from nowhere. Everyone was tweeting: politicians, movie stars, dog catchers, sports personalities and regular folk were sending out their observations to the whole universe. Twitter began—in some important ways—to become a substitute platform for newscasts and weather reports. Often it was more up to the minute than the most up-to-the-minute television, radio and web offerings.

YouTube had also burst onto the scene with explosive energy. Suddenly everyone was uploading every kind of video: dancing dogs, children's antics, old music videos, whole TV shows. The number of people who viewed these was astonishing. Tens, sometimes hundreds of millions of viewers watched children bite each other's fingers, Justin Bieber dance and sing, and dogs express displeasure at seeing their food given to cats. Big stars became bigger still. Weird events took on lives of their own. Individuals popped out of nowhere into international celebrity. The big media companies took note. CBS, BBC and others started uploading their shows to YouTube. Then YouTube was bought by an even greater monster, Google.

At the same time, the traditional cable companies had begun deploying video on demand (VOD). Whereas in the past a popular show was only available on Tuesday night at 9:00 PM, now shows began to appear on VOD platforms. Miss the show on Tuesday night, no problem. Watch it on Wednesday night or Thursday night or whenever you want. The tyranny of time-based network schedules was being broken.

The cable companies themselves were being challenged. A host of newcomers began to offer TV shows on demand over the Internet. People could go to Apple's iTunes Store and buy their favourite shows. They could subscribe to Netflix and access a wealth of movies and older TV shows for a modest monthly fee. Their Xbox game consoles suddenly morphed into TV platforms. Everywhere, new entrants came on the scene: Apple TV, Google TV, Sony TV. Television appeared on tablets and smart phones. These new businesses came to be known within the broadcasting world as over-the-top offers, because they completely bypassed the cable companies by going "over the top" of them with TV shows via the Internet.

Everywhere, everyone was crossing boundaries and moving into old media's territory. What had been fixed was increasingly fluid. What was a television platform? What was a schedule? Who was a producer? Who was a distributor? Who was just around the corner ready to stand everything on its ear one more time? The speed and scope of the changes taking place was convulsive. They challenged the most basic assumptions about the traditional media businesses.

The CBC had historically controlled the distribution of its shows. It owned its own transmission infrastructure of towers beaming out radio waves. The transmissions were picked up by cable and satellite companies and retransmitted to the audiences unchanged, with the shows still scheduled in the time-honoured blocks of morning, daytime, prime time and late night. But now it was all going away. The CBC did not own the new transmission platforms. It did not own YouTube or Facebook or Twitter or iTunes or Xbox or Netflix or

Google TV or any of the others. If it were going to make its shows available in these new environments, it would have to develop partnerships with people operating novel platforms.

But more than that, the plethora of new ways of distributing television and radio raised the deeper question of what kind of company CBC really was. When particular kinds of content were "tethered" to particular platforms, the answer was clear. When TV shows only appeared on TV, a company that bought, made and scheduled TV shows was clearly in the TV business. But if the shows could appear "untethered" on all sorts of new platforms, however the viewer wanted to watch them, was it wise to continue to think of oneself as being in the TV business? Or would it be better to think of oneself as being in the content business?

When we began redeveloping news, we took the view that we were no longer in the television, radio or online news businesses. We were simply in the news business. The Hub would provide editorially integrated, coherent news across all the different ways Canadians might want to consume it. The news remained on television and radio and online, but it also moved on to smart phones, tablets and Twitter. It moved onto screens everywhere: on planes, in airports, on billboards. The CBC's job was news. The CBC's job was content.

Similar thinking underpinned the ongoing reform of Radio 2. What was Radio 2? Traditionally, it was thought to be a transcontinental FM radio network. It was certainly that, but was it something else besides? Was it in fact simply one part of a much larger music offer? Was the CBC's job Canadian contemporary music, rather than radio? In this view, all the Corporation's music activities should be pulled together in one place, as had happened with news, and reconceived as a music department. Radio 2 might be seen not as a stand-alone radio network but as simply one among a number of distribution platforms, and perhaps the one that acted as the principal barker and promoter of all the rest.

Understanding that the CBC was not really a TV or radio company but a content company opened up new ways of thinking about the Corporation. If it is a content company, then what are the key content genres? A traditional TV company would choose shows according to the time of day: small children in the morning, lifestyle in the afternoon, news at supper, entertainment in the evening and news and talk late at night. But if the CBC is a content company, its genre choices should be dictated exclusively by the requirements of Canadian culture rather than those of a television company's schedule, which might lead to different answers.

Should the CBC be in children's programming for preschoolers? The morning TV schedule may say yes, but the landscape may say no. There was a whole channel—Treehouse TV—devoted exclusively to non-commercial preschool children's shows. In Ontario, it was supplemented by TVOntario and throughout the rest of the country by PBS and its brilliant *Sesame Street*. It was true that only the CBC focused on distinctively Canadian characters—Saumon de Champlain and Mamma Yamma (a yam that lives in Kensington Market in Toronto). But was that enough? Should one of the CBC's key genres be kids?

When it came to entertainment, the argument seemed much clearer. Nobody else would devote significant financial and network resources to the creation of distinctively Canadian drama, comedy or reality shows. The other big broadcasters simply could not. If there was ever a major market failure, entertainment was it. One of the CBC's key genre priorities must therefore be entertainment.

Thinking about the CBC as a content company also raised important questions about who its partners should be. If its focus was getting its content as widely distributed as possible, then it needed to make friends with all the great platform providers. It needed to ensure that it had good relations with everyone, from the traditional cable and satellite companies to the new entrants. It needed to make sure its content was available—and in a prominent position—on the platforms of Apple, Google, Netflix, RIM, Facebook. It needed to ensure that it could manage and build these relationships as effectively as it managed its transmission towers.

The head of digital strategy and business development, Steve Billinger, had been busy pursuing those relationships for some time.

He had come to the CBC with extensive experience in the area, having worked variously for BSkyB in the United Kingdom, Microsoft, Bell Digital and ExtendMedia. He had, over the course of the previous three years, engineered on-demand and multi-platform (online and wireless) deals with Rogers and Bell. He had concluded an arrangement to bring Current TV, the user-generated digital TV content network founded by Al Gore, to Canada. He had rebuilt the CBC website and created all of the Corporation's digital video distribution platforms.

One of the most interesting deals he made was to have the CBC become Apple's preferred content partner in Canada. Apple would show us their road map for the evolution of their iPhones, and we would build apps that showed off the phones' new functionality. Apple would then promote our app and feature it prominently. One of the first and most successful was the radio app. It allowed listeners to stream any CBC radio station on their iPhone or iPad. If you were in Calgary and wanted to listen to CBC radio originating in Yellowknife or Montreal, no problem. This significantly expanded the CBC's footprint and better served its listeners.

The content strategy also raised questions of whether the CBC should have other content partners. For example, we knew that our business news was weak, so it seemed a good idea to find a sophisticated partner. We made an arrangement with the *National Post*, whose financial section is one of the two great daily financial papers in the country: they provided access to their financial reporting, and in exchange we provided access to our sports news. Their audience was better served, as was ours.

The transition to a content company meant that we would have to plan the future of the CBC quite differently from how it might have been considered in the past. The first order of business was not to specify what our television or radio services should look like in 2015 or 2016. It was rather to say, here are the major content areas that should constitute CBC's priorities for the next several years—news, entertainment, music, whatever—and here is why the CBC needs to be in these areas. Here is the reason the private sector cannot cover these content areas adequately. Here are the market failures in our national cultural life that require the intervention of a public broadcaster.

The CBC also had to be very conscious of its competitive environment. Whether we liked it or not, we competed with the private broadcasters for audiences, revenue and talent. Our traditional competitors had become stronger still. The CTV of Ivan Fecan had been formidable before, but it was now even more intimidating. Its purchase by Bell meant that it not only had a parent with deep pockets, it had one that controlled extremely important platforms for the distribution of CBC services. Bell owned ExpressVu, the biggest satellite TV company in Canada, and Fibe, its alternative to the cable companies in Ontario and Quebec. It was now a frenemy, both a partner and a rival.

The same was true of Shaw. Just after the CanWest empire collapsed into bankruptcy, Shaw bought the CBC's other major competitor, Global, out of receivership. This recapitalized Global, which meant it was no longer the weak, struggling thing it had been. To the contrary, like CTV, it now had a parent with very deep pockets. It had a parent that owned the second-largest cable company in the country. This group was another frenemy to the CBC.

The other big groups were similar. Rogers, the cable and wireless giant, owned Citytv and Sportsnet. Vidéotron, the Quebec-based cable and wireless company, owned TVA (Radio-Canada's great competitor), as well as a host of newspapers, such as *Le Journal de Montréal*, and other content assets. They were, like Shaw/Global and Bell/CTV, integrated telecommunications/broadcasting/cable/wireless groups. They were immensely well capitalized and kicked off enormous quantities of free cash. They were intimidating frenemies.

With the emergence of these big groups, the situation of the CBC changed radically. The Corporation was more alone than ever. It confronted much better-financed and more powerful competitors, who in most cases believed that the CBC's success came at their expense. Global was certainly not happy that CBC television beat it in prime time. It wanted its share back. It would make aggressive efforts to recover it. And now, refinanced and with a new parent, it was in a position to mount a serious comeback.

The emergence of these groups required that the CBC be more daring and aggressive. If it attempted to sit still, act timidly or be cautious, it would be steamrollered. The only chance the Corporation had was to be more imaginative, take greater risks, make better shows and push even harder than it had in the last few years. With rivals of this size, it had to become absolutely essential to Canadians.

A plan for the future of the CBC also needed to resolve the contradictions of the Corporation itself. The tensions and uncertainties— whether the CBC was a vehicle for popular culture or the higher arts, small towns or large ones, popular music or classical, advertising or ad-free—needed to be explicitly addressed and resolved one way or another. Until it was absolutely clear what the CBC was about and how it wanted to move forward, it would be impossible to produce a sensible or coherent approach. The CBC needed a plan with teeth.

To have teeth, the plan would have to be described in great financial detail. It would have to indicate exactly what the Corporation would do if it was resourced at any given level—if the CBC has less money, it will cut the following activities; if it has the same amount, it will stay the course; if it has more, it will do the following new things.

And in each case, the plan would have to indicate why the Corporation would cut or initiate the new activities. It would do so against the backdrop of the environment it confronted, the content genres that were its priorities, the partners it needed and the situation of its competitors. This would allow everyone—the government, the employees, the media and the public at large—to understand the consequences of changes in the CBC's financing. It would allow everyone to have a coherent and transparent debate on the CBC's future.

TOWARD THE END of 2009, the board voted to engage strategy consultants to help CBC/Radio-Canada formulate a proper plan. Requests for proposals were sent out to the usual suspects. After a rigorous process of shortlisting, interviewing and vetting, we settled on Bain & Company. Bain describes itself as "one of the world's leading consulting firms. We work with top executives to help them make better decisions, convert those decisions into actions and deliver the sustainable success they desire. For forty years, we've been passionate about achieving better results for our clients—results that go beyond financial and are uniquely tailored, pragmatic, holistic and enduring." It claims to have a particular expertise in the media industries.

CBC/Radio-Canada had contracted strategy consultants before. When Perrin Beatty was president he had hired McKinsey & Company to help figure out what to do about the Chrétien-Martin cuts. Apparently, the McKinsey consultants ran around the Corporation studying all sorts of things, interviewing people, looking at the external environment and applying their advanced consulting tools. And then... nothing much.

The whole effort was declared a waste of time by those who had lived through it. After spending large amounts of money on McKinsey in the mid-1990s, CBC television continued to decline. The collapse in audiences that had been going on for thirty years continued. Between 1994 and 2004, the CBC lost almost half its share, falling from 12.3 to its all-time low of 6.7. Whatever the results of the McKinsey effort, clearly it had not produced "sustainable success."

To avoid the same fate for our new planning exercise, I felt that it was important that we agree to examine everything at the CBC, challenge everything. We had to ensure that all aspects of the Corporation were on the table, no matter how ancient, how deeply ingrained, how sacred. We had to be prepared to reconsider everything, even if the resulting changes would lead to controversy and outrage. We had to be prepared to be really daring if we were to develop a plan that would allow CBC/Radio-Canada to grow in the extremely challenging environment that confronted it. We had to be prepared to reconsider all the traditional ways of doing things if we were to find a way through to greatness.

And greatness was what the senior executives claimed they wanted for the future of the Corporation. In early 2010, Hubert Lacroix had organized a pair of retreats with his Senior Executive Team (SET): Sylvain Lafrance, the CFO, the head of human resources, the vice-president of corporate communications, the head of the legal department, the head of business development and me. He wanted to ensure that everyone was aligned and that we would function as a "high performing" team.

We retreated to a remote hotel on the banks of the St. Lawrence in the Montreal suburb of Vaudreuil. The purpose of the meeting was to make sure that we all agreed on how—in the most general terms—we wanted to work together and move forward. For my part, I thought it would also be a good opportunity to see if we could set some tough benchmarks for the development of the Strategic Plan with Bain.

"Do we want to be great?" I asked.

The question seemed to catch the other members of the SET a little off-guard.

"Do we want to be great?" I repeated.

"What do you mean?" one member asked.

"Just what I said. Are we prepared to make the really difficult and daring decisions that could allow the Corporation to be great?"

"Well, of course," another said. "Of course we should try to be great."

"But you know that if we do, we will inevitably create controversy. You know that we will be heavily criticized. You know that we will be pilloried. Are we prepared for that?"

The members of the SET dug into the topic. They talked extensively about whether they really wanted to set such a standard. After a couple of intense days of debate, on February 17, we all signed a sort of manifesto. In it, we committed ourselves "to seek greatness" for the Corporation and "to act boldly" to make it happen.

At the time, I was not convinced that everyone was sincere about "seeking greatness" or "acting boldly," but I was pleased that people seemed prepared to at least pay lip service to such an ambitious goal. I was afraid, however, that we would ultimately be ground down by the inherent caution of the CBC's corporate culture. I was afraid that when it became clear that the price of greatness would inevitably be paid in the coin of controversy, everyone would back off and we would fall back to the wearying incrementalism that had so damaged the Corporation in the past. But that possibility was for the future. We were at least starting with a grand and daring goal in mind.

When Hubert, Sylvain and I discussed with Bain the process we wanted, we were very clear that we were prepared to explore and reassess everything. Nothing was sacrosanct. Putting advertising on radio, changing the 60/40 split between English and French services, closing stations, getting out of sports, selling Radio 2—everything was on the table. We would, as well, look at the constraints on the Corporation: our inability to borrow money or access the capital markets, the limits of our capacity to buy and sell shares in other companies, the strange governance of the place. We wanted to ensure that the resulting plan would create the best possible circumstances for the Corporation's success.

And however it came out, it had to be exciting and compelling. We wanted to produce a plan sufficiently bold that it would command the attention of the Canadian public, a plan that would make absolutely clear why the CBC was essential to the future of the country. We wanted a plan that would stir the cultural imagination of the country. We wanted a plan that crackled with energy and sparks, a plan that would define greatness and show what was required to achieve it. We wanted a future for the Corporation that was soaring and wild with ambition. We knew that if we produced it, a national debate about the future of the Corporation would inevitably follow. In fact, the clearer and bolder the plan, the greater the debate that was likely to ensue.

IN SETTING TO work on the plan, my principal concern was the board's mindset. During the fall of 2009, we had explained the English television programming strategy at a long meeting in November. We had explained that television was really about entertainment. We had reviewed the chronic failure of English Canada to produce popular Canadian dramas, comedies and reality shows. We had noted that we were the only industrialized country in the world to prefer foreign shows to our own. We had reviewed the schedules of BBC, the Australian public broadcaster and the French public broadcaster to demonstrate that they were pursuing similar strategies. We had taken them through the success we had already achieved. We showed them that we continued to receive the same number of prizes and awards for quality. We showed them that Canadians' attitude toward the CBC had grown significantly more positive. We showed them all of the arguments about how the strategy was right and was actually working.

And yet the board was not happy. They talked about wanting "higher-quality" shows. They wondered why the arts were not on television, why there was no opera or ballet. Their attitude was puzzling. If a drama was produced on a stage, it was art; if it was produced on a sound stage, it was not. At one point, Sylvain Lafrance said to the board, "You know, television is also an art form." But to no particular effect.

At best, the board seemed to like news and current affairs. They seemed to feel that CBC television would be better if it had more news, current affairs and documentaries; the fact that there was lots of news available elsewhere seemed unimportant to them. The fact that we were the only broadcaster that did documentaries and current affairs in prime time also seemed to cut no ice. They clearly thought that information programming generally was the core of the CBC. I had the impression that they would have been happiest if CBC television was nothing but news, current affairs, performing arts and Shakespeare.

There is a wonderful observation attributed to Tony Manera. Just after he was appointed president of the CBC in 1994, he was asked what he wanted to see on television. He said that what he wanted did not matter. If CBC TV reflected his tastes, it would consist of nothing but operas and gardening shows, hardly a recipe for success.

The board asked for another opportunity to discuss programming strategy. Doubtless they hoped that their dissatisfaction with our earlier efforts would lead to an improved performance. In January 2010, there was a long conversation on the subject. Sylvain started this time.

"*La clé*," Sylvain *a commencé*, "*est la marque*."

"The key," Sylvain began in French, "is the brand."

The board members put on their headphones to listen to the simultaneous translation.

"And what is the brand of Radio-Canada?" he asked rhetorically. "It's culture and democracy. The great pillars of Radio-Canada's programming strategy are culture and democracy."

The board members turned up the sound on their translation devices. They nodded enthusiastically.

"Our job is to contribute to the building and exploration of Canadian culture in French. We seek to speak to our loftiest aspirations, to strengthening drama, music and the arts."

The board leaned in further.

"We seek to reinforce the foundations of democracy, to ensure that Canadians are well informed and can participate actively and fully as citizens.

"In a sea of increasing choice, we need a strong brand. The brand is everything. If it is trusted and admired, people will come to us in the future. If we stand for the great pillars of democracy and culture, the brand will be strong and the future secure."

Sylvain went on in this general vein for some time, in his charming and eloquent way, promising that Radio-Canada would stand for the Higher Things in Life. The board members looked a little giddy. At one point, I thought they might burst into applause.

When my turn came, the board members removed their headphones and turned off the simultaneous translation. They looked at me sadly. The plodder was about to begin. It seemed harsh to have to follow the scholarship student.

I ran through my traditional arguments. I noted that there was little to choose between the schedules of Radio-Canada and those of the CBC. The board members looked sadder still.

"But, Richard, where is the mandate programming?"

"Where are the high-quality shows? Shouldn't we be appealing to Canadians' higher cultural ambitions?"

I felt a wave of despair go through me.

"Perhaps," one of the board members said helpfully, "it's the ads. They are forcing us to make lower-quality shows. If we got rid of them, we would be freed from the tyranny of ratings. Then we would be free to be a real public broadcaster."

A number of the board members nodded.

"Maybe then we could do what we should be doing."

My heart sank. I no longer had any idea where to go. The fact that there were ads on Radio-Canada seemed to make no difference. The fact that there was almost little to choose between Radio-Canada's television offering and CBC's was irrelevant. The question remained: How was it that the French were successful at discharging their mandate as a public broadcaster and the English were not?

The president was in a tough spot. The board was not happy. They did not agree with the direction of English services. Some members had started speaking to the press. Jeffrey Simpson of the *Globe and Mail* reported that, "... (some) CBC board members sharply disagree with this direction, but they have been beaten down." They wanted something quite different from what we had been doing. I was totally opposed to their view. I seemed incapable of explaining the strategy in a way they found convincing and compelling. Things were getting tense.

"You need to show the board you're listening," Hubert Lacroix said to me one day.

"Listening?" I replied.

"Yes. You need to talk more like Sylvain."

"More culture and democracy."

"Yes. And mandate. And public broadcasting."

"God, Hubert. You know how I hate that talk. It's just that sort of gibberish that got the CBC into trouble in the past. All high-flown talk to cover up poor results."

"That doesn't matter. You need better public broadcasting language."

That was probably sound advice, but I hated the idea of it and feared the consequences for the culture of English services if I started to use the language of old.

"And give them three or four high culture events a year."

"Like *Mulroney: The Opera*?"

"Of course not like *Mulroney: The Opera*. Do something with the Toronto Symphony like Sylvain does with the Montreal Symphony."

"He does that before the television season really begins," I noted.

I hated the thought of making these concessions. In the last three years, we had proved that we could reverse thirty years of decline by focusing on audiences. In the last year, as we cut $80 million and four hundred jobs out of English services, we had still posted the best numbers, arguably ever. Television's share was up by more than 50 percent in prime time, and radio was enjoying its highest share ever.

And the employees loved it. They were thrilled that Canadians were watching and listening with such pleasure and enthusiasm. Not only were 74 percent "optimistic about the future of English services" compared to 41 percent three years earlier, but when asked if their staff was "on board" with the direction of English services," 60 percent said yes compared to 37 percent three years earlier. When asked if "attracting large audiences is an important objective of English services," almost 90 percent said yes compared to just over 60 percent three years earlier. When asked if they were proud to work for English services, 90 percent said yes.

What was I supposed to say to everyone who worked there? Just kidding? All the stuff about audiences and the nature of TV and serving the public and making great shows? All the stuff that everyone had bought and now agreed with and revelled in? All the success? Just kidding: I really mean we should put classical music on TV and not take it off radio. I really mean we should go back to *Opening Night*, with two hours of performing arts every Thursday evening. I really mean we should revert to local current affairs instead of hard news. I really mean we should talk about mandate shows instead of audiences. I hated the message I would send if I did what the board and Hubert Lacroix wanted.

But I agreed to do so. I agreed because I knew that everyone found me difficult and prickly and arrogant. The president could reasonably expect me to do what I was told. So too the board. They were appointed by the government to run the place. I was not. I was also getting tired of arguing with everyone. Perhaps Lacroix was right. If I made some compromises, everything would move along much more easily. Perhaps. At any event, despite my misgivings, I said okay. Three to four high cultural events per year and more mandate language.

THE BOARD ESTABLISHED a sub-committee to work on the strategic plan with Bain, the president and the executive team. The first order of business was to agree on the role of the CBC: what it should do and then how it would measure its success in doing it. The key was to establish the CBC's mission. For my part, I thought we should define the mission by reviewing the major market failures the CBC needed to address. The point of departure should be to define very clearly those content areas the private sector did not and could not address. After all, we were planning the future of the *public* broadcaster. For its part, the board preferred to begin with the Broadcasting Act.

This is not a simple matter. The Broadcasting Act provides very little direction. It says simply that the job of the Corporation is to "provide radio and television services incorporating a wide range of programming that informs, enlightens and entertains." The programming should be "predominantly and distinctively Canadian... reflect Canada and its regions, and... reflect the multicultural and multiracial nature of Canada." That is pretty much it. The act is silent on whether the CBC should be in sports, news, drama, lifestyle, reality, music or talk. It makes no comment on the importance of making popular shows. It offers no guidance on how the resources available should be split between English and French or the regional and national services. The question of whether there should be advertising on radio or television is not addressed. The act provides almost no guidance whatsoever on any of the main questions that have bedevilled the CBC over the years.

The only real hint in the act on programming strategy is the phrase "a wide range of programming that informs, enlightens and entertains," which became the basis for extensive board discussions on how to build a mission statement for the CBC.

Through many meetings, the members of the sub-committee engaged in an almost Talmudic exegesis of the words. The most puzzling and enigmatic was, of course, *enlightens*. Enlightens? I explained to the members of the sub-committee that I knew something of this matter, since I had been involved in drafting the act as assistant deputy minister of communications. The government originally wanted the formulation to be "informs, *educates* and entertains," but could not use the word *educates* because education falls into provincial jurisdiction. Thus, I explained, a proper understanding of *enlightens* is that it really means "educates." None of the board members found this helpful. They pointed out that while my account may be historically accurate, the act still says "enlightens." That is what parliament agreed and that is what must be parsed.

Dictionaries were sent for. Enlighten? According to the Oxford dictionary, it means "to give someone greater knowledge or understanding about a subject or situation." That hardly seemed satisfactory. *Enlighten* seemed little different from *inform*. Surely *enlightened* carried with it some sense of "enlightenment," the Enlightenment, the Age of Reason, Voltaire, Locke, Rousseau, that sort of thing. Or perhaps it was more a Buddhist sort of enlightenment, a flash of satori that strips away the veil of maya that blinds us to the truth. Whatever the case, it must mean more than "inform." If it was the same as inform, why bother to include both?

The French text of the act was consulted. In French, the formulation was *éclairer*: "*rendre quelque chose plus clair, plus compréhensible, l'expliquer.*" Hmm. It sounded suspiciously like the English. Further researches were undertaken: "*répandre de la lumière, s'allumer, briller.*" *Briller.* To shine. Something shining. Something bright, something brilliant. Yes. Yes. The Talmudists carried on. More parsing. More research. I understood one of the board's in-camera dinners was wholly devoted to the meaning of "enlightenment." Mercifully, I was not there.

As these discussions progressed, the sub-committee moved to address the vexatious question of "quality." The board was agreed that they wanted "higher-quality" shows, but what did that mean? What was "quality"? Who decided? How was it measured? If you could not define it, you could hardly demand it. Further researches were undertaken.

We explained that the BBC defined "quality" as being what the British public took to be "quality." That seemed to alarm the board. The public defining quality? Surely that could not be right. If you let the public define "quality," would it not imply that the popular shows would be deemed of "high quality"? Would it not mean that the disjunction between popular and high-quality would collapse? But then again, the sainted BBC must know something about the matter.

What the BBC knew, and what most cultural observers knew, was that the idea that the higher arts were of higher quality and the popular arts were of lower quality was wrong-headed. There were terrible operas and ballets, as there were terrible reality shows and situation comedies. There were terrific operas and ballets, as there were terrific reality shows and situation comedies. The trick was to judge each medium on its own terms. Situation comedies should be judged by the standards of situation comedies, reality shows by the standards of reality shows. And it appeared that the most popular situation comedies were also the best written, acted and produced. The most popular situation comedies were the highest-quality situation comedies.

We could see that this was true from our internal research. For years, the CBC had conducted a study called FIATS (the Fully Integrated Attitude Tracking Study) that asked Canadians what they thought about the CBC on a number of different dimensions. They asked whether the CBC was "essential," whether the shows were "distinctively Canadian" and most importantly whether they were of "high quality." Interestingly, as the audiences grew with the success of the new entertainment shows, public perceptions of the Corporation strengthened as well.

As the CBC's share of prime-time viewership increased, Canadians said that they thought the quality of the shows was improving too. Only 34 percent of Canadians thought that CBC programming was of high quality in 2006–07, and by March 2010 that number had risen to 44 percent. At the same time, when we looked at how Canadians ranked the quality of CBC's shows compared to those of

CTV, Global, Citytv and the then A-Channel, they picked CBC above all the others (even if only marginally so when compared to Global and CTV and their beautiful American shows).

When it came to how "distinctively Canadian" the CBC was, Canadians also thought the network was becoming more so. In 2006–07, 56 percent of the population thought CBC was distinctively Canadian, and 63 percent thought so in 2010. Not surprisingly, the CBC clobbered the other networks on this dimension, with only 27 percent thinking Global was, and 31 percent thinking CTV was. CBC was seen as twice as distinctive as the other two big networks.

This was extremely encouraging. The data seemed to show that we could make distinctive Canadian shows without sacrificing quality or popularity. In fact, the three seemed to vary together. The higher the quality and the more distinctive the shows, the more popular they were. That should come as no surprise. The level of competition in the television markets is so intense that poorly made, undistinguished fare will simply not survive. Nobody will watch rubbish.

All of that should have been reassuring to the board, but it was not. They continued on their dissection of "enlightenment" and "quality." Hours of management and board time were consumed in the quest. The board believed that the definition and measurement of these terms was key to the development of the mission and the future directions of the Corporation. They would provide us clear guidelines by which to tell which shows should stay and which should go. The mission statement would reveal all. It was exhausting.

While the board continued to work, subtle and not-so-subtle messages were sent. At one point, James Moore, the minister of heritage, was to meet with the board and discuss future directions. The meeting was ultimately cancelled, but the minister went on *Tout le monde en parle*, Radio-Canada's most popular talk show. He said: "Frankly I can tell you I don't like it when I see CBC cancelling Canadian content and we see *Jeopardy!*"

The fact that no Canadian content had been cancelled for *Jeopardy!* was neither here nor there. The fact that *Jeopardy!* had provided a powerful lead-in to our prime time Canadian shows was neither here nor there. The message about *Jeopardy!* was a message about direction. It was read as a symbol: Return to the mandate!

As these conversations unfolded, other work was moving ahead. One of the first areas we considered was the regions. We had to decide what we were really doing locally. Were we trying to give the largest number of Canadians local CBC services or were we trying to serve Canadians who had no service at all? What was our policy?

The question was even more pressing when we compared the costs of local French and English service. The fact that it cost three times more to provide local French service in Regina or Calgary than it did to serve the North in English raised questions of equity with a particular pertinence. What was our policy? Should we wind up French Regina and serve English Hamilton? What was the rule of thumb? How much should we reasonably spend per capita, whether for French local services or English ones?

In February 2010, I sat down with the president to review the relative costs of local service in French and English. He was startled. They suggested that Radio-Canada had too much money compared to CBC for its regional services. How could we defend full French local television and radio services in Regina and Halifax when we had no local English services at all in London or Hamilton? Maybe it was time to revisit the 60/40 split of the parliamentary appropriation between English and French services.

Taking on the 60/40 split is, of course, political dynamite, both internally and externally. If it were made more equitable, a torrent of criticism and anger would be unleashed.

"Only a French president can take this on," I said to Hubert Lacroix. "An English president could never survive an attempt to change it."

He looked at me thoughtfully.

"We agreed that everything was on the table," I reminded him.

"We did," he agreed. "Perhaps you're right," he went on. "Perhaps it is time to reconsider the 60/40 split."

This was one of the two or three most difficult questions we needed to face in building the plan. At a lunch, Sylvain Lafrance,

Lacroix and I discussed the matter. Sylvain was understandably concerned about changing the split. He was not sure that he could survive as the head of Radio-Canada if it changed. He would lose the confidence of his employees. He might have to resign.

Foolishly I agreed that we should not reconsider the split. Sylvain and the president looked relieved.

It was a mistake to have taken it off the table. I realized later that as much as I liked and admired Sylvain, it was wrong to let personal feelings confuse the matter. I returned to the president and told him I had reconsidered. He looked dark.

"You agreed at lunch not to raise it again," he said.

"That's true, but I was wrong."

"Well, it's too late. You agreed. We cannot reopen it."

And that was that.

Later I returned with a proposal to ameliorate the situation somewhat. I proposed that for television, we merge all the news resources in the regions. The trucks, cameras, technicians, reporters and producers, whether originally French or English, would be placed in a common pool. This would allow us to extract the synergies by avoiding duplicate infrastructure and efforts. After all, the local news in Regina is the local news, whether the viewer is French or English. It is the same weather, the same city council, the same fires and crimes and the same problems with the parks. Only the language of reporting is different.

To make it work, I suggested that we should manage the common news resources in all the English markets and produce the local French newscast for Radio-Canada. The reverse would be true in Quebec. There the French would control the common resources and produce the English supper-hour news for us in Montreal. Not surprisingly, this suggestion was not well received. It meant that the French employees would have to work in English (which, of course, all of them spoke fluently if they lived in Regina or Vancouver). It meant that we would not be sensitive to French cultural issues. It meant that the Radio-Canada news department would lose resources. The idea never went anywhere.

The matter of the regions was not just about the French. It was, of course, also about English services—whether to provide local service to the largest possible number of Canadians or to those with no private-sector service. The two ideas contradicted each other. If the correct policy was to provide service to the underserved towns, then the CBC should wind up its local operations in Toronto and Vancouver, where there are many alternatives, and redeploy the resources to Wawa and Sturgeon Falls. On the other hand, if the correct policy was to provide local CBC service to as many Canadians as possible, then Sydney, Corner Brook and Thomson should go and these resources be used to open London or Hamilton.

The matter was further confused by the situation in the North. The CBC was there to provide local service because the region was remote. At the same time, it operated not only in English but also in eight aboriginal languages. But why did the CBC broadcast in aboriginal languages there and nowhere else? Far more aboriginal language speakers lived in the rest of Canada than in the North. In fact, of the three great aboriginal language groups that are likely to survive—Cree, Inuit and Ojibwe—the CBC broadcasts only in the first two, and only in the North. What was the right policy here? Why favour marginal languages that are almost extinct, like Gwich'in and Dogrib, and not help preserve Ojibwe?

The local issue went back and forth, round and round, as it had during the cuts exercise. Bain & Company provided graphs and maps. Finally it was concluded that while no existing small stations would be closed, new ones would be opened in the largest unserved markets first. This was progress, even if only of a limited kind. We were, at least, going to be clear that the CBC's policy was to provide the largest number of Canadians with local CBC service and not to favour remote and underserved areas.

The North was another matter. Although it was extremely expensive to provide service for small numbers of people, there was a strong feeling that it was a special case. It was so remote that nobody—not even me at my most truculent—could imagine the CBC not being there. But the question of native languages was never concluded. The Dené would receive CBC service for their dwindling and aging population, while the vibrant southern communities of Ojibwe and Cree would not.

As the planning process ground on, certain subjects were never considered, despite our promises to look at everything. Was it a good idea to put advertising back on radio? The evidence from television was very clear that while people prefer shows without ads, they will watch the attractive shows with ads over poor shows without them, every time. The CBC radio shows were excellent. They dominated their category. People would not turn off CBC radio if there were ads. Where would they go? To the second-rate private stations that also had ads? Listeners would complain, of course, but they would not leave.

Putting advertising on CBC Radio One might be worth as much as $100 million, almost the total cost of the network. With an extra $100 million, local radio stations could have been opened in all the large underserved markets. The quality and level of local journalism and talk could be increased everywhere. We would not face the hard choice of cutting back the independent news coverage in Saint John, where there is nothing else but the Irving empire. Even if ads were placed only in the local drive shows, tens of millions could be raised. For radio, $10 million or $20 million is a great deal of money.

But the matter was never discussed. It was too controversial. There was no point even thinking about it. What, after all, is the point of spending time on something when the conclusion is forgone? Better to leave it undisturbed and not cause pointless alarm.

Other subjects were addressed but did not seem to go anywhere. For some time, it had been clear that CBC needed more specialty channels, to diversify our revenue streams and amortize our costs. The News Network was enormously important to CBC news as a whole. We knew from our experiences in sports that if we were to hold our major properties, we needed a CBC sports channel. Radio-Canada had lost *La Soirée du hockey* precisely because they did not have a sports specialty channel. The NHL and the Canadiens had said they wanted all the Montreal games on one channel. The Réseau des sports, owned by CTV and Ivan Fecan, could accommodate them, but Radio-Canada never could. Putting all of the games on the main network would displace Radio-Canada's prime-time schedule completely. Without a sports channel, Radio-Canada could not mount a bid.

In English services we had applied for and been given a specialty sports licence by the CRTC. We had not launched it, because we did not have the money to do so and could not go to the capital markets to raise it. Without it, however, the future of CBC sports—what remained of it—was in jeopardy.

The same was true of all the major genres. If we were to stay in kids, we needed a kids' channel to complement the morning shows on the main network. We certainly needed an entertainment channel to complement our entertainment offer. Ideally the CBC would have a specialty channel to support and diversify each of its major content areas.

At the same time, we recognized that it was also important for our content to be on the emerging new platforms, whether video-on-demand with the cable companies or iTunes or Apple TV or Netflix or Xbox. Like the specialty channels, they promised to extend access to our audiences while strengthening the CBC's revenues. It was important that we understand these issues, and that we determine what we had to do to remain competitive in the future and how much it would cost us.

We asked Bain & Company to look into these matters. We asked them to build business models to estimate how the pieces might fit together and how we should approach them. If there was a way of diversifying the CBC's revenues, reducing its dependence on government and moving successfully into the future, it was here. This, presumably, was the core of Bain's competency. They were strategic advisors on managing business challenges. We asked them to treat this set of questions as a priority.

Then, nothing much. Astonishingly to me, they seemed to have no particular insight into these matters. They appeared to have no studies from other jurisdictions. They asked us—in the time-honoured way of consultants—whether we had any ideas or data. We explained, as gently as we could, that if we knew the answers to the questions we would not have hired them.

Frustration with the process and the Bain consultants mounted through the first few months of 2010. The top executives in English services grew increasingly impatient. Scott Moore, the head of sales, was particularly annoyed when he explained to Bain that CBC's advertising inventory was underpriced, only to have them turn around and trumpet it as a discovery they had made. The clever head of digital strategy and business development, Steve Billinger, was annoyed to be lectured by thirty-year-olds with MBAS on subjects that he knew more profoundly than they did. Moore's and Billinger's frustration was echoed in all the other areas of English services. The most senior managers grumbled about the time they had spent with Bain.

To try and help get the process back on a sensible footing, I met with Hubert Lacroix on April 13. We had breakfast. I explained that there was great frustration with Bain. The management of English services worried that we were going nowhere. They feared that we would end up with the status quo, not the exciting, daring plan for the CBC's future that everyone wanted. We needed to more clearly frame for Bain and the board what was required.

I volunteered to take a crack at an outline of what might constitute a five-year plan to transform CBC into a content company. It would define the key content areas that we needed to be in, the platforms we needed to be on, the partnerships required and the financial resources necessary to hold it all together. If we could agree on what the plan should ultimately look like, perhaps we could make faster progress. A new approach might let us put aside, at least for a while, some of the most difficult and wearying of the CBC's contradictions.

Over the next couple of weeks, the senior management of English services pulled together a complete view of what we might look like as a content company. It was based on our own experience, our sense of where CBC needed to be and the success we had had to date. We began by defining the principal content areas: news and information, entertainment, kids, sports, music and smart talk. They were chosen because they are the areas with a particular need for a public broadcaster, whether because the private sector cannot work in the area (as with entertainment and smart talk) or the CBC brings something unique (news, kids, music) or the area is fundamental to the Corporation's financing (sports). The choice also implied what the CBC would not do. It would not cover lifestyle, how-to, performing arts, teenagers, tweens, pets. The content areas would define what the CBC was about and where it would put its energy and resources.

The next step was to define where we wanted our content to appear. If we wanted to serve our audiences wherever they were and however they wanted to watch, listen or read, we needed to ensure we could do so. It was pretty clear, for example, that we needed complementary specialty channels in the areas of sports, kids and entertainment if we were to compete for rights in the future and more effectively manage our costs. Beyond specialty channels, we needed to understand and have solid relationships with the video-on-demand operators at Shaw and Rogers, the Apples, Googles and Xboxes, the Spotifys, Facebooks and Pandoras, the Siriuses, Twitters and Netflixes, and all the other denizens of the new digital universe.

On April 21, I walked the board through the approach we had developed at English services. I explained how we might shift from being a public broadcaster to a public content company. The executives in English services had worked very hard on defining the conceptual shift and the key initiatives that would be required to drive it forward. The board members listened politely, but not, it seemed, with much enthusiasm. I was a little surprised. We had discussed the transition to a content company on many occasions.

Things were getting worse all around. The president and the board were still preoccupied with the mission statement. They continued to research "enlightenment" and "quality." I pushed for a focus on content models and the financial requirements of the new platforms. We were working at complete cross-purposes. Bain was frustrated. The board was frustrated. The president was frustrated. I was frustrated.

On April 27, Hubert Lacroix and I met again. This time he raised the stakes.

"You remember our agreement?" he asked.

"I do. If I don't agree with the plan, I go."

"Exactly."

"Well, first we need a plan."

"So we do."

We sat in Lacroix's stripped-down office. It is a little forbidding.

"You need to deliver the plan," he said.

"I thought you, me and Sylvain owned the plan," I replied.

"We do. But you need to ensure that we actually have one."

That seemed a little tough.

"And," he went on, "if we do not have a plan, you have to go. Okay?"

Okay? It did not sound like a question or a proposal to which he was seeking my assent.

"So we are clear," he said. "No plan. You go. A plan you do not agree with, you go."

There seemed little more to say.

AS THE FISCAL year ended, it was time to evaluate the performance of the senior management and the various services. Like all big companies, CBC has a formalized evaluation process. Objectives are agreed at the beginning of the year, and people are ranked against them at the end. The rankings are made on a three-point scale: not met, met, exceeded. Bonuses are paid out on the basis of where one falls on the scale. The heads of the French and English services receive two rankings: one for how they performed personally and one for how their service performed. Once the rankings are established, the president recommends them to the board. The board reviews the recommendations. The decisions are then used to calculate the relevant bonuses.

The fiscal year end for 2009-10 was March 31, 2010. By the end of April, once the final numbers were available, we were well advanced in our conversation about my personal ranking and the ranking of English services. I took the view that we had "exceeded." We had eliminated four hundred jobs, reduced expenditures by $80 million and landed the best ratings for CBC radio in history and certainly the best performance for CBC television in a decade, and arguably ever. If that did not merit an "exceeded," it was not clear what did.

Despite our differences of view and the increasing rancour of our relationship, the president agreed and proposed that I receive an "exceeded" and that English service receive an "exceeded." The board agreed too. In fact, they went further. They decided to establish a long-term compensation package, designed to incentivize me to stay in my job. If I stayed for another three years, I would be rewarded.

On June 2, 2010, I met the president, who reviewed the board's decision on the rankings and the long-term compensation plan. This seemed encouraging. Surely it meant that the president and the board had made their peace with me. Despite the difficulties of the cuts and the planning process, they were apparently prepared to judge performance based on results rather than personal feelings. I was, of course, quite wrong.

Over the course of the next month, the endless meetings on the strategic plan continued, and the real world drifted further and further out of focus. We continued to be lost in conversations about "enlightenment" and "quality." The Canadiens' run for the Stanley Cup, the preparations for the G20 Summit in Toronto, the ongoing conversations about upcoming shows and deals, the preparations for the CBC's seventy-fifth anniversary, the day-to-day work of running CBC English services—all was increasingly lost in the fog of the planning exercise. I felt like a man unmoored from his life. The days passed in anonymous boardrooms engaged in Thomist reflections. "I said it was three angels." "Don't be absurd. Anyone can see it is five." "The pin can probably accommodate upwards of eight or nine."

There was nothing left to talk about. The conversation had shrunk to the status quo. Nothing could be changed. Nothing could be imagined. The promises we had made to ourselves to "seek greatness" and "act boldly" had evaporated. Basically we had spent six months and millions of dollars on Bain to conclude that we had no fresh ideas. I felt utterly lost and demoralized.

During my summer holidays, I reflected on where we were. There was no apparent appetite to push forward aggressively, to explore new and compelling futures for the Corporation. I was at a loss. If the best we could imagine was the status quo, I would have to leave the CBC. I had told the president I would not stay if I did not agree with the plan, and so far there seemed to be no plan to agree with. If on my return there was still no appetite for something "great," something "bold," I would have to pack my belongings, fold my tents and prepare to leave.

In early August, the conversation began again. I had not seen Hubert Lacroix for about six weeks. I was rejuvenated by the warmth of the Mediterranean and looking forward to picking up the debate one more time. If I was going to have to leave the job that I had loved more than any other in my life, at least I would go out pushing for a bigger, bolder CBC. I would argue one last time that we should plan a daring future for the Corporation, one with swagger, confidence and fun. I would say, one last time, with all the grunt I could command, that it was only about the audiences.

Our job was simple. We should make great Canadian content for Canadians. Nothing more. We would know whether we had won or lost based on whether Canadians watched, listened or read what we made. They were the only judges who counted. Enough with all the drivel of "mandates" and "quality" and "higher purposes." It was time to commit ourselves completely to the essential thing, the brutally hard thing, the only thing that could ever count: making content that Canadians found compelling. And there could be only one way to know we had succeeded: audiences. Everything else was self-absorption and entitlement.

On August 5, Hubert Lacroix, Sylvain Lafrance and the other members of the Senior Executive Team took up the conversation one last time. We reviewed where we were on the Strategic Plan. There was another tussle over the direction, exactly the same conversation we had had six weeks earlier. Let's dream. Let's not. Let's be big. Let's not. Let's be great. Let's not. Let's be bold. Let's not. I felt myself once again sinking into the quicksand of the CBC.

I once again raised the idea of moving *The National* to 11:00 PM so that we could air new Canadian dramas at 10:00 PM. The room froze. The spectre of *The One* returned. The anger of the Constituency would be unbounded. Time slowed down.

The president looked exceptionally dark. I was at my post-holiday, insistent worst. He told me that it was a very bad idea and we would not raise it with the board. We exchanged harsh words. He looked at me with the exhaustion of one who has borne a great burden for too long.

Where there had been ambiguity, everything suddenly became clear. Where accommodation had seemed possible, it now evaporated. We stared at each other across an impossible gulf. It was stark and obvious. Hubert Lacroix wanted the mandate CBC that I detested. He had lost all patience with my insubordination and arrogance.

When the meeting broke up, I walked back to my office with Christine Wilson, the deputy head of the Network Program Office. She had been with me through the whole unpleasant strategic planning exercise, the squandering of all those millions on that process. She looked breathless and frightened.

"You are so fired," she said.

"No," I replied. "He cannot fire me yet."

"Why not?"

"He and the board just gave me and English services their highest rating. They would look like fools to dump me now."

"You're wrong," she went on. "You were too high-handed. Nobody could keep you now."

Christine did not know that Hubert Lacroix and I had agreed I would go if I could not live with the plan. So far there was no plan. Our agreement provided that I would not leave until the plan was done. Only then would we know whether my time was up.

My mood was very dark. After six years of abuse and success, of working until late in the night and waking with anxiety, of loving the great undisciplined beast, I was damned if I would go gently. I was far too invested in the CBC, in its importance and centrality to our cultural life, its history and its weirdness, to go easily. Perhaps Christine was right. Perhaps I would be fired. But whatever else, I would not go unless I was forced to leave.

Around 4:30 that afternoon, Hubert Lacroix came to my office. He said, "We are parting ways."

"Really," I replied as insouciantly as possible. "Are you leaving?"

He looked darker than ever.

What happened after this, I cannot say. The terms of my separation agreement forbid me from describing the moment.

> ⚡ To achieve the impossible,
> one must attempt the absurd.
> Miguel de Unamuno

ten
THE END

I WAS DISMISSED while sitting in the office that I had inhabited for six years. It was filled with memorabilia. Stuffed in the bookcase was an official CFL football, signed by Tom Wright when he was the commissioner. On the coffee table was the Don Cherry action figure with Blue that had so preoccupied me when I told Jennifer McGuire she would have to cut millions of dollars from the news department. On my desk was a plastic statuette of Sir John A. Macdonald standing beside a Victorian table with a gin bottle on it. The whiteboard beside the conference table was covered with calculations about how to finance a new 10:00 PM drama strategy. I looked around at the office I had loved, packed my briefcase and left.

Outside, in the ante-chamber, were pictures of some of my favourite moments. Rick Mercer was being tucked into bed by Prime Minister Stephen Harper during his famous sleepover at 24 Sussex Drive. Mamma Yamma, the orange tuber, was kissing me on the set of her children's show. Show posters lined the corridors: *Little Mosque on the Prairie, Being Erica, Dragons' Den, Battle of the Blades, Heartland*. There were photographs of the stars: Peter Mansbridge, looking serious and authoritative; Wendy Mesley, smiling perkily; Jian Ghomeshi, staring thoughtfully into the camera;

313

George Stroumboulopoulos; Michael Enright; Heather Hiscox; on and on. I looked at them individually as I walked out, touching gently the ones I liked best.

I took the elevator from the seventh floor down to the atrium that is the architectural centrepiece of the Toronto Broadcast Centre. It had changed completely since I had arrived. The player piano from *The Happy Gang* was long gone. The trophy case with the medals from the Lucerne Television Festival of 1962 had been sidelined. The atrium was instead a riot of giant posters featuring the big shows and stars. The cast from *Little Mosque* were walking Beatles-like across Abbey Road. The Dragons were engulfed in flame, Kevin O'Leary staring balefully into the near distance. Don Cherry and Ron MacLean stood together, Cherry scowling, his thumb up and his collars stiff as a nun's wimple. The radiant Erin Karpluk from *Being Erica* looked down over her glamorous shoulder.

I walked out the main doors onto Front Street. It was a warm and welcoming evening, the air still and dense. I walked around the Broadcast Centre, looking at it one last time. I went west past the statue of Glenn Gould, sitting hunched and scarfed, in front of the Glenn Gould Studio, turned right at John Street, past the billboards showing posters for Ivan Fecan's U.S. shows, along to Wellington Street, east again past the enormous parking garage with the news trucks rolling in and out, and right one more time into Simcoe Park, which adjoins the building. The park was full of couples taking in the summer night, sitting on benches and holding hands.

THE 2010–11 SEASON was really my last, even though I was already gone. The shows had already been commissioned and made. The trajectory for the revamped news was set and agreed. Radio moved along. It is impossible to change schedules or shows in a short period of time. It takes at least a year or two to begin to shift an organization as large and complex as the CBC, and four to five years to remake it completely.

The 2010–11 season was another excellent one for the Corporation. The prime-time television schedule continued to perform extremely well, making a 9.3 share, just as it had the previous year.

Radio One's numbers were equally impressive, matching and in some cases surpassing those of its previous record year. The news continued to strengthen. CBC News Network became more dominant, while the local newscasts attracted more viewers and carried along their slow but steady expansion. It was gratifying to see things going well, although I regretted, sometimes bitterly, that I was not there anymore.

ABOUT A WEEK after I was dismissed, I received a call from an unnameable source (not producer Larry Weinstein) saying that the CBC wanted to dump *Mulroney: The Opera*. They were prepared to walk away from the money that had already been invested and insisted that there must never be any acknowledgment the Corporation had been involved with it. What did I think?

I was surprised. I thought it was unwise. Everyone in the arts community knew about *The Opera*. It had been five years in the making. If the CBC walked away and ordered a gag, everyone would know. It would be compromising the Corporation's freedom of expression, the most important value it stands for. It would all come out in the press. The damage to the CBC's reputation would be much worse than any fallout from the Gilbert and Sullivan-like qualities of *Mulroney: The Opera*.

Astonishingly, although the CBC's involvement was well known, none of the press—let alone the CBC's news department—ferreted out the story. Aside from some partial reporting by Martin Knelman at the *Toronto Star*, nobody seemed capable of connecting the dots. It seemed weird that a gag order by Canada's most important cultural organization did not cause any significant controversy, let alone criticism.

The cancellation of *Mulroney: The Opera* (and presumably the Chrétien one as well) was only the beginning. Shortly thereafter, the Feature Film Program was cancelled, I can only speculate because of complaints by the pay-television operators and the feature film distributors. The pay-TV companies never liked the idea in the first place, and the distributors worry about anything that seems novel or risky.

My successor at Telefilm, Wayne Clarkson, had described the Feature Film Program as one of the things he was most proud of during his time there. He felt, like me, that it could have an enormously beneficial effect on the sluggish English-Canadian movie business. Certainly nothing that had been done in the past had made much impact. But the forces of caution and stasis triumphed here as well. Beyond *Midnight's Children*, we will not see any more films come out of it.

Along with the abandonment of the operas and the movie strategy, the Corporation moved quickly to announce that it would not be renewing *Jeopardy!* Although it still had two seasons to run and had provided a million-viewer lead-in to the prime-time schedule, it was to be axed well in advance of its due date. The CBC said it would be replaced by a Canadian show, even though a non-news daily Canadian show has never made a million viewers every night.

Small initiatives were announced to return more mandate-oriented programming. Shows that had been cancelled because they made poor TV were being revived. The Giller, the country's most prestigious literary prize, was back on CBC television, everyone in evening dress, listening to speeches and thanks from happy talking heads.

Apart from these changes to television, the speed and tempo of things seemed to shift subtly. The changes to Radio 2 appeared to grind to a halt. The peculiar hybrid of contemporary and classical music carried on. The creation of the Home of Music and the simultaneous relaunch of Radio 2 as a modern network seemed to be on hold.

The deals with the *National Post* appeared to come undone. We had made plans to expand our relationship and start to work together at the local level. We hoped to replicate some of the successes we had had nationally by exploring how to share content between the local newscasts and the papers of the Southam chain. We thought there could be excellent opportunities to strengthen both parties, but this too seemed to have stalled.

The language within the organization also began to change. The top people started to say that audiences were nice but not everything. They started to revive the language of quality. Audience considerations sometimes had to be trumped by meeting the public broadcaster's mandate.

The next few years are likely to prove exceptionally challenging for the CBC. The sales of Global, CTV and Citytv to Shaw, Bell and Rogers respectively mean that the Corporation now confronts much better-capitalized rivals. Already they have been spending more than ever on the purchase and promotion of U.S. shows. They are determined to expand their prime-time share.

In approving the transactions that created the new, vertically integrated broadcasting and television conglomerates, the CRTC extracted public benefits concessions representing roughly 10 percent of the total value of the transactions. The concessions require that the companies spend more than $400 million over the next seven years to strengthen the Canadian broadcasting system. Among other things, the CRTC ordered them to spend more money than they normally would on Canadian entertainment shows and local news, the two areas the CBC has particularly emphasized over the last little while.

More recently, Rogers and Bell have combined to purchase Maple Leaf Sports and Entertainment, the company that controls the Maple Leafs, the Raptors and the Toronto FC. They paid over $500 million each. They did so principally to secure the local Maple Leafs rights for their television, online and wireless platforms. They seem convinced that hockey is more important to them than anything else, and are prepared to pay accordingly.

ONE OF THE CBC's looming challenges is extending the NHL agreements after the last year of the current contract, the 2013–14 season. Rogers and Bell Media will almost certainly bid on the rights. They have already demonstrated that their powerful sports specialty networks can draw as many viewers as the CBC. The last Grey Cup on TSN, for example, drew more viewers than CBC's Grey Cup coverage ever had.

In bidding against the CBC, they would have the advantage of recovering their costs through two revenue streams: the fees that they receive from the cable and satellite companies and their advertising revenues. The CBC, for its part, cannot use its public subsidy to support its bid. It must rely exclusively on advertising revenues.

Even if the contest were more equal and based on advertising revenues alone, both Rogers and Bell Media have more platforms off which they can realize revenue. They have not just television but online and mobile as well. Their online and mobile offerings add significantly more viewers to their bases.

Bell Media has also shown that it is prepared to pay significant premiums for sporting properties, even if it means taking a loss. We saw that when CTV paid substantially more than CBC could ever justify for the 2010–12 Olympic Games. More recently, they paid a hefty premium for the FIFA World Cups of 2018 and 2022 to take them away from the CBC.

The next round of negotiations with the NHL will likely begin in 2012. This time the forces arrayed against the CBC will be much more powerful than they were in 2006–07. The private broadcasters will continue to lean on the government, arguing that whatever happens, the CBC should get "back to basics" and get out of bidding for hockey. As the years go by, their arguments seem to gain more and more traction. It's no longer just minor Senate committees recommending that the CBC exit professional sports; it's increasingly all the other media, which—with the exception of Postmedia, the *Toronto Star* and the *Globe and Mail*—are all controlled by CBC's competitors. It's hard to imagine any government having much appetite to resist the biggest media groups in the country.

When—as seems likely—the CBC loses *Hockey Night in Canada*, the loss will mark not just the end of the oldest media property in the world, it may also cut the CBC's ties with those Canadians who often see the Corporation as foreign, remote and patronizing. Losing the Corporation's tie to the Game, losing Don Cherry, losing the memories of pond hockey and frozen winter nights, losing the most loved and remembered sport in Canada will inevitably diminish the Corporation.

This is quite apart from the financial issues associated with replacing *Hockey Night in Canada*. If those hundreds of hours of programming were to be replaced by original Canadian drama, documentaries, comedy and public affairs, the cost would be hundreds of millions more in public subsidies. The CBC has not received a permanent increase in its funding in more than thirty years. It seems unlikely to happen now.

The only alternative would be to replace the lost hours with repeats of Canadian shows. Saturday nights would become Repeat Night in Canada, with third and fourth runs of the CBC's primetime schedule, which would profoundly erode the CBC's share and damage its relationship with advertisers.

The loss of hockey would result not only in a huge financial and programming challenges, it would—in effect—mark the end of CBC sports. Hockey is the last great property left. Now that TSN has curling, the CFL, FIFA and the Olympics, the loss of hockey would drive the final nail into the coffin.

THE NEWS DEPARTMENT also faces significant challenges. It is halfway through its renewal. The reversal of the news department's plunging audiences was only the first part of the renewal, although it remains critical to its future success. Unfortunately for the CBC, a portion of the public benefits mandated in the Shaw/Global and Bell/CTV buyouts are to be spent strengthening those networks' local news offers. Together they will spend almost $75 million more than they would have done, beefing up their offerings in Halifax, Montreal, Toronto, Winnipeg, Regina, Edmonton, Calgary and Vancouver—the very markets where CBC has been attempting to strengthen its local news.

The second part of CBC's news renewal involves demonstrating that *CBC is making a contribution to the public debate that is not only valuable but that would not otherwise occur.* This is the unfinished business. If CBC news cannot demonstrate that it is delivering news that Canadians would not otherwise receive from the private sector, the rationale for its existence breaks down. Why spend public money on what the privates are prepared to do?

The standard is difficult, but essential to the future of CBC news. It means a number of things. First, for the Now part of Well Informed

Now, the CBC must break news that the privates do not have. It has to cover the big stories that everyone needs to cover but it must also break stories that nobody else has. And this needs to be done not occasionally, but continuously. In John Cruickshank's lovely phrase, CBC's journalists must be "news breakers, not news takers."

An excellent example of what this means is the Canadian Press bureau in Ottawa. It breaks more stories in Ottawa than anyone else. Its knowledgeable and competitive boss, Rob Russo, explained his method to me once at lunch. "Every morning," he said, "I sit down with all the journalists and I ask them one question. I say, 'Tell me something I don't know.' We go around the table and each one tells me what he has. If I can describe for them what it's about and where I saw it, they lose. If I've never heard of it, they win. It's fun. It's like a game that keeps everyone sharp."

Tell me something I don't know. Perfect. The question appeals to the intensely competitive instincts of great journalists. It puts a premium on being first.

Adopting this attitude will be a challenge for CBC news. It is more aggressive now than it was, but the challenge will be to become the most competitive news organization in the country. It has to be if it is going to start meeting the test of doing what the privates cannot.

But that is not enough. Like ratings, breaking news is really the price of entry to having a great and essential news department. Its coverage also has to be wider than the private sector's if it is to meet the promise of Well Informed. It has to cover fires, weather, crime and politics, but it has to be broader than that. It needs to cover the subjects that the private sector cannot or will not.

For example, the CBC should be the leading purveyor of international news in Canada. Covering other countries is not, however, a matter of simply reporting on events abroad. It is much more fundamentally about covering the world from a Canadian point of view. This means finding the stories abroad that matter to people at home. These very often will not be the stories that appear in the local press of the foreign country being covered.

If a CBC journalist is covering France, for example, the interesting issues for Canadians may not be the ones that matter to the French.

The internal politics of the Socialist party are likely to be of little concern, even though they are exhaustively covered in the French press. Rather, Canadians need to know why the French medical system works so much better than the Canadian one. It is a public system like ours, but without the astonishingly long wait times for treatment and hopelessly overcrowded emergency rooms. What have the French done that we can learn? This issue will not appear in the French press. Their medical system is not a story in France, because it works.

The same point applies to covering the United States, but here the situation is different again. Canadians interested in U.S. developments have easy access to all the news that Americans get. They can watch CNN, MSNBC, Fox, ABC, CBS, NBC. The CBC cannot, nor would it make any sense for it to try to, cover U.S. news better than the Americans. Rather the CBC has to cover the United States in light of one question: what does this mean for Canada?

The Well Informed must also include reaching beyond the Corporation's normal orbit. We felt strongly, for example, that CBC's business coverage was terrible. We decided, therefore, to try and steal the Business News Network's show, with hosts Amanda Lang and Kevin O'Leary. It was not easy. Kevin O'Leary was concerned that if the show came to CBC, the banks and financial analysts would worry that it was going to the Communist network, which would be bad for his credibility and the show's.

In the same way, we wanted to expand the range of political commentary to ensure that we covered the right wing fairly. At one point, I asked Kory Teneycke, Prime Minister Stephen Harper's former head of communications, if he would work as an analyst for us. He is very clever, very right-wing and very articulate. He was ideal for television.

"Work for the CBC?" he asked.

"Yes, indeed."

"Why would I want to work for the Communist network? It would be bad for my reputation."

"Well," I replied, "if you won't come, how are we to rebalance its leftist slant?"

"A good point," he admitted.

Eventually he came and provided a stimulating and provocative point of view.

All of these approaches are outside the CBC comfort zone. They require aggressively searching out stories, getting to them faster than the privates, drilling deeply into difficult and complex questions and reaching out to unfamiliar topics and people beyond the CBC's normal interests and acquaintances. These changes will not happen of their own accord. They will happen only if the journalists and producers are pushed, measured and rewarded for doing them. Top management of the news department and the Corporation more generally must insist that CBC news make good on its promise of Well Informed Now. If they do, the CBC will genuinely *make a contribution to the public debate that is not only valuable but would not otherwise occur.*

CBC'S ENTERTAINMENT department will also face challenges. The private sector not only has more money to spend on Canadian shows, it is beginning to produce some very good ones. A few years ago, CTV commissioned *Flashpoint*, a police procedural set in Toronto. It is now in its fourth season and has more viewers than any CBC entertainment show except *Dragons' Den* and *Battle of the Blades*.

Global has begun to awaken from its slumber. Recently it has commissioned two strong shows: *Combat Hospital*, a medical procedural set in the Canadian military base at Kandahar, Afghanistan, and *Rookie Blue*, a police drama. These two did well with Canadian viewers, even though they were aired principally in the summer.

At the same time, the public benefits in the Shaw/Global and Bell/CTV transactions will increase the amount of money those conglomerates can spend on Canadian entertainment shows—between them, they will spend almost $200 million more than they otherwise would have on the development, production and promotion of Canadian drama. They will compete more aggressively with CBC for scripts, talent, directors and show runners. The CBC will need to bring all of its resources to bear to avoid losing its position as the number one network for Canadian entertainment. It ceded that position to CTV in the early part of this century, and that could happen again. It would be doubly ignominious if it happened at the hands of Global.

All of this, in conjunction with the dramatic evolution of the digital environment and the emergence of altogether new platforms—Netflix, Google, Facebook—means the Corporation will find itself in very stormy seas. To succeed, it will have to be daring, clear in how it responds to the new environment and absolutely relentless in its focus. It must have an exceptional plan to move forward and the will to execute it fully.

The CBC issued its five-year plan a few months after I left. It is called "2015: Everyone, Every Way." It is seven pages long.

Not surprisingly, it makes a meal of Culture and Democracy. It states the CBC's new Mission, finally derived from those endless months of the board's parsing of the words *enlightenment* and *quality*: "CBC/Radio-Canada will be the recognized leader in expressing Canadian culture and will enrich the democratic life of all Canadians."

The plan rests on three pillars. First, the CBC "will produce and air ten 'signature events' per year on both our English and French networks. Events of significant meaning to Canadians. Programs or initiatives that leave their mark." According to the Corporation's progress report to Canadians, by the end of 2011 they had had three signature events, two in English and one in French. The English ones were: *Live Right Now*, a television show about how to have a healthy lifestyle and lose weight; the other was *Hockey Day in Canada*. On the French side, they did a Christmas concert.

The second pillar was "to strengthen our footprint in the regions." The Corporation has announced that it will add some radio and online services in Kamloops, Kelowna, Kitchener, London and Hamilton. It will also expand its local coverage in some other places.

The third pillar was a commitment to a gradual increase in spending "on new technology to fund innovation and development of our live platforms." They have announced a redesigned website.

There it is. After almost two years of work and the expenditure of millions of dollars with Bain & Company, not to mention thousands of hours of management and board time, the CBC has produced its plan, the plan that will guide it through what promises to be the most convulsive, competitive and turbulent period in its history: "2015: Everyone, Every Way."

AFTER I LEFT the CBC, many people from within and without the Corporation called to talk about what had happened and ask how I was doing. Perhaps the most remarkable was Dan Oldfield, one of the original members of the Central Committee during the lockout. Five years after the vilification of the Gang of Four, he was phoning to say goodbye.

Many things had changed since these terrible days in 2005. A new process had been initiated with the union to see whether the 2009 contract could be negotiated without industrial action. George Smith had led an altogether novel set of discussions with Oldfield and other members of the Canadian Media Guild. Amazingly, by the end of 2008, fully three months before the expiration of the contract, a new deal was reached and signed.

Oldfield said that he was sorry I was gone.

"We may not have agreed on everything, Richard, but I always thought you wanted the best for the CBC and its employees."

I was a little stunned.

"I don't know if you will ever need a reference from a union leader, but if you do, I'm happy to provide it."

Then he asked me to lunch.

We ate at a restaurant on King Street in Toronto called the Kit Kat. It is a well-known CBC haunt. The walls are covered in mirrors so everyone can see everyone else. A couple of booths away, Peter Mansbridge was having lunch with the head of the News Network. I went over to say hello. He asked in a slightly strangled voice why Dan and I were having lunch. I explained that he had offered me a job with the CMG and that I had accepted. For a moment, Peter seemed to believe it.

ACKNOWLEDGMENTS

I WOULD LIKE to acknowledge the assistance of the following people: Suzanne dePoe, my agent, who showed me how to approach writing a book and selling it; Trena White, the associate publisher at Douglas & McIntyre, who was wonderfully patient and supportive with a first-time writer and taught me a great deal about story structure; Robert Rabinovitch, George Smith, Scott Moore, Derwyn Smith and Steve Billinger, all of whom read parts of the book in draft and provided helpful comments and suggestions; and Gerard MacNeil, who suggested the title.

INDEX

RICHARD STURSBERG was head of CBC's English services—television, online and radio—from 2004 to 2010. Before that, he was executive director of Telefilm Canada, where he achieved the largest share for Canadian movies at the domestic box office in history. He has also been chair of the Canadian Television Fund, CEO of the satellite television company Starchoice, president of the Canadian Cable Television Association and assistant deputy minister for Culture and Broadcasting. He has been a member of the boards of the Canadian Film Centre, the Banff Television Festival and the Sectoral Advisory Group on International Trade in Cultural Products. He lives in Toronto.